Raymond M. Berger, PhD

Gay and Gray:
The Older Homosexual Man
Second Edition

Pre-publication
REVIEWS,
COMMENTARIES,
EVALUATIONS . . .

"**B**uilding on previous research, Berger explodes myths about the older homosexual man. An important book for everyone interested in the study of aging as well as those more specifically interested in gay studies."

Martin S. Weinberg, PhD
Co-Author of *Dual Attraction: Understanding Bisexuality*

"**W**hen *Gay and Gray: The Older Homosexual Man* appeared more than a decade ago, Ray Berger challenged and irrevocably refuted the received wisdom that older gay men were lonely, isolated, and desperate souls. Out of print for a time, this landmark book in gay studies is now available again in a second edition. The original text and transcripts are all here, and now helpfully bracketed with a reflective prologue by Berger and his colleague James Kelley, and four concluding papers that add other perspectives to the subject of gay aging.

This book is must reading for mental health professionals in all disciplines who work with gay men. The original text and the new chapters provide a vital corrective analysis about what happens to gay men as they age. There are too many myths about many aspects of the gay experience. Berger deserves accolades for putting to rest one of the most enduring and pernicious. The return of *Gay and Gray* in this second edition is welcome news, indeed."

Gary A. Lloyd, PhD
Professor and Coordinator,
Institute for Research and Training
in HIV/AIDS Counseling,
School of Social Work,
Tulane University

Harrington Park Press
An Imprint of The Haworth Press, Inc.

Gay and Gray
The Older Homosexual Man
Second Edition

HAWORTH Gay & Lesbian Studies
John P. De Cecco, PhD
Editor in Chief

Gay and Gray
The Older Homosexual Man
Second Edition

Raymond M. Berger, PhD

Harrington Park Press
An Imprint of The Haworth Press, Inc.
New York • London

Harrington Park Press, an imprint of The Haworth Press, Inc., 10 Alice Street, Binghamton, NY 13904-1580

Library of Congress Cataloging-in-Publication Data

Berger, Raymond M. (Raymond), 1950-
  Gay and gray : the older homosexual man / Raymond M. Berger.–2nd ed.
      p.   cm.
  Includes bibliographical references and index.
  ISBN 1-56023-875-5 (pbk. : alk. paper).
    1. Aged gay men–United States–Social conditions. 2. Aged gay men–United States–Interviews. I. Title.
HQ76.B475 1995
305.26–dc20

95-23223
CIP

CONTENTS

ABOUT THE AUTHOR

Raymond M. Berger, PhD, MSSW, has conducted research and written widely in the areas of aging, homosexuality, and social work practice and is the author of a popular social work research textbook. He has over fifteen years of teaching experience, serving on the faculties of the University of Illinois at Urbana-Champaign and California State University, Long Beach. In recognition of his scholarly and community work on behalf of older gay men, Dr. Berger received the Evelyn Hooker Research Award of the Gay Academic Union and the Humanitarian of the Year Award from the Dade County (Florida) Coalition for Human Rights.

Foreword

When Mr. Berger asked me to write a foreword to his excellent book, I was delighted (and honored), first because I so greatly admire his work and second because it deals with a subject about which I am so conspicuously equipped to write.

For gay men, they are indeed not long–the days of wine and roses; as Mr. Dowson put it. As soon as one can no longer be described as a boy, one's social and sexual life is finished.

I have sat with groups of middle-aged gay men who are discussing a guest who had not yet arrived at some gathering. Such phrases as, "Mind you, he used to be sensational" fell from their haggard lips. When the individual in question arrived, he turned out not to be some stooping, shuffling person. He was a young man of about twenty-eight years of age but he could no longer be described as "a boy."

This problem cannot be applied to a woman. When she can no longer be called a girl, she remains a woman and can be admired as a picturesque ruin. She can be cheered on in her progress toward the grave with such condescending phrases as "terribly well preserved" but, in the portly gentleman in a three-piece suit who has become part of some impressive corporate structure, there is no vestige–nothing–of the exotic, bejewelled perfumed youth that was all the rage in some city's gay community. If he attempts to describe the romantic triumphs of his youth, he is openly mocked or quietly despised.

The false value set on conventional good looks and youth by gay men is as universal as it is fatuous. It never seems to occur to anyone that he might enjoy a longer-lasting, friendlier, or more sexually satisfying relationship with a potbellied man of forty than with some gilded though not gelded Adonis with whom he is always fighting for a position in front of the mirror. The desire is not so much to engage seriously with such a person as to be seen standing next to him in a gay bar or, better still, to be observed leaving the place with him.

Mr. Berger is to be congratulated on having found men to interview for this book—men who did not suffer from this school-girlish obsession with cuteness and who are not bristling with their "rights" because they did not enter the gay world until they were middle-aged. They are of a species that must have been difficult to interrogate and even more difficult to understand. As one reads their absorbing histories, one cannot help wondering, if they could acquit themselves successfully in marriage and could produce a brood of children, why they wanted to endure the dangers, the discomforts, and the sheer nastiness of homosexual intercourse. I could not help suspecting that they wanted extramarital sexual experience without the complications of an "affair," a courtship, a scandal—to say nothing of illegitimate offspring that pursuing a woman would entail. They wanted instant sex that we all know can never equal in flavor or in nutritional content of the old-fashioned stuff you had to peel and bring to the boil.

Loss of youth in these smash and grab sexual raids was never in question. These men suffered the indignities of senility elsewhere, in the real world—the inability to run to catch a bus, the difficulty in kneeling, the impossibility of getting up again, the petty ills that flesh is heir to, the general feeling that one's body has become a heavy and uncomfortable coat that one cannot shed, but these handicaps have nothing to do with being gay.

I am far older than any of the individuals questioned in this book and am quite frankly waiting for death which seems to be a hell of a time arriving. I am only not lonely because I now live in America where, like Miss Dubois, I find that I can always rely on the kindness of strangers. In Manhattan everybody speaks to everybody.

The inevitable conclusion to be drawn from *Gay and Gray* is that, if homosexual men were not so obsessed with their sex lives, the problems of old age would be no greater for them than for anyone else.

Quentin Crisp

Preface to the First Edition

When I entered graduate school, several well-meaning friends and teachers cautioned me to moderate my academic interest in homosexuality. Becoming identified with this topic was dangerous; it could lead to ostracism, academic difficulties, and future employment problems. When I took my first permanent teaching position, my new boss sternly advised me to keep a "low profile" on this issue. When I moved up to another position at a more prestigious university, I was encouraged to continue supplementing my publications on homosexuality with others on "safe" topics.

Back in my early graduate school days, when I pondered writing my first term paper on gay couples, I could never have envisioned the incredible four-year experience which was to culminate in the publication of *Gay and Gray*. In retrospect, I am glad that I ignored the well-meaning advice. For it has always seemed to me that homosexuality is not only a legitimate field of interest, but one which sorely needs more serious study and research. I would somehow have felt dishonest avoiding this most fascinating of human experiences because of fear of unknown consequences.

In this process of pursuing the topic of homosexuality my life has been enriched. I believe I can recall every individual, every workshop, every group meeting in which I have been involved, and I also believe that I gained something from each encounter. I have had complete strangers approach me with their life's burdens; old people have shared with me secrets revealed to no one else; I have counseled desperate teenagers and middle-aged men. I have seen new aspects of myself reflected in other people's joys and sorrows; I have been challenged and threatened; I have received hate mail; I have been named Humanitarian of the Year for my work with older gays. I have been shocked, amused, disgusted, and amazed. How many researchers can say as much?

Perhaps it is the social worker in me who identifies with the underdog and seeks to redress societal grievances. In my studies the greatest grievance, it seems to me, has been the way older gay men and lesbians have been relegated to a land from where they are never seen nor heard from. Like the Amerasian child of the conflict in Southeast Asia, the older homosexual is not wanted by either side—by the gerontologists or the homosexuals. Having completed this study, I feel more disturbed than ever about the fact that *almost every* gerontological researcher and commentator has chosen to ignore older folks who happen to be homosexual. Can these researchers believe that homosexuals self-destruct at the age of forty? Or have they simply been unaware of the millions of older persons who are homosexual? And have the gay male and lesbian communities been so oblivious to their own futures that they have succeeded in excluding older persons from their bars, their organizations, their literature, and their social activism? Because it is true, as one commentator has noted, that the elderly are one minority group we all aspire to join, this exclusion has served the gay and lesbian communities badly.

The situation is beginning to change, although slowly. Since I began formulating my ideas for this book five years ago, a number of scholarly journal articles on older homosexuals have appeared, as have popular articles. In addition, a small number of educational and social service programs for this special group have been established or significantly expanded. As the largely young gay and lesbian activists of the 1970s grow older, I expect this trend to continue.

Acknowledgments

Every book represents the efforts of many people in addition to the author. This is especially true of *Gay and Gray.*

The ten older gay men who agreed to be interviewed for this study deserve special thanks for their openness and willingness to share with others.

In the course of writing this book I received what seemed at times to be inexhaustible personal and professional support, including critical readings of drafts and valuable suggestions. For this I thank Anthony Canta, Jim Kelly, Nancy Weinberg, and Frederick Suppe.

The staff at the University of Illinois Press, especially Richard L. Wentworth, Ann Lowry Weir, and Christie B. Schuetz, have all been knowledgeable, patient, and always there to help.

I thank Don Brieland and Lela Costin for their encouragement, and especially for providing me with a crash course on "Everything You Always Wanted to Know about Publishing." Beatrice Saunders's contribution was substantial, although she may not know it. Learning about the publishing world from Bea was learning from a pro, and one of the best. Her guidance certainly helped me to become a better writer.

Several directors and volunteers of agencies serving older gay men and women spent many hours sharing their experiences with me. For that I am grateful.

Yvonne Bacarisse provided the administrative support which enabled me to complete work on the early phases of this study; gracias. The many revisions were ably typed by Tina Fisher, Jeannette Ingram, Lina Monel, Marta Sellick, and Peggy Swanson.

Rosita Perez was one of the nicest things that happened to me while writing this book. She used her guitar and her personal charm to motivate older gay men and women to respond to our pleas for participation in the study. She was more than a research assistant. She took this project on as her own, even though she had had no prior exposure to homosexuals. And she did it with an openness and sense of enthusiasm that touched me in a special way.

Prologue:
Gay and Gray Revisited

No one should try to prove that older gay men are happy and well adjusted. That is an impossible task.

The publication of *Gay and Gray: The Older Homosexual Man* in 1982 was notable in that it was one of the first widely distributed research reports to suggest that older gay men might not be the lonely and self-tortured lot described by earlier writers on homosexuality. There were inklings that this might be true even before the book's publication. In 1969, sociologists Simon and Gagnon suggested that older gay men might be able to mitigate the negative effects of aging by drawing on support from friends.

A year later, Weinberg (1970) reported the results of a comparison of younger (under 26 years of age) and older (over 45) gay men based on a large survey conducted in the late 1960s by the famed Institute for Sex Research. Although Weinberg noted that older gay men were less actively involved in the gay community, and had fewer sexual contacts, they appeared to be no less well adjusted than their younger peers–for example, older gays were no more lonely, depressed, or unhappy. And in several ways they showed higher levels of adjustment. For example, older gay men were less worried about being "exposed," more self-accepting, had more stable self-concepts, fewer negative feelings in general, and less interpersonal awkwardness.

Contrary to popular stereotypes, these men had come into their own as they aged. Weinberg even suggested that the aging process had been facilitated for these gay men by their lowered life expectations, and their willingness to accept their lot in life–characteristics of aging that are thought to be universal.

1

At the time that Berger began work on the study that led to *Gay and Gray,* only a very few writers had dared to argue that older gay men might not face a terrible and lonely old age after all (Francher and Henkin, 1973; Friend, 1980; Kelly, 1974). *Gay and Gray* promoted this more optimistic view and buttressed it with data from questionnaires and in-depth interviews. Subsequent studies and essays echoed this new "gay positive" view of older homosexuals (Dawson, 1982; Friend, 1987, 1989; Lipman, 1986; Pope and Schulz, 1990).

Had these gay-positive researchers and scholars established definitively that older gay men are happy? Perhaps not. In response to *Gay and Gray,* Lee (1987, 1989, 1991) accused the gay positive researchers of going overboard: In our zeal to correct years of misinformation, we had painted "too rosy" a picture of gay aging. Many or most older gays, Lee argued, were left out of the newly liberated world of younger gays, and were often rejected by them. Gay liberation had in fact robbed the older gay man of his special place among gays. Unlike younger gays, who eschewed secrecy, many older gays were locked firmly in their closets, where they preferred to be. And they often faced severe social, emotional, and other problems. To make matters worse, the younger gay community's lack of interest in older men, and older men's lack of organization, meant that these men could not turn to their own community for help. Few organizations existed to provide them with services.

Debate about the realities of gay aging are salutary. They alert us to critical issues that gay men face as they grow older, and they enlighten us about the widely divergent ways in which older gay men set about creating their lives. But focusing on a narrow answer to the question, "Are older gay men happy?" is based on a fallacy about the studies of gay positive researchers. None of these studies set out to prove that older gay men are well-adjusted. That is, none of them could claim that they had described what life is like for older gay men generally.

In order to accurately describe the characteristics of any group of people, it is necessary to study a *representative* sample of that group. This is often possible in social science research. But it is not possible in any study of gay people. The phenomenon of homosexuality, and the life situations of gay people, are so complex and shifting, that we can never hope to recruit a sample that will be representative of a supposed population of gays. For example, there are problems of definition that can never be resolved: Is a middle-aged man who recently left his wife and three children to live with a male lover, a member of the gay population in the same way as the single male who has been integrated into an urban gay community since his teen years? How do we classify the complex changes in self-identity that occur over the life span of many individuals, who may see themselves as representing different "orientations" at different points in their lives? And how can we possibly include in our studies the large numbers of persons who may be gay in some sense, but never participate in any gay group, organization, activity, or social network, and therefore are entirely inaccessible to researchers?

For these reasons alone, the studies of aging of gay positive researchers can never describe the elusive "older gay man." More significant, studies published to date do not even attempt to do so–they are almost all based on relatively small samples, often collected in one region, and limited to traditional sources of sociological and psychological research: organizations, clubs, mailing lists, and the like.

This does not mean that existing research on older gay men is of little use–the contrary is true. It means rather, that this research must be judged in light of goals that it was capable of achieving. These studies were not designed to answer questions about older gay men generally; they had a more narrow but still vital purpose. By describing groups of older gay men who challenged entrenched negative views of gay aging, they illustrated the fallacy of these views as universal descriptions. In the real world, older gay men–like other groups of people–cannot be described in simplistic terms. The desperately lonely gay man whom Stearn (1961) described as "beating the walls in anguish," certainly exists, and merits our attention. But for the first time in the modern era, social science studies point to the inescapable fact that there is a more sanguine alternative for older gay men. And many have achieved it.

GAY AND GRAY: ADVANTAGE OR NOT?

Gay and Gray helped to promote the novel idea that being gay can actually be an advantage in adapting to the aging experience.

Every gardener knows that placing his seedlings in the harsh outdoors early in the season creates plants that are better able than the
greenhouse variety to withstand the stressors of the growing season.
So it is with people, the gay positive scholars have argued. Early
weathering promotes survival. Two central ideas are "crisis competence" and "mastery of stigma."

crisis competence

    In the former case, the young gay man realizes that, unlike his
heterosexual counterparts, he cannot always rely on a family or
wife to be there for him. When he leaves his home of origin he is
less likely to replace it with a family, at least a traditional one. And
he certainly cannot take the approval of others for granted–after all,
being homosexual is not an automatic ticket to social approval.
Although it is not unusual for a heterosexual male to go directly
from being cared for by mother, to being cared for by wife (a
perennial complaint of wives), gay men rarely have such a smooth
transition. As a result of this crisis of competence, gay men learn to
be independent at the commencement of their adult years. Later,
when faced with the losses of old age–loss of job, status, friends–the
older gay man can draw upon the skills and attitudes that he learned
as a young adult.

mastery of stigma

    The gay positive researchers also argue that the young gay man
must also face a crisis of stigma. As the young man develops a gay
self-identity, he must come to terms with the potential and real
negative reactions of everyone around him–family, friends, employers, and strangers. Although embedded in a homophobic culture, he must somehow come to view himself as a worthwhile
individual, in spite of, and even as a result of, his minority status. In
Gay and Gray, Matthew's story best illustrates this mastery of
stigma. After a long period of self-doubt he finds that he can rely
only on himself for the self-worth that will sustain him throughout
his life. In Matthew's words, "I came to believe that I was born like
everybody else and that my life, too, had come from God" (p. 56).
This self-created adaptation exemplifies the early life mastery of
crisis that facilitates adaptation to aging. For entry into the status of
"old person," like entry into the status of "homosexual," calls for
the individual to develop strategies for coping with an identity that
is widely viewed in a negative manner. Who then can be better
prepared than the gay man to adapt to this aspect of growing older?

In defense of his argument that gay positive researchers have promoted an incorrect view of gay aging, Lee (1987) reported on an intriguing interview study of forty-seven gay men between the ages of fifty and eighty. One of his purposes was to test the notions of crisis competence and mastery of stigma. Does the resolution of early adult crises really help gay men to adapt better to growing old?

Lee presented his older gay respondents with a list of stress-causing life events developed by Huyck (1974). To these general life crises he added crisis events typical of homosexual men, such as problems in coming out, extended periods of self-doubt, and losing a job because of one's homosexuality. He counted the number of life stressors cited by his respondents, as well as their intensity, and then cross-tabulated these with a standard measure of life satisfaction.

The results of these analyses failed to confirm the hypotheses of crisis competence and mastery of stigma. Contrary to the predictions in *Gay and Gray,* those men most satisfied with their lives reported the fewest major life crises. This was true for the homosexually oriented crisis items as well as Huyck's (1974) general crises. Lee found for example, that gay men who reported the "fewest recalled fears or events of discovery"–those who avoided long periods of self-doubt, and those for whom acceptance of homosexuality came most easily–were the most likely to report greater current life satisfaction as older men. Lee concluded that the best route to a well-adjusted old age for gay men is not to face and master crises, but rather to avoid them (Lee, 1987, p. 56).

The crisis competence and mastery of stigma hypotheses have become a bit commonplace among gay positive gerontology writers. Surprisingly, no one other than Lee has thought to subject these hypotheses to test. So gay gerontologists can only be grateful for his attempt. However, the design of Lee's study invalidates it as a test of these hypotheses.

Central to the crisis hypotheses is the statement of a *difference* between older heterosexual and homosexual men. Both older heterosexuals and homosexuals may be expected to react to the stressors of old age–but homosexuals have certain differences in their life histories that should make their adaptation to aging different, easier. Therefore, any adequate test of these hypotheses requires a comparison between these two groups, a feature lacking in Lee's homosexual-only study. Additionally, the predictor variables that differentiate gay from heterosexual men are the unique stressors that gay men face. A test of the hypotheses then, need examine only those stressors that differentiate the two groups, and not stressors that are common to both groups.

A more serious problem is that Lee failed to use an appropriate measure of outcome. According to Berger's thesis set forth in *Gay and Gray*, adjustment in old age is facilitated not simply by the number or intensity of crises, but by the success with which these crises are resolved—something that Lee did not measure. Even a single crisis, if it is well resolved with the adoption of coping attitudes and behaviors, can contribute greatly to the individual's subsequent well-being. For example, a young gay man who resolves an early crisis of identity may work through that crisis by developing strong self-affirming attitudes, greater faith, and better practical coping skills—very much as Matthew did in the first case study of *Gay and Gray*. It is these attitudes and skills that foster good adaptation later in life, not merely the number of crises experienced.

The experience of multiple crises, far from predicting good adjustment, may predict just the opposite. If these crises are not quickly and effectively resolved, they may wear down the individual, deplete his social and emotional resources, and make him more vulnerable to subsequent stressors throughout his lifetime. (This is amply illustrated in the literature on childhood trauma, in which children who experience multiple long-term stressors carry their trauma into their adult lives.) This perspective on multiple crises is consistent with the crisis hypotheses, and illustrates the inadequacy of Lee's test.

Admittedly, it is much harder to measure the success of crisis resolution than it is to count the number of crises. Any test of the crisis hypothesis is also hampered by the difficulties of respondent recall of early life events that may be thirty or more years in the past. There is, for example, the tendency for more optimistic individuals to recall fewer difficulties in early life.

Oddly, Lee chose only one variable as a measure of adjustment to aging: life satisfaction. Adjustment to aging is of course multidimensional. The few studies of older gay men have all used multiple measures. These have included psychological factors related to self-perception, for example, self-acceptance, and stability of self-concept. They have also included standardized measures of mental health, such as assessments for depression and psychosomatic symptoms, as well as questions to assess characteristics such as the individual's desire for mental health treatment. Conceivably, a comprehensive study of adjustment among older gay men would include behavioral assessments as well: Does the older man relate well to age peers? Is he well integrated into friendship networks? Are his finances adequate? and so on.

A proper test of the crisis hypotheses is a task that has not yet been fulfilled. It will certainly present a challenge to future researchers of gay aging.

IS THERE A GENERATION GAP BETWEEN OLDER AND YOUNGER GAY MEN?

Casual observers have sometimes described "gay life" as youth-oriented. And some scholars have observed that older people have little place in gay life (e.g., Hooker, 1965; Lee, 1989). Indeed, many of the public institutions of the gay community seem to be dominated by the twenty- and thirty-somethings. But is there truly an antipathy between younger and older gay men? Are there conflicting interests?

Gay and Gray was perhaps the first study to ask older gay men about their attitudes toward their younger counterparts. Most of these men had few younger friends, and most preferred to socialize with age peers. It was of course hard to tell if this preference reflected the unavailability or unwillingness of younger gays to involve themselves with older gays. The older gay man's preference for age peers may reflect his accommodation to this social reality. More telling was the finding that many older gay men believed–accurately or not–that younger gay men held negative attitudes toward them. After all, it has been a truism among gay men that growing older is no particular advantage in attracting others.

This issue has received only limited attention in the literature, with the exception of the writings of John Alan Lee, a gay Canadian gerontologist. Lee (1987) has argued for a classical model of "asymmetrical-age relationships." This particular view conforms to predominant stereotypes of homosexual relationships, based perhaps on the Greek model of older mentor and younger protégé. Drawing on exchange theory, Lee posits that the younger gay man exchanges his good looks for the older man's wealth and social standing. This view has also been promoted by Steinman (1991).

One aspect of Lee's model strikes us as strange. He argues that in the preliberation era (before the Stonewall riots of 1969), young gay men were coerced to provide sexual favors to the older men who "controlled" the secret society of the homosexual world. Young entrants could only gain access to the secret gay world–with its parties and other social events–by winning the favor of older homosexuals, and thereby their willingness to provide introductions. According to Lee, this antiquated system still exists in less urbanized areas. Many older homosexual men, Lee further argues, have opposed the new openness of gay liberation because it forced them to give up the power they traditionally held over younger gay men. Presumably, after gay liberation, younger gay men no longer needed the older men for access to other gays. They now had their own social and civil rights organizations, and a new openness about their identities that allowed them to identify and interact easily with other gays.

This is a troubling model of intergenerational relations. It provides grist for the anti-civil rights mills of reactionary groups, who are fond of calling forth images of younger men being manipulated by older homosexuals. This image, for example, was used with great success in the late 1970s by Anita Bryant's "Save Our Children" campaign, which overturned a Miami, Florida civil rights ordinance and launched the nationwide anti-gay campaign of right-wing religious groups that continues to this day.

The exchange theory model of intergenerational gay relations is disheartening in that it depicts a crass and mean-spirited gay life. And it suggests wrongly that many or most older gay men are opposed to gay liberation. My own research and experience suggest the opposite. Most older gay men (at least the ones who appear in the organized community– the churches, bars, social clubs, political organizations, and social service agencies) favor gay rights and gay rights activities just as heartily as younger gays. And, as Berger argued in *Gay and Gray,* many older men feel a greater freedom than younger men to be open about their sexual identity, and hence are more free to work openly for gay rights. Many of the leaders of current gay rights groups are older gay men.

The "exchange theory" world of a gay society controlled by affluent older homosexuals probably never existed, outside of a few social networks in large cities. Young gay men always have used their considerable resourcefulness to gain access to other gay men. This is evidenced by the many historical reports of gay liaisons and networks that arose spontaneously even in the most hostile environments (e.g., Katz, 1976).

The generation gap is a thoroughly modern idea. There were never "gaps" between generations during earlier eras when social change was gradual. But in today's fast-changing world, each generation is exposed to new social realities–hence, the gerontologists' accurate claim about the importance of "cohort effects." For example, today's generation of older gay men were shaped by the Great Depression, the Second World War, and the anti-homosexual witch hunts of the McCarthy era. In the current era, the AIDS pandemic will shape future relations among age cohorts in the gay community. It is intriguing to speculate about the dimensions this social phenomenon is likely to take.

Statistically, the cohort most affected by the AIDS pandemic are gay men who today are in their thirties and forties. Disease incidence is highest in these groups. Although there has been some increase in infection among adolescents, the prevalence of infection in this cohort is not likely to reach the levels of the hardest hit age groups. Having come of age in an era of safer sex education, this younger cohort has had the opportunity, not available to the preceding generation, to avoid infection. Similarly, the "old old" among gay men–those currently in their sixties and above–have also shown much lower rates of infection, and there is no reason to believe that this will change. In addition to information about safer sex practices, this cohort is also protected by age related changes in sexual activity: Older gay men tend to have less frequent sex, fewer sex partners, and a more narrow (hence safer) sexual repertoire (Bell and Weinberg, 1978, pp. 86, 107-108; Weinberg, 1970; Weinberg and Williams, 1975).

These epidemiological facts leave the current cohort of thirty- and forty-somethings in the middle of a bad situation. While this middle cohort struggles to survive in the face of devastation of its social networks, the younger and older cohorts on either side may be expected to react with some resentment. The sexual revolution of the 1970s was all well and good, the young might say, but now they may add the complaint, "You had too much sex then, so we can't have any now." The sixty-plussers may have their own view: "We are entering the age where we need supportive programs. These were never too plentiful in the first place. Now, with the energy of the community drained by the AIDS problem, there seems to be no room for our needs."

ARE OLDER GAYS REALLY MORE SECRETIVE?

According to those who argue that gay liberation has opened a chasm between older gay men (who purportedly oppose it) and younger gay men (who are said to support it), the primary point of contention between the generations is the issue of passing. Passing is the time-honored means of survival by which gay people conceal their sexual orientation in order to avoid discrimination and ostracism. They "pass" as heterosexual, much like some light-skinned African Americans passed as white, and some Jews in Nazi-controlled Europe passed as gentiles. As a strategy, it certainly has its advantages.

In her review, Adelman (1991) noted that several studies concluded that successful adjustment is associated with greater involvement with other gays and with wider self-disclosure (p. 9). This was true for adolescents, adults, and middle-aged gays. In the *Gay and Gray* study Berger reported that high integration into the gay community, and less concern about concealment of sexual orientation, were related to good adjustment for gay men over forty.

Surprisingly, Adelman (1991) found just the opposite in her own study of heterosexual and homosexual men and women sixty years of age and older. She reported that among gay men, low disclosure and low involvement with other gays were associated with good adjustment. (Specifically, Adelman found that low disclosure at work was related to higher life satisfaction; and low disclosure to relatives was associated with lower self-criticism.)

Based on the interview study cited earlier, Lee (1987) argued that for older gay men, remaining in the closet was more likely to lead to a happy old age. Staying in the closet, Lee argued, "is one way to avoid [life's] storms" (p. 57). However, according to Lee's report, he found no correlation between how widely a person was known as gay and that person's self-rated life satisfaction. If this is so, then a more accurate conclusion is that whether one stayed in the closet or came out, made no difference in one's subsequent life satisfaction. How can we make sense of these contradictory findings?

We believe that in order to understand the socioemotional effects of passing or disclosure, we need to include an additional variable that takes account of the individual's social context. Being openly gay can be personally liberating, but it is not adaptive in every situation. Passing may help the individual to avoid negative social consequences, but exacts its toll in the stresses due to secrecy. The deciding factor in selecting an optimal strategy may be the *supportiveness of the individual's environment.*

In its simplest terms, this idea states that being open is adaptive for individuals in environments that support a gay self-identity, and maladaptive in environments that do not. However, assessing the supportiveness of an individual's environment is a complex task. The assessment needs to consider more than just the social and political climate of the particular locale. For example, even in an enlightened urban environment, rich with supportive services and liberal attitudes, if the individual's family, social, and work networks are homophobic, the individual's environment can be said to be unsupportive. The converse holds true for repressive rural locales. This may explain the ease with which some gay people have openly gay relationships in very conservative rural areas. In assessing the supportiveness of the environment, we will want to consider such factors as the presence of social or work network members who hold homophobic attitudes; the values of the individual's family; and the effects of religious, cultural, or ethnic beliefs and attitudes about homosexuality on the gay person and on those around him.

Adding to the complexity of assessing the supportiveness of the individual's environment is the observation that individuals are embedded in multiple, overlapping environments that may differ in their supportiveness toward homosexuality. For example, many gay men who have highly supportive family and social networks, may also interact within homophobic work environments. That is why so many gay men employ a "selective" coming out strategy. Thus, in addition to assessing the supportiveness of the individual's environment, it is also necessary to consider the groups to whom the individual is "out."

In *Gay and Gray* Berger first suggested the novel idea that older gay men may actually be freer to be open in their various environments. For example, they are less likely to have parents still living, or parents who would view the news of their son's homosexuality as a crisis. Hence they are more free within their families. They also may be freer to reveal their orientation in work settings where they are sufficiently well established to deflect potential harm; or as retirees, these concerns may simply not be relevant to them. This pattern would explain Berger's finding in *Gay and Gray*, that contrary to popular conceptions, compared to younger gay men, older gays were more widely known to others as gay, and were less worried about being exposed as homosexual.

Of course, as Lee (1987) noted, one must also consider cohort effects in assessing the role of passing in the lives of older gay men. Given their unique histories, the experiences of future cohorts may be different. For example, the last decade of this century represents the first time that gay men who have not experienced the severe homophobia of the first half of this century, will be entering their fifties. In the future, fewer and fewer gay men of all ages may be willing to pass as heterosexual.

WHY ARE THERE SO FEW ORGANIZATIONS AND SERVICES FOR OLDER GAY MEN?

With some chagrin, John Alan Lee (1989) noted that older homosexuals are "invisible," even in the gay community itself. Lee described the failure of emerging support groups for older gay men to attract participation, and their resulting demise. He bemoaned the dearth of age-specific social service groups and community organizations for older gay men. Although Lee was describing his experience in Toronto, the same can be said for American cities. The absence of groups for older gay men is especially notable, given the great number and variety of groups for younger gay men (Lee, 1989, p. 92).

Lee (1989) criticized the notion that homosexuals have advantages over heterosexuals in aging. He asked, "If gay elders are so 'advantaged' then why do they have such difficulty getting organized and developing a niche for themselves in 'liberated' gay communities?" (p. 81).

But of course, there is no logical connection between the advantages of gay aging and the presence of senior-specific organizations. In fact, it could be argued that if gay men adapt well to aging–even better than their heterosexual counterparts–then senior-specific gay organizations may not have developed because there has been little need for them. Still, we cannot easily dismiss Lee's observation.

There are probably many reasons for the absence of senior-specific organizations in the gay community. It is not necessarily due, as Lee implies, to the socioemotional difficulties faced by gay men who have grown old, nor to the reluctance of younger gay men to associate with older gay men. It may be due in part to the more general phenomenon of disengagement from active participation in community life. This explanation reflects the gerontological perspective called disengagement theory (Cumming and Henry, 1961). It is also consistent with Berger's finding in *Gay and Gray* that older gay men were less likely than younger ones to participate in public aspects of the gay community.

On the other hand, Lee presented at least some evidence that the invisibility of older gay men may be due less to disengagement and more to other factors. Among his forty-seven older respondents, although two-thirds were involved in at least one non-gay organization, fewer than a third participated in a gay organization.

So it is quite possible that older gay men become invisible because they are rejected, or more likely ignored, by younger gays. As Berger noted in *Gay and Gray,* this tendency is fueled by the prevalent belief among older gay men themselves that younger gays will reject them. Expecting rejection, they may find it. Or they simply may not try to join what appears to them to be a youth-dominated community.

Although this sort of mutual avoidance and rejection certainly goes on, we are not sure how much of it there is. We suspect that the most important reason for the absence of senior-specific groups is that increasingly, older gay individuals are finding their places in the burgeoning groups and service agencies within the gay community.

It is true that some parts of the gay community have been inhospitable to older gays–most notably the sexual marketplace settings such as bars, bathhouses, and some social clubs. But most other parts of the gay community are attracting increasing numbers of older gay men. And as the gay community becomes more diverse, the older gay man is able to choose from a wider range of options. To the churches, political organizations, social service agencies, and clubs have been added a dizzying array of groups formed to meet the interests of subgroups in the gay community. These include, for example, such interest groups as computer bulletin board clubs, travel services, fathers' support groups, science fiction clubs, gay Toastmasters, and so on. It is inevitable that older gay men will take advantage of these options. And of course, as today's actively participating gay men grow older themselves, gay community groups are likely to continue to see the participation of older members.

DO OLDER GAY MEN HAVE MORE IN COMMON WITH OLDER HETEROSEXUAL MEN THAN WITH OLDER WOMEN?

After many years of observing and participating in the gay community we are struck by a surprising reality: Age and gender are more important than sexual orientation in determining most behaviors and attitudes.

For example, despite differences between older gays and older heterosexuals, the factors that determine happiness in one's later years appear to be the same for both groups. Older persons fare best when they have sufficient finances, good health, and enough social and family contact to avoid isolation and loneliness. In a study of gay men over fifty, Gray and Dressel (1985) concluded that identical cultural- and age-related factors affect older gay and heterosexual men. For example, the emphasis on youth in both the gay subculture and society-at-large may cause some homosexual and heterosexual older men to feel negatively about their own age and the physical changes that accompany it. (Although, Gray and Dressel reported that the majority of older gay men managed to express some positive feelings about growing older and about their appearance.)

The sexual activity of both older gay and heterosexual men may be determined more by what Gray and Dressel (1985) call subcultural opportunity, than it is by sexual orientation. They note that compared to younger gay men, older gays are more likely to have had a wider age range of partners, and are more likely to have paid for sex. But this is likely due to the fact that older gays have been homosexually active for a longer period of time, and have therefore had greater opportunities to experience a full range of diverse sexual options. These factors also determine the sexual experience of heterosexuals. So, older heterosexuals, like older gay men, are more likely than their younger counterparts to have histories of sexual experience with younger partners. Although the culture at large tends to look with alarm at "May-December" relationships among gay men, such relationships are accepted among heterosexuals, at least when the man is older. In fact, the older man-younger woman liaison is almost a cultural institution. Gray and Dressel suggest that the factors that underlie these age-diverse relationships are not so different for gay men.

One finding of the *Gay and Gray* study that surprised us was the continued high levels of sexual activity among gay men over forty. On the face of it, this may seem like a characteristic that distinguishes older gay men from older heterosexuals. But ironically, it may be a characteristically male approach to sexuality that underlies this phenomenon.

Men–homosexual and heterosexual–approach the issue of sexual attraction and sexual activity with a similar mentality that is quite distinct from the approach of women. Men are more sexually aggressive than women. They often feel that they must initiate sexual contact, and that sustained sexuality activity is a test of masculinity and self-concept. While this "conquest" mentality is common among men, it is rare among women.

Changes in sexual functioning that accompany aging are potentially traumatic for both homosexual and heterosexual men, who share a common adherence to a virile identity, and the common problem of maintaining this virile self-image in the face of the "feminizing" changes of age-related diminished capacity. Men are more likely than women to define sexual desirability in their partners in terms of physical appearance, conformance to a physical ideal, and possession of youth. Despite propaganda that demonizes the "dirty old gay man," the high levels of sexual activity among this group may be due to the dynamics that inevitably ensue in a situation where men–with their particular approach to sexuality– choose other men as objects of sexual choice.

WHAT WILL THE FUTURE BE LIKE?

Prognostication is a dangerous business. And we profess no special skills in predicting what life will be like for older gay men in the future. However, we have observed several trends, that if continued, will lead to dramatic changes for gay people. In this prologue we have space only to suggest what some of these changes may be.

1. Chronic Illness Will Play an Increasing Role in the Lives of Gay Men of All Ages.

With the increases in life expectancy achieved in the first part of this century, as well as more recent advances in medicine, we have created an increasingly large population of older persons with chronic medical conditions. Currently, older persons comprise the age group most likely to have chronic illnesses. But in the future, chronic illnesses may affect all age groups. AIDS comes to mind. As treatments improve, and as a cure continues to elude scientists, AIDS will become more of a chronic, rather than a terminal illness. But other medical conditions are likely to follow.

The current cohort of thirty to fifty year olds is the first generation exposed to the new chemical age that began shortly after the Second World War. Through its exposure to pesticides, industrial chemicals, ozone depletion, and a host of other influences, this generation, and those following it, are likely to experience higher levels of chronic illness than has been the case in the past.

As a result of these changes, the gay community and the larger society will have a much greater awareness of health behaviors, and there will be a great deal of community education on this topic. Our own chronic illnesses and those of our friends and loved ones will teach us powerful lessons about human dignity and coping. There will be renewed interest in issues of death and dying, not just among gerontologists, but among everyone.

2. Lesbians Will Assume an Increasing Role in the Leadership of Gay Community Groups and Lesbian Participation in the Gay Community Will Increase Dramatically.

This has already happened, as many gay men, including community leaders, have fallen ill and died of AIDS. This change has also been fueled by the increased participation of lesbians in the many social service networks created within the last decade in order to care for persons with AIDS.

Gay men, including older gay men, will be interacting a great deal more with lesbians and with lesbian community institutions. This, combined with lesbian women's greater intolerance of sexism, will force gay men to confront their own sexist and anti-lesbian attitudes. They will need to do this on a personal level, to allow them to work successfully side-by-side with lesbians; and they will need to re-orient their community education, social services, and recreational organizations to accommodate lesbians.

In the future, the particular health concerns of lesbians, long ignored by gay men, will come to the fore. The most apparent example of this is the insistence of many lesbian organizers that the gay community focus as much attention on the epidemic of breast cancer as they currently do on AIDS. There is potential for polarization and factionalizing between gay men and lesbians, as each group pursues its particular community health concerns.

3. Older Gay Men Will Become a Large Part of Gay Community Institutions.

Early gay liberation groups in the 1970s were dominated by young gay men. This first generation of gay activists is now entering middle age. The general aging of the larger population will be reflected in the gay community. As older gay men become more common in the public institutions of the gay community, they will also become more accepted. Even the traditionally youth-oriented bars and social clubs will increasingly cater to the more numerous and affluent older gay men.

4. Gay Men Will Increasingly Adopt Traditional "Family Values."

This trend will be most pronounced among gay men beginning in their middle aged years. The AIDS pandemic has already changed the approach of many gay men toward sexuality and relationships. It has revived the notions of sexual exclusivity and relationship building. Gay men and gay community education will focus less on recreational sex and more on finding and maintaining relationships. These trends reflect greater concerns about avoiding the infections that result from multiple sexual contacts. But they also reflect changing values as the gay men who survive the AIDS epidemic reevaluate their attitudes toward other gay men as sexual objects versus friends and family. In a crisis, only friends and family count.

More and more gay men will become parents. They will be creative in the methods they use to create nontraditional families. Many will form family units with lesbians who also desire children. Complex issues will need to be resolved related to: adoptions, foster care, sperm donation, artificial insemination by donor, child support, and child rearing responsibilities.

5. Senior-Specific Gay Social Service Agencies Will Continue to be Rare.

Rather than turning to senior-specific aging services, older gay men will be able to obtain services from both gay and mainstream social service agencies in their own communities. Gay agencies will expand their outreach and service delivery to older gays. But the most significant change will be that mainstream agencies will "discover" that among the senior citizens they have traditionally served, are many gay and lesbian clients. These clients will continue to be served, but they will be more open about their sexual identities, and senior service agencies will, for the first time, include them in their planning, outreach, education, and service programs.

6. The Aging of the Gay Population Will Enhance the Political Clout of Urban Gay Communities.

The greater tendency for older persons to vote will enhance "gay power," but this will be offset somewhat by the effect of AIDS mortality in decreasing the numbers of gay men. Lesbians will grow as a political force. More openly gay and lesbian persons, including older persons, will run for political office. These politicians will need to convince voters that they represent a much broader range of interests than those specific to the gay community. This will "normalize" the gay and lesbian political block and make gay constituencies much like the more traditional constituencies of ethnic and racial groups.

7. Older Gays Will Play an Increasing Role in the Environmental Movement.

The link between environmental degradation, immune dysfunction, and human illness has not yet entered the public consciousness in any significant way. Because gay men have been disproportionately affected by AIDS–the first major public health threat clearly identified with immune dysfunction–they are likely to be among the first to understand the connection between environmental change and human health. They will be prompted by lesbian groups, some of whom are already addressing other health issues linked to immune dysfunction and environmental pollution–most notably Chronic Fatigue Syndrome and Multiple Chemical Sensitivities, immune dysfunctions that have hit hardest in the women's community. Older gays and lesbians, particularly those who are retired and have the time for political activity, will become an important force in the larger environmental movement.

CONCLUSION

What is it like to be gay and gray? We are better prepared to answer this question today than we were over a decade ago when *Gay and Gray* was first published. But we are still confronted with many questions. Why is aging a process of fulfillment for some gay men and a nightmare for others? How do, and how should, older gay men and young gay men interact with one another? What are the benefits and costs of concealing our sexual orientation and preserving our privacy? Why have older gay men been loathe to organize? How do gender, age, and sexual orientation combine to create our life experiences? Is being gay really an advantage in adjusting to old age? And what about the very old–those seventy and above–who have only been studied in very small numbers, while researchers have focused on the more resilient young-old. What do we know of the very old? And what will the future bring for all of us?

It is one of the prerogatives of youth to believe that old age will bring with it the answers for which we long. But old age brings with it instead many new questions, and hopefully, the dignity to ponder them, unanswered.

SECOND EDITION

In this second edition of *Gay and Gray* we have reprinted four chapters that present additional perspectives on the reality of gay aging. All but the first were published in 1990, eight years after the publication of the first edition of *Gay and Gray*.

The first chapter, by Fred Minnigerode, is a classic. Berger discovered this work on age-status labeling in homosexual men, several years before he wrote *Gay and Gray*. He subsequently met with Dr. Minnigerode to discuss his findings. These experiences sparked his interest in gay aging and ultimately led him to conduct the research study described in *Gay and Gray*. Based on interviews with gay men of all ages, Dr. Minnigerode showed that older gay men did not perceive themselves as growing older faster any more than did their heterosexual counterparts. This study also showed that the age of forty was a watershed for most gay men: It was the age at which most gay men believed that the label "young" no longer applied. This led Berger and other researchers to define "older" gay men as those over forty.

In *Gay and Gray*, interview respondents described what their lives had been like as gay men. But the book did not explore the cultural divide between today's older gay man and his younger counterpart. John Grube's chapter on the interaction of older gay men with younger gay liberationists fills this gap. In this study of older gay men, Grube argues that these men made up a "traditional gay community," distinct in values and attitudes from today's "lib-

erated" or "organized gay community." As we have suggested
earlier in this prologue, this dichotomy between "pre-liberation"
and "post-liberation" cultures is overdrawn. It nevertheless provides us with a glimpse into the histories of the older men presented
in *Gay and Gray,* and helps us to understand the attitudes of at least
some of today's older gay men toward the gay community.

As Berger did in *Gay and Gray,* Mark Pope and Richard Schulz
asked older gay men to report on and evaluate their sex lives. We are
all to be excused for prying into this private domain. But it is a most
intriguing inquiry, especially in light of the stereotype of the sexless
and unhappy older gay man. Happily, Pope and Schulz confirmed
Berger's finding that for most gay men a continuation of sexual activity and sexual enjoyment is the norm. Unfortunately, both this study
and *Gay and Gray* were based on data gathered prior to the AIDS
epidemic. A study of the sexual behavior of this group in the AIDS era
is sorely needed, particularly since advanced age confers no protection
against infection. In addition, neither study shed much light on the
sexual adjustment of the very old–those seventy-five and older.

Richard Friend's chapter on a theory of successful gay aging is a
fitting conclusion to this second edition of *Gay and Gray.* Friend
summarizes much of current thinking about gay aging. He proposes
that, for gay men and lesbians, the aging process may take any one
of three routes. There are "stereotypic" older gays and lesbians
who internalize society's homophobia; "affirmative" older gays
who hold positive, accepting self-concepts; and "passing" older
gays who fall somewhere in between. Our own instincts tell us that
this model is too simple to describe the full range of experiences we
have discovered in coming to know many older gay men and
women. Nevertheless, Friend's model is a good starting point for
research, and perhaps a good model for understanding the needs of
this group and for designing appropriate services. In a broad but
appealing way, Friend goes on to tie together knowledge from several areas–individual psychology, social and interpersonal experiences, and political advocacy–into a comprehensive theory of successful gay aging.

When *Gay and Gray* was first published in 1982, there were
almost no studies or scholarly papers on this topic. That is no longer
true today. The papers reprinted here, and the continued interest in

Gay and Gray over a decade after its first appearance, attest to the fascination that both scholars and lay readers attach to this topic. It is a fascination that will never end for us.

Raymond M. Berger, PhD

James J. Kelly, PhD
Director and Professor,
Department of Social Work,
California State University,
Long Beach

CHAPTER 1

Introduction

*On the outside we are old and
shriveled, but on the inside we are
twenty-two years old.*

Dispel fear through understanding.

In 1962 Michael Harrington startled the nation with publication of *The Other America,* which revealed that millions of Americans lived in extreme poverty. Somehow, only the poor themselves had noticed. The situation of older homosexuals today is analogous in that they, as a large minority, are usually ignored. The increasing attention which is now being paid to the elderly, and to homosexuals as a group, has not extended to older homosexuals. When gerontologists talk about the elderly, they mean heterosexual elderly; when gay rights advocates talk about homosexuals, they mean young homosexuals. The homosexuals who began to disclose their identities publicly on a large scale in the 1970s were mostly young; they now constitute the public stereotype of the homosexual, while large numbers of their elders continue their lives unnoticed.

Despite the predominance of younger people in the public gay community–the bars, clubs, social and political organizations–there are as many older as younger homosexuals (Kinsey, Pomeroy, and Martin, 1948). If we assume that 10 percent of the adult male population is homosexual (Kimmel, 1978), then there are nearly a million homosexual men over the age of sixty-five in our country today.

There are, of course, many older lesbians as well. The older female homosexual has remained hidden to an even greater extent than has her male counterpart; this is reflected in the newly emerging literature on the older homosexual, which focuses primarily on the male. The older women are simply less accessible to the probing eye of the researcher. As Chapter 9 explains, we were unable to collect sufficient information on the older lesbian and therefore decided to limit *Gay and Gray* to males. In so doing we do not intend to contribute to the trend to ignore this group. Some female researchers have been more successful in studying the older lesbian (e.g., Robinson, 1979; Wolf, 1978) and the task of enlightening us about this group may have to be left to them.

The invisibility of the older homosexual is unfortunate for a number of reasons. First, although homosexuals contribute as taxpayers throughout their working lives, they are shortchanged when it comes to publicly funded social services. This has become more apparent as the variety and availability of services for the elderly have increased–services such as day care, bereavement counseling, and nursing home placement.

Consider the older homosexual whose lover of thirty years dies. As we will show later, most homosexuals make special efforts to maintain friendships which may substitute for kin relations in providing support during crises. But for a variety of reasons these friendship supports may be unavailable, or the older man may face special emotional or legal problems that require professional help. Many agencies which serve the elderly recognize these needs for the elderly heterosexual and provide services such as bereavement counseling, widows' support groups, and legal assistance. However, the presumption that all elderly persons are heterosexual leaves these agencies unprepared to deal with the unique situation of the older homosexual.

Will helping professionals be too shocked or uncomfortable with older homosexual clients to be of help? Will they be familiar with homosexual lifestyles and relationship patterns so that their interventions will be based on knowledge, rather than on stereotypes? Will they be aware of the limited resources available in the gay community for their older clients?

Second, the invisibility of older homosexuals within the gay community itself is unfortunate. As our research and that of others shows, older homosexuals are less likely to be involved in the civil rights organizations, social clubs, bars, and bathhouses of the gay community. Part of this is due to the older person's desire to disengage from active participation in the community, and part is due to the lack of hospitality afforded to older homosexuals by their younger counterparts who dominate the public gay community. In any case, the results are clear. The gay community does not have the opportunity to take advantage of the knowledge and leadership skills of older people, and younger gays do not have role models of successful gay aging to counter the myths about the horrors of being gay and gray.

Third, older homosexuals are isolated from each other. In organizing a support group for older homosexual men, we became aware of the great need for these men to associate with their peers and of the absence of such opportunities. We met several couples and individuals who had spent years trying unsuccessfully to meet other older homosexuals; they felt they had little in common with the heterosexual elderly and with younger gays at the bars and in political groups, yet they had not figured out how to meet older homosexuals in other settings.

The older homosexual, however, has not remained totally invisible. Unfortunately, where he has been described, stereotypes predominate: he becomes increasingly effeminate with age, he is alienated from friends and family alike, and he lives alone, not by choice but by necessity. At thirty he is old. Since he is no longer sexually attractive to other homosexuals, he is forced to prey on children and to pursue anonymous sexual contacts in public places such as restrooms and parks. He is desperately unhappy.

Even within the gay community the older homosexual is despised and feared: "I never knew his name. He lived somewhere on the floor above us, rather anonymously. . . . I only know a few things about him. He wore too many rings. He liked cats and Mozart. He was gentle-mannered and fastidious, and he scared me half to death. That was because he was everything I was afraid I was going to be: an 'auntie'" (Kantrowitz, 1976).

These stereotypes serve a social control function. They are a deterrent to selection of a homosexual lifestyle, particularly for young people who have no role models of successful homosexual elders. Saghir and Robins (1973), for instance, found that most homosexual men were apprehensive about aging and did not believe they would grow old "gracefully." So the elderly homosexual remains a tragic figure, both in the professional literature and in the popular media.

However, in the past few years several researchers have unearthed some startling findings about the older homosexual. Weinberg and Williams (1975), in a questionnaire study of 1,117 homosexual men, found that although homosexuals over forty-five did not differ from younger homosexuals in most aspects of psychological adjustment, in some ways the older men were healthier; they were less worried about exposure of their homosexuality, less likely to desire psychiatric treatment, and had more stable self-concepts. Kelly (1977) found that few homosexual men over sixty-five fit prevailing negative stereotypes, and that most reported satisfactory social and sex lives. A comparative study of older homosexual and heterosexual men and women by Minnigerode and Adelman (1976) showed that these groups did not differ in morale, although homosexual men and women were lonely more often. Minnigerode (1976), asking ninety-five homosexual men of all ages to describe themselves as "young," "middle-aged," or "old," found no evidence that homosexual men perceived themselves as aging sooner than heterosexuals. A similar conclusion was reached by Laner (1978), based on analysis of "personals" advertisements by homosexual men. She also found that homosexuals were no more likely than heterosexuals to seek younger partners.

Our study intended to examine the situation of the older homosexual male in light of stereotypes of gay aging, and to do this more thoroughly than earlier researchers had. Although a great deal of research has described older people and homosexuals, our intention was to extend this knowledge to people who are both older *and* homosexual. In addition, we wanted to determine the level of psychological adjustment of this group, and to identify factors associated with good adjustment.

In order to gain a comprehensive understanding of older gay men, we used two methods to collect information. We asked 112 men to complete an extensive questionnaire, and from this group we selected ten men to be interviewed. In selecting these ten men we attempted to reflect the wide diversity of backgrounds and lifestyles which characterizes this group. The questionnaire findings provided us with statistical information from which we drew generalizations about older gay men. While these data are certainly important, we chose to go beyond a questionnaire so that we could examine the depth and complexity of gay aging, bringing to life the uniqueness of each man we came to know in the course of this study.

Part I presents the findings of the interview study. Chapter 2 describes the interview process and summarizes what we learned by comparing and contrasting interviewees. Chapters 3 to 8 contain the life stories and perspectives of six interviewees, again chosen for their diversity. Each man is unique, yet these stories are tied together by the common theme of a lifelong struggle for self-acceptance in an unaccepting world. The stories are reproduced for the reader much the way they were told to us. While details are altered to guarantee anonymity, the respondents' own words are used throughout.

The questionnaire study and its findings are the subject of Part II. Chapter 9 describes the questionnaire as well as the procedures used to recruit respondents, while Chapters 10 and 11 contain a detailed presentation and discussion of the questionnaire findings. Chapter 10 focuses on describing older gay men in terms of demographic information and a range of social psychological variables such as sexual orientation, living situation, relationships, psychological adjustment, and concealment of homosexuality. Within the perspective of societal reaction theory and earlier research on homosexuality, Chapter 11 attempts to identify personal characteristics associated with positive adaptation to aging for gay men. Chapter 12 summarizes our findings about gay aging and discusses their implications in relation to the diversity of this group, prejudice, adaptation to aging, psychosocial problems, and service and policy considerations.

PART I: THE INTERVIEW STUDY

CHAPTER 2

The Interview
Respondents

I would be very frustrated if I were perpetually young. It would be boring to stay the same, just as it would be boring if it were summer all the time.

I was working out every day to get my figure back in shape. One day my son said to me, "Daddy, what good is it going to be? Who wants to have an eighteen-year-old body and a sixty-year-old face?"

The best thing about growing older is all the special privileges you get. Instead of being blamed, you are excused.

This chapter presents our findings from in-depth interviews with ten older homosexual men. My research assistant and I conducted the interviews individually in 1978, in locations selected by the interviewees. We listened to the stories of these men while sitting on stools at a gay bar that had not yet opened for business early one Sunday morning. We recorded conversations in lovely homes and humble apartments; we met in the privacy of a small university office, and in a meeting room of a local gay organization. The interviews lasted from one to one and three-quarter hours. All sessions were tape recorded, and a brief introduction was read to each interviewee to explain the purpose of the interview and to give assurance of anonymity.

Many of the questions on the interview schedule also appeared in similar form on the questionnaire, which is discussed in Part II. However, in the interview, the respondent was asked to elaborate on the question. For instance, both the questionnaire and the interview schedule asked him to *describe* his current social life, but the interview schedule also asked him to discuss how he *felt* about his social life and to explore ways in which it might be different.

The interview schedule consisted of open-ended questions grouped into fourteen clusters, each cluster relating to one topic (such as "coming out," or involvement with family). The least personal question clusters (concerning social life, involvement with homosexual community) were generally presented first in order to establish rapport, while more personal questions (about coming out and sex life) appeared later in the interview schedule. However, the order of questions varied in each interview, since the interviewer followed topics as they were introduced by the respondent, in order to maintain the natural flow of the interview. Questions asking the interviewee to evaluate his life and to share his thoughts about the aging process came at the end and provided closure.

For clarity in the following discussion, the question clusters appear as follows. First we present some general observations and demographic data on age, marital status, presence of a lover, current living arrangements, retirement status, and health. We then discuss the coming-out process, explain the variety of definitions attributed to this term, and review events such as the first sexual experience, self-realization, and being open with others. Involvement with immediate family (parents, siblings, spouse, and children) is explored next, followed by a description of involvement in gay organizations, bars, and other aspects of the public gay community. Discussion of social life focuses on the extent to which the interviewees socialize with heterosexuals versus homosexuals, and with age peers versus younger people. We then look at their current sex lives: relationship to partner or partners, changes brought about by age, and level of satisfaction. Next we examine feelings about younger gays and beliefs about how young and old regard each other. We describe instances of discrimination based on both sexual preference and age. Finally, we present life-review material: how these men evaluate their lives, how they view the aging process, and how they believe gay men can adapt more easily to that process. (See Appendix B for a copy of the interview schedule.)

GENERAL OBSERVATIONS AND DEMOGRAPHIC DATA

Each older man we interviewed was singular in some way. Each had a unique perspective or life experience to share, and each contributed to our understanding. The case histories presented in the next six chapters allow us to share with readers the uniqueness and complexity of human experience. These stories add depth to the questionnaire study findings presented in Chapters 10 and 11.

Some of the men shared fascinating stories. Most shared feelings. Some concentrated on the present; others chose to speak more of the past. Although all were asked the same questions, we allowed each to set his own pace. Each respondent was encouraged to focus on and elaborate on those aspects of his story which were most significant to him. As a result, some interviewees omitted or glossed over topics or events that would have provided a more complete picture. For instance, one man who left his wife for a male lover provided little detail on his wife's reaction. It is impossible to determine whether this omission was due to the issue's unimportance to him, or to painful feelings associated with the separation. In defense of our method, we believe that by allowing each man to tell his own story we produced a highly accurate account of how older homosexual men view themselves, thereby fulfilling the purpose of the interviews. More systematic study of selected issues was left to the questionnaire study.

In the interviews we appreciated the ways in which these men helped us to understand their innermost feelings. This was often done by reminiscing. One man recalled, "Let me see if I can help you understand. When I was young and I'd go to a movie involving a girl and a fellow in love, sometimes I'd come out crying like a fool . . . and not because it ended sadly. It was because I was as much in love with that handsome man on the screen as Bette Davis was. So I wasn't crying for her. I was crying *with* her."

Some statements by the same person may appear contradictory. That should not hamper our understanding, however, if we keep in mind the aspects of our own lives about which we ourselves may not be completely clear.

One frequently expressed thought was that homosexuality was accepted when a man operated from an internal feeling that loving another person could not be bad. The culprit was not his love, but society's lack of love. No doubt all would have agreed with the observation of a soldier dishonorably discharged for being a homosexual: "The army gave me a medal for killing a man and threw me out for loving one."

The men we interviewed ranged in age from forty-four to seventy-two years. Seven had never been married, and two had experienced lengthy and difficult divorces in their attempts to assume gay lifestyles after years of marriage. In one case the decision to live a gay life was made when the individual was in his forties; the other was in his fifties. One man was currently married and chose to keep his gay life separate from his family life–neither his wife of thirty years nor his young adult children knew of his homosexuality. But none of our other respondents felt the need to manage identities in two different worlds, as suggested by some stereotypes of homosexual men. Most of them would probably agree with one man who said, "I don't feel a need to show other people I'm gay. But if anyone asked, I'd tell them right out!"

The interview study illustrates that the stereotype of the lonely, unwanted, and isolated older gay man is inaccurate. Half of the men we interviewed currently had lovers of long standing. One man boasted that, the day after the interview, he and his "mate" would be celebrating eighteen years together. All five of these men lived with their lovers–one on a part-time basis, since his lover had to be in another city for business regularly. The remaining five did not currently have lovers, but all except one had had a lover for at least a year, and often for many years. In some cases lovers had drifted apart, separated for personal reasons, or died. The one man who had never had a male lover was heterosexually married and limited his contacts to brief relationships so as not to threaten his marriage.

Living alone was not the norm. In fact, none of our interviewees could really be described as living alone. Four lived with a lover on a regular basis, and one did so on a part-time basis. One man lived alone, but his ex-lover, who remained a close personal friend, lived in an adjoining apartment. The remaining men lived with one or more gay roommates.

Four of the men were fully retired. Two conducted business from their own homes and were able to partially retire. All of these men enjoyed retirement and expressed satisfaction at being able to pursue interests they had developed earlier in life. Four men were working fulltime, and all liked their jobs. Two had low-status employment (such as unskilled laborer), seven held medium-status jobs (such as sales clerk), and one held a high-status professional position. In the case histories which follow, the interviewees' occupations were modified to preserve their anonymity.

All the men were in good health, except two in their seventies who had chronic health problems associated with advanced age.

COMING OUT

The men were asked about their experiences in coming out as homosexuals. Because there are a variety of definitions for "coming out," we began by asking our interviewees to specify what "coming out" meant to them. Three related definitions emerged. Some believed that coming out referred to one's first sexual encounter with another man. Others felt it referred to being open with others about one's homosexuality. This openness might be limited to family or close friends, or it might extend to all situations. This stance was described as "openness and honesty with others," "exposing oneself as a homosexual to the outside world," and "being ready to acknowledge in any social situation that one is gay." The third definition focused on self-recognition and self-acceptance. Sometimes recognizing one's homosexuality occurred long after having sex with another man; for example, one man who had a lengthy and passionate affair with a college buddy didn't come to recognize himself as a homosexual until years later. But self-recognition is only the first part of a process leading to self-acceptance. To one man, coming out was "knowing who I am and accepting myself the way I am."

All interviewees felt that coming out was one of their most significant life experiences. It could also be a very difficult and frightening step that was taken only after years of soul-searching. As one man expressed it, "Coming out is the easiest thing in the world to do. The hardest part is thinking about it."

We asked these men to describe their first same-sex sexual experience. All except one had the first such experience during early puberty or in adolescence. One man had his first experience at age twenty-one. Despite these early experiences, three of the men pursued heterosexual interests, married, and raised children before returning to same-sex interests in their forties and fifties. Contrary to the popular misconception that boys are recruited into homosexuality through the seduction of an older man, seven of these men had their first experiences with peers, usually friends from school or the neighborhood. Three men did have their first same-sex experience with an older man: one began having anal intercourse with his father at age thirteen, another engaged in mutual masturbation with a stepfather, and one had oral sex with a middle-aged man when he was seventeen. In all three instances the older man was remembered with kindness and without any hint of anger. The first man said of his father, "He was a very sexy man. He was the sweetest, kindest man I ever knew."

In asking our interviewees for their personal definitions of coming out, it became clear that there was often a gap between actual homosexual experience and self-labeling as homosexual. There may also be a gap between recognizing attraction to other men or boys and self-labeling. Particularly for older homosexuals, self-labeling may have been impeded because of secrecy surrounding this topic and the absence of role models. For instance, several interviewees described long periods of self-doubt during which each believed he was the only person in the world with such feelings.

In order to understand how these men came to be the way they are, we asked them to describe when they first realized they were attracted to the same sex, when they first admitted to themselves that they were gay, and when they began to know other gay people. Most of them remember being attracted to other boys at a very early age, usually during early adolescence. One man remembered being attracted to the male sex organ at the age of four or five. Most of them were aware of their attraction by age fifteen, one at seventeen, and one at twenty-one. One man was not in touch with these feelings until he "came out" in his fifties. All except for the latter came to identify themselves as homosexual by their early twenties. The oldest men in this group tended to reach self-identification as homosexual at a later age. This may be due to the bars, moviehouses, and other outlets which first appeared after World War II and coincided with the early adolescence of the younger men. The oldest men were forced to come to terms with their feelings when contact with other homosexuals was not readily available. Lacking contact with other self-identified homosexuals, they were less likely to think of themselves as homosexual.

Even same-sex experiences and self-recognition as a person attracted to men did not guarantee a clear homosexual identity. For this it was necessary for these men to associate with other self-identified homosexuals. Just as there was often a gap between same-sex behavior and self-identification, there may also have been a time lag between self-identification and integration into the homosexual community. This is particularly important, for (as we will show in the questionnaire study) being well integrated into a homosexual community is closely related to good psychological and social adaptation for older homosexual men–as it may be for younger men, too. The peer network serves as a source of emotional support and tends to validate the legitimacy of a homosexual lifestyle. One interviewee took advantage of his "older" appearance at the age of fourteen to attend gay bars and moviehouses where sex with other men was readily available. Two men, both heterosexually married, did not get to know other gay people until their forties and fifties respectively. The other interviewees became acquainted with other gay men during late adolescence or their twenties.

While associating with self-identified homosexuals can be a major factor in helping a man assume the self-definition of homosexual, such association is not always necessary. Although two of the married men did not meet other gays until their middle age, both realized their interests before seeking out the homosexual community. Still, finding other homosexual men who have "put the pieces of the puzzle together" certainly facilitates the process, as was illustrated by the touching story of one interviewee. After struggling through adolescence with fears of being a freak, he accidentally discovered that his own father, long dead, had also been homosexual. This discovery led to a meeting with his father's former lover which served as a turning point in this man's self-identification and self-acceptance.

INVOLVEMENT WITH FAMILY AND COMMUNITY

In recent years increasing attention has been paid to the gay person's family and the role it plays in impeding or enhancing the gay person's adjustment (Silverstein, 1977). How did the homosexuality of these men affect their family relationships? We asked our interviewees to describe their immediate families. Did these family members know of the interviewee's homosexuality and, if so, how had this affected the relationship?

Six of the men had never shared their homosexuality with their families. In two cases parents had died long before the individual was aware of his own sexuality. One man had made a conscious decision years earlier to hide his homosexuality from his wife and children: "I can handle it, but they couldn't. It would be selfish of me to confront them." Four men had openly revealed their homosexuality to parents or a spouse. One had a mother and father who were both supportive; another had had regular sex relations with his father while his mother, aware of the situation, had remained silent. Two of the men had revealed their homosexuality to their wives. Although their openness was beneficial in the long run, both were faced with hostile, unaccepting wives who used the revelation as a weapon. One wife spread gossip which damaged her husband's career; the other used her husband's homosexuality to win a divorce and to prevent his visitation with the children. Although these sorts of reactions may not be typical, they do illustrate the vulnerability of gay people, especially in situations where they are extricating themselves from unhappy marriages.

As we noted earlier, integration into a homosexual community is an important factor in the adaptation of older male homosexuals. We asked our interviewees if they were involved in gay rights groups, social service organizations, or churches. Hundreds of such organizations have sprung up all over the country in the past ten years, and they serve as an important source of social contact for homosexuals. All the men had participated regularly in one or more of these gay community institutions. One was a board member of a local gay rights group and devoted many hours each week to the organization. Another attended weekly meetings of this group "mostly as a social thing," although he had never been actively involved in a leadership position or attended a public rally. Two of the men had been very active in organizing gay rights groups, but both had left in protest, upset over the directions of their respective organizations. One objected to infighting, poor organization, and the preponderance of "low elements" (the unemployed, militants, etc.) in the organization. The other man was part of a religious group intended to provide support to gays; he left the organization feeling that some of the group's religious leaders actually condemned homosexuals.

Gay churches have been among the most successful gay organizations. The largest of these is the Metropolitan Community Church (MCC), which attracts worshipers of several denominations, primarily Protestant. MCC was first established by an openly gay minister, Troy Perry, in Los Angeles in the late 1960s. Today MCC has member churches in dozens of towns and cities across the country. More of our interviewees (five) participated in MCC activities than in any other gay organization; one was a member of Integrity, a counterpart church for Episcopalians. The church, with its emphasis on spiritual values and community life, provides an environment much more hospitable to older gay people than do the youth-oriented civil rights groups. One will usually meet more older gays by visiting a church service or function than by visiting a civil rights group meeting, bar, or bathhouse.

Except for the two men who left their organizations under unhappy circumstances, interviewees tended to attach a great deal of importance to these fledgling gay community institutions. Although the limitations and problems of these organizations were recognized (particularly political infighting and poor organizational leadership), the organizations themselves were seen as vital to an awakening gay consciousness. As one man noted, "These civic organizations serve the gay community in the same way that other civic groups serve the straight community. We need to pull together all the different segments of the gay community–the lesbians and gay men, minorities, the S&M crowd, old and young–to work toward a common goal."

We also asked whether our interviewees frequented gay bars, bathhouses, and "cruising areas." These outlets have a much more sexual atmosphere in that they are used as resources for meeting other men, often (if not usually) for sexual contact. In a bar contacts can easily be limited to social purposes, whereas bathhouses and cruising areas are oriented quite specifically to sexual contact. In fact, three interviewees preferred the bathhouse to the bar because they disliked the game-playing and extended conversations that had to precede sexual contact in the "bar scene." In the bathhouse, sexual contact is made easily and quickly by men wandering into and out of steam rooms, pools, and orgy rooms. It is done without conversation and with minimal signaling. The participants generally go their separate ways afterward. Cruising areas are places in parks, on beaches, or in other public places where gay men come to pursue anonymous sex. The sex may take place behind a bush, in a car, or at the home of one of the participants. Men who prefer bathhouses to bars often frequent public cruising areas as well. Four interviewees frequented gay bathhouses regularly; these men also enjoyed bars on occasion. Two went to gay bars regularly but avoided the baths. Four rarely went to either, preferring to limit their sexual contact to a lover; if they could not have sex within the context of a relationship, they preferred to avoid it altogether.

SOCIAL AND SEX LIFE

Since contact with other gays is so important to the older gay man's adjustment, and since stereotypes about the absence of a social life are so prevalent, we were interested in learning about the social lives of these men. We found a very strong preference for socializing with other homosexuals, almost exclusively males. Five of the ten men reported that all of their friends were gay. The others did have some straight friends, but they made it clear that they socialized mostly with other gays. All of these men provided some rationale for the presence of straight friends–i.e., their business required socializing with heterosexual clients, they had made some straight friends at work, or all their straight friends were from a time before they came out.

Seven of the interviewees socialized only or mostly with age peers. Some felt they had nothing in common with younger people: "Why should they invite me to the park with them? I'm not interested in playing frisbee!" Some felt that younger people, especially those under twenty-five, were shallow or self-centered and hence not pleasant to be with. Others said that, although all their friends were age peers, they would like to meet younger people; they simply had not had the opportunity. Three of the men had extensive contacts with younger men. One man in his forties was involved with a series of men in their twenties; he paid for their sexual favors or provided living space for them. Another man socialized with many younger gays through his active involvement in a gay human rights group. The third man reported that he simply enjoyed the company of younger men and socialized equally with younger and older men.

The picture of the unhappy, isolated older gay man did not portray reality. Eight men said they were reasonably or very satisfied with their social lives. One felt that his social life would be improved if he met men of a higher caliber, professionals like himself, while the tenth felt that his jealous lover prevented him from socializing as widely as he would have liked.

We asked questions about sex lives as well. While one man had stopped having regular sexual relations due to surgery and related health problems, all the others continued to have sex with other men. These men fell into two groups. One group (six men) had sexual relations on a frequent basis, often daily or two or three times a week. Several of these men had regular relations with a steady lover and also with other men picked up in a bar, bathhouse, or cruising area. (These casual partners were referred to as "tricks.") The four men who regularly visited bathhouses might have sex with a number of men on one occasion or over the course of several visits in one month. Some contacts were also made through social functions and friendship networks.

The other group (three men) had sex infrequently. Typical was a man who had sex only about once a month, each time with his lover. One man said he limited his sex life because he was only interested in having sexual relations within the context of a meaningful relationship. One man also limited his sexual relations to close friends but felt that he would have sex more frequently if he had a car which would give him access to the bars.

We were interested in looking at the effects of age on the nature of gay men's sex lives. We asked our interviewees how their current sex lives compared with their sex lives as younger men. As in earlier studies (Bell and Weinberg, 1978; Weinberg and Williams, 1975), age seemed to be associated with a lower frequency of sexual relations. Six interviewees said they were having sex less often than in their younger days. Various reasons were given: difficulty due to illness, a jealous lover, inability to frequent bars. The most common sentiment expressed was, "The feelings and drives are just the same. Only the frequency is less." One man felt that although he now had sex less frequently, it was "just as enjoyable and meaningful as ever." Another reported that he was having as much sex with men in his newfound gay life as he did when living with his wife and having homosexual relations on the sly. Interestingly, three men reported that their current sex lives were *more* active. One attributed this to his positive attitude when meeting young men and his ability to attract them with attention and money. Another attributed his increased sex life to abandonment of his wife and assumption of a gay lifestyle. The third felt that the "bath era" made possible more sex than ever before.

Six respondents were satisfied with their current sex lives, among them men who had sex frequently and men who did not. Two who did not have sex frequently were satisfied because "sex is a low priority in my life" or because they "rarely thought about it." Four men expressed dissatisfaction with their current sex lives; three of these men complained that they would like to have sex more often. One man traced his dissatisfaction to the fact that he had not been able to find "true love" in a relationship.

We found a relatively high level of continuing sexual interest and activity in these older gay men, as well as a great range in frequency of sexual relations.

INTERGENERATIONAL ATTITUDES

A series of questions asked how younger gay people feel toward older gays, and vice versa. This is an important issue, since beliefs about others' evaluations can affect one's psychological adjustment (Weinberg and Williams, 1975). Age segregation in the gay community often prevents older and younger gay men from checking out their possibly erroneous assumptions about each other. Since most interviewees told us they socialized only or mostly with age peers, we were not surprised to find that half of them strongly believed that young gay men held negative attitudes toward their elders: "They don't want anything to do with us," "They think our sexual capacity is worn out," "They think we are old relics that ought to be stored away."

One older man who had no younger friends said he didn't have enough contact with younger gays to know how they felt. Two felt that younger gays were usually open to them, and they enjoyed the regular company of younger men. One believed that many younger gays had a "father fixation," i.e., that they sought older men as lovers to replace their own fathers. Another remembered that, as a young man, he had always felt attracted to older men, and that the young gays he met seemed to treat him nicely. One pointed out that although younger men might seem unfriendly at first, once approached they quickly became responsive.

It would be interesting to speculate on the reasons for such divergent perceptions of the young. It appears that those who made an effort to reach out to younger men found them receptive; those who avoided them could continue believing that the young are not interested in their elders. The older men who did socialize with younger gays noted the importance of a positive attitude: "Many older gay men are always lonely because they are afraid to take the risk of being rejected. If you take a cheerful and positive attitude, younger gays will be vying for your attention."

Five of our interviewees believed that most older gay men have negative attitudes toward younger gays. (Three of these men also believed that the young react negatively to older gays.) Two men talked about how the older man's physical attraction to young men can be coupled with negative feelings. These negative reactions were due to the belief that younger gays made older gays feel left out by ignoring them or not including them, and to the feeling that younger men often turn out to be physically attractive but boring company. A commonly expressed thought was, "A twenty-year-old hasn't been anywhere or done anything. What would we talk about?" On the other hand, three interviewees seemed to take a special delight in associating with younger men: "Most older gays love younger ones. They like to serve as guides or teachers to those with less experience"; "I almost prefer the company of gay men under twenty-five. They are more open and honest about their homosexuality, while many older gays are still hiding in the closet."

DISCRIMINATION

We asked these men to tell us whether they had been victims of discrimination due to sexual preference or age. Older gay men are the most likely to have been discriminated against on the basis of sexual preference, at some time in their lives. With age they have had the greatest number of opportunities to experience discrimination, and having lived through the intense homophobia of the 1940s and 1950s, they were most likely to have suffered its effects. Three men described specific instances of discrimination. One was denied a previously approved job promotion when his embittered wife spread gossip about his homosexuality. Two were dishonorably discharged from the military, one due to rumors and the other because of a conversation overheard by an officer. Another narrowly escaped a similar fate; he was reprieved by a military officer who happened to be homosexual himself.

One of the men who had been discharged from the military also described a series of other, more recent episodes of discrimination. Although this man was very "straight appearing," he experienced much discrimination because he was very open and at times assertive about his homosexuality and his relationship with his lover. He reported that he and his lover had been denied rental units on many occasions, that they had had difficulty securing joint charge accounts in local department stores, and that they had experienced harassment from some neighbors in their conservative working-class neighborhood. This man also felt that he had lost several jobs when his employers had learned that he was gay.

Most of the other men attributed their success in avoiding sexual-preference discrimination to their "straight" appearance and to the fact that they hid their homosexuality from "certain people," mostly employers and work associates. In fact, two of the interviewees were clearly offended by homosexuals who "flaunted their sexuality" (i.e., were effeminate or "obvious" in dress and appearance) and felt that such men deserved it if they were discriminated against. (This attitude was more common up through the 1960s, when secrecy was a prerequisite to survival. Any member of a secret homosexual clique who became "obvious" constituted a threat to others in the group, and was therefore excluded [Leznoff and Westley, 1967].) Two of the men attributed their lack of difficulty to the fact that men in their professions were commonly assumed to be homosexual, so no one seemed to care. In fact, one of these men, an interior designer, often had to deal with men (usually married) who made their business contingent on sexual relations.

But homosexuality had unanticipated effects in other arenas as well. Two men felt that their homosexuality was an asset in the military. As one explained, "There was a great society of homosexual men in the military, both enlisted men and officers. Knowing a gay officer could get you a promotion." This was not an isolated instance. During the course of the study, we were invited to a respondent's home to view a home movie; taken toward the end of World War II, it depicted a social gathering of homosexuals stationed in a certain area. The party was attended by well over a hundred soldiers.

Age can be a stigma just as difficult to bear as homosexuality. Four interviewees felt that they had been discriminated against due to age. In every instance the discrimination centered around an employer's refusal to hire our interviewee and in no instance was the man's sexual orientation known to the employer. One man now in his early seventies recalled the difficulty he had in finding a new job at age forty. The other three men were in their forties and fifties; all found that employers were reluctant to hire anyone over forty. Apparently employers believed that a younger employee could be hired for less money, that it would take longer to train an older person, and that the older employee would leave sooner, particularly if he was already close to retirement. Some employers even stated openly, "We want a younger person for the job." These men were bitter and resentful about age discrimination, and they felt that the assets of older workers were not sufficiently appreciated. In some ways age discrimination was actually *worse* than discrimination based on sexual preference. Men could hide the latter, but not the former.

LIFE REVIEW

In an attempt to understand how these men viewed their lives, we asked each to identify his most important personal accomplishment. This sort of life review or reminiscence has been identified as a necessary component of adjustment to aging (Pincus, 1970). Some men had obviously done this "reminiscing work" and were able to produce immediate answers; others took several minutes to decide. Two men quickly identified their relationship with a lover as their most important accomplishment. In both cases the relationships spanned two decades. Two of the men identified a career as their most important accomplishment. In both instances the important aspect was not career advancement or "success" measured in traditional terms, but the feeling of having helped others. Other responses were varied: "living up to my obligations to others," "the gay social service organization I helped to organize," "getting a few younger people started in life," "graduating from Alcoholics Anonymous and staying sober for ten years," and "raising three children and making them into fine human beings."

We also asked these men to identify the least satisfying aspect of their lives. Four men named issues related to the family. One man regretted that he had never become close to his brothers and sisters. Another felt that a bitter divorce, in which his wife brought his homosexuality into court, was the low point in his life. Still another– who lost both parents when he was six, and who had many years later learned that his father was gay–regretted not having known his parents. One man who carefully hid his homosexuality from his wife and adult children regretted the need for this charade. As one of these men said, "The homosexual is not readily accepted into his family. That is perhaps the greatest tragedy of being a homosexual. We need a right to belong to the families of the world."

Other least satisfying aspects of these men's lives included "flunking out of Weight Watchers," "never experiencing a total emotional commitment to another person," "being rejected by my church because I am homosexual," "not having accomplished what I had hoped to in my profession," and "having to go through years playing the role of a heterosexual just to please my family."

We were also interested in finding out how older gay men perceive the aging process. We asked them to tell us the worst and the best things about growing older. The most salient negative aspect centered around the physical losses that accompany old age. Seven men said deteriorating health, physical limitations, and loss of input from the senses were the worst aspects of growing older: "You can't do the things you did before. You can't get your things out of the bottom drawer of the dresser. You have to use the siderail to get up the stairs. You need glasses to read and you can't get around as quickly as you used to." Other negative aspects of aging were also mentioned: "Realizing that time is limited. It's like being forced to leave a party before the rest of the guests go," "watching my lover deteriorate after his stroke," "losing everyone you love," "losing your patience with things, feeling you've heard or seen it all before," "not being able to work after you are sixty-five," and "worrying about growing older."

But there are also many positive aspects about growing older, and in fact most of our interviewees seemed to take a special interest in talking about these. Most men mentioned what could be called the "privileges of age." As one man put it, when you are older, "you don't get blamed; you get excused." You are permitted to make mistakes and to forget things. You are offered special courtesies, such as the front seat of the car or the first place in line. Others come to you for advice and recognize the wisdom you have accrued over the years. You change from an active producer into a resource to whom others turn for information. One man recognized this with a touch of cynicism: "People make the rather silly assumption that because one has lived a lot, one knows a lot. I'm looking forward to using this more and more as I get older."

The interviewees also gave us insights into ways gay men become more self-accepting with age: "All the things that mattered so much when I was younger, all the little things that upset me, don't seem important any longer." "As I grow older I worry less and less about what others think." "Now I'm less frantic to get things done. I think to myself, I've gone through all that and thank God I don't have to face it again." "I'm more sure of myself now because I am able to draw on past experiences to help me out. I know myself better."

ADAPTATION

Since a major purpose of our study was to find out what makes gay men adjust well to growing older, we went right to the point and asked that question. Every interviewee stressed the need for a positive attitude toward the aging process; such an attitude about oneself was said to ease the pains of growing older. It is easier to stay active and involved with others if you project positive feelings, and this involvement helps in adjusting to age. The interviewees admonished other older gays to "tear the calendar off the wall. Don't celebrate birthdays, get beyond the age hang-up." "Don't assume that just because you are growing older that your social life or your sex life will fall apart." "Set goals for yourself and work toward them. Think positive." "If you think of yourself as a poor old man, you will become one." "Think of the future, don't live in the past."

Another major theme in response to this question was that there is no difference between heterosexuals and homosexuals in adjusting to age. They face the same issues: "Whether you are gay or straight doesn't make a difference. It's your attitude that makes the difference." Another man noted, "Any person who hasn't adjusted well to other aspects of his life won't adjust well to aging, either. Being gay is just the icing on the cake." These comments are particularly interesting in light of the sometimes intense propaganda which claims that aging is much worse for homosexuals than for heterosexuals. Apparently these ten older homosexual men have rejected such stereotypical notions.

Two interviewees felt that older persons can ease their adjustment by not restricting their activities to older people. They should remain open to younger people and learn to accept their differences as aspects of a different generation, raised in different times. As one of these men explained, "Going out and meeting younger people keeps *you* young." One interviewee, however, did not agree with this advice. He felt that pursuing younger people would only lead to frustration; attempts to relate to younger gays would only lead to rejection, since they are not interested in older men. This man felt it was best to socialize with age peers who are more likely to share common interests.

Several men stressed the importance of accepting the changes that come with age, rather than trying to fight them. "Accept your age. Don't lie to yourself or your friends about your age. If you need to use the siderail to get up the stairs–go ahead and use it. If it's time to go to bed, do it. Be honest with yourself about the changes as you grow older." "Accept the fact that other, younger people are taking over." "Realize that you may no longer be beautiful on the outside. It's time to work on the inside." Other practical advice was suggested: "Become interested in things other than your job." "Don't think only about yourself. Learn to get out of the spotlight." "Plan your retirement," and "Keep up a good sense of humor."

FOLLOW UP

After the interviews, these men were contacted in order to obtain written permission to use their stories. As before, our conversations with them revealed wide differences in values. In one case, when we explained that names, places, and occupations would be altered to ensure respondents' anonymity, we were assured that it would be unnecessary: "I'm gay. I've worked too long to accept that fact. At this point in my life, I don't care who knows." That view contrasted sharply with that of another man, who said, "You can only use my story if I see what you write first, and if you mix it up with someone else's story so that I cannot be identified."

In contacting these men by phone we had the opportunity to ask how things were going almost a year after the interviews had taken place. One man's health was causing him concern; another had suffered a mild stroke and had consequently curtailed many of his activities. A third was excited at the prospect of traveling to Europe within a few days, and one man reported that he was now a minister in a gay church with a membership that had grown respectably within the past year.

No man described in these case histories bears much resemblance to the popular image of the older homosexual. But then, stereotypes never reveal the true depth and complexity of any group of people. What does emerge from the case studies is a picture of a group of men with rich and generally rewarding lives. While they share a common interest in other men, they are as different, one from the other, as any group of ten men might be. Each has chosen a separate path in living his life as a homosexual—and now, as an older person.

CHAPTER 3

Matthew

Matthew greeted the interviewer at the door of his modest but comfortable home. The neighborhood had long since become "dangerous," but, in his characteristic way, Matthew was determined to remain in this place in which he had invested so much effort and love. The Persian rugs, overstuffed chairs, and antique furniture lent a warm feeling to the living room, and the interviewer immediately felt at ease. With his slight drawl and genteel manner, Matthew was the picture of a southern gentleman. There was an air of calmly achieved success about him. The interviewer could not help but think, "What a lovely grandfather this man would make."

It was during the 1918 flu epidemic that I lost both parents. I was eleven at the time, and my only brother was ten. Father was a physician in the army, stationed at a base in a neighboring state, and Mother was a nurse who had assisted Father in his duties as a country doctor before he was conscripted into the service. Most people today wouldn't understand how tragic a flu epidemic was in those days. Hardly a family was left untouched.

While Father was away, Mother went into the military stockade in our little town to administer aid to the men who had taken ill. She was highly criticized for going in among the men, for that was something ladies in that little Georgia town just didn't do in those days. She was so selfless she never bothered to think of herself, until she became ill. Father got a leave and returned home to care for her because it was just impossible to get a doctor to travel out from the city. They were just too busy with the epidemic everywhere.

I saw Father the first night he was home and I didn't see him again until he was sick with pneumonia. Father died and was buried one Sunday, and Mother died and was buried the next Sunday.

51

There was a considerable fuss between Mother's and Father's sides of the family as to who would have my brother and me. It wasn't a case of not being wanted; rather, too many people wanted us. There was quite a family council for several days. It was finally agreed that my uncle, Father's brother, would be the guardian and administrator of the estate, and he was so appointed by the courts. But my grandfather on the maternal side would not give in to it until my uncle signed papers that said we would live half of our time with Mother's people. Consequently, every Friday my brother John and I would change homes. We went to the same school each week but caught different buses.

Unhappily for us, Father had been of one religion and Mother of another. So each week, in addition to the experience of a different family, we got alternate doses of two religions. Each time we switched homes we were exposed to a different church and a different minister. This experience made me begin to question organized religion. What the two ministers said often did not agree, and this prompted a crisis in me as to who was the real authority. How much *can* you regard a minister, and just what is his authority? As I grew older I realized that a minister preaches doctrine; he is not preaching religion. My faith is with God, not with a particular church.

By the time I was in high school I knew I was attracted to other boys, but I had no idea that there was anyone else like me. This was the early 1920s in a small Georgia town and boys were expected to date girls, so I did. Dating a girl meant nothing more than having the companionship of someone for the prom, dinner parties, or the like. I always thought girls were pretty and led charming lives–I envied them. I was fascinated by their clothes and jewelry and their freedom to have all the things boys were not allowed to have.

When I was little Father would indulge me in the sorts of things that were considered appropriate only for girls. In retrospect, I understand why he did this. He bought me a dollhouse the size of a small room, complete with tiny furniture and running water and gas lights. It was a wonderful thing. I'm sure I was the only boy in Georgia who had a two-story dollhouse. When Father died, my uncle wouldn't hear of allowing me to keep it. I lost my treasure when the property was sold shortly after Father's death. The only thing I have left is a little tea set that was inadvertently packed along with the china instead of with the toys. That was saved for me.

There were other times when Father indulged my taste for feminine things. When I was nine our parents took us to see our first musical comedy, and it had a chorus line of girls with enormous ostrich-plume fans. They waved the fans and danced and sang the song "Every Little Movement Has a Meaning of Its Own." To me this was the epitome of everything lovely and beautiful in life. Well, Christmas was approaching, and it was time for our annual visit to the store to pick out our Christmas presents. You see, we were not brought up on myths. There was no Santa Claus in our lives; instead, we were taken to the store and allowed to pick out just one present. One day shortly before Christmas I accompanied Mother on an errand to the department store in town, and in the front window they had a display with big feather fans like the ones in the musical. I tried to get Mother to buy them for me but she refused. Later that day we met Father for lunch, and when he asked me what we had done and if I had seen anything I wanted for Christmas, I told him about the fans. This led to quite a heated discussion between Mother and Father. Mother said I shouldn't be indulged and that the fans were far too costly anyway. Finally Daddy said, "We won't discuss it anymore."

That was the last I heard about the fans until I went downstairs on Christmas morning and found a set of fans under my Christmas tree. I loved Daddy for that. I think that the worst thing that ever happened to me was his death. If he had lived, I would have had more opportunities–he would have seen to that.

Life went on without our parents, and in high school I did so well that I was sent off to college at some distance from home, at the age of sixteen. By then I had discovered masturbation, but I had never had a sexual experience with another person. In college I was attracted to several men and I knew they were attracted to me. I had a crush on one fellow in particular, and I recall being miserable whenever he had something else to do than to be with me.

It happened that one of my favorite high school professors came from the town where I went to college, and the summer after my freshman year I met him there. Mr. Bailey invited me to visit him at his mother's house, where he was staying for summer vacation. He was a young man, I would guess in his early thirties at that time. Of course to me he was an older man. We had dinner and afterward sat on the porch talking. He said, "There were things I could never talk to you about when you were in high school." We talked about how well we had gotten along, and I told him that he had been my favorite professor and that I used to sit and get pleasure just watching him. He replied, "Well, I'm right then—you are a homosexual."

I was thunderstruck. I had never spoken to another human being about such things. I told him that I had just heard of that word only a few months ago, that I didn't really know about it, and that I would appreciate it if he would explain it to me. I sat there and listened to him for a long time. He was very informative and even explained the various ways two men could make love. When he finished he said something for which I was not prepared. He told me, "If you ever want me for a sex partner, I will be available." That left me feeling so uncomfortable that I soon made an excuse and left abruptly.

As I was walking home, I regretted this terribly and said to myself, "You're not being honest with yourself." I was afraid that he would feel I had rejected him and think that I didn't want him. So I walked back and we talked. But there was still a great hurt between us. I really had the feeling that I wanted this man to love me, but, not being experienced, I rejected the whole idea. I felt that I had hurt him and felt guilty about this.

After that day I decided that I would see Mr. Bailey again, but this time I would make the overtures and we would have sex. This never came to pass.

I had my first sexual experience back home during the next Christmas holiday. It was quite unexpected. There was a man who lived in our small town from the earliest time I can remember. Father had hired him as manager of a farm that he owned in the adjacent countryside. When Father died he got a job in town. He was an older man by this time, I would guess in his forties or early fifties. He lived in a small house back of my grandfather's place with his elderly mother.

I passed him in town one day and he invited me to visit him. He said he rarely got out these days because of his mother's poor health. So the following week I got on a horse and rode out to his place. I said, "What did you want with me?" He said, "My, you've grown up to be a pretty young thing." I asked, "Is that what you wanted to tell me?" and he said, "Yes."

He talked about a lot of events from the past. When we were small children he would take a group of us swimming together, or sometimes he would mind us when the other adults were busy. He was a sort of caretaker for us boys. In retrospect, I'm sure he enjoyed looking at our bodies, but he never made any advances.

We talked about the good times we had at the swimming hole where we would all take off our clothes and dive in. Then he asked me if I would take off my clothes so he could look at me again. Now, there had been several years while I was in high school and then college that I had had nothing to do with this man–he was a stranger. But I was ready to experience this new thing that Mr. Bailey had talked about. I removed my clothes and the old caretaker went down on me.

I didn't really feel any desire, and I certainly was not attracted to this man, but the experience was not unpleasant. I felt a great deal of kindness toward him. After it was over I had to deal with the consequences. This was the first time I had actually had a sexual experience. All that year back in college I had been hounded with temptation, but I had held my feelings in check because of the fear that this was something terribly wrong. The one fellow of whom I was so fond asked me for a "Christmas kiss" before he left for vacation, and I complied; then I worried about whether I had done something evil. Now, after the experience with the old man, I knew I had done something really serious.

Had I committed a terrible sin? Was this behavior acceptable in the eyes of God?–Or was I some sort of freak? Did I just happen to meet two people who are this way? So I decided that the following summer when I returned home I would try to locate a minister who could answer my questions.

That summer I decided I had to find a minister in another town. I wouldn't dare talk to anyone who knew Mother's or Father's families. In those days the railroads would have one-day excursions to various cities. During the summer months the rates were lower than the regular fare, and you could leave in the morning and return at night. I took the excursion to Columbus, where I found a Methodist minister who unfortunately turned out to be a double-crosser. I lost faith in ministers because of him. He managed to find out where I lived, and he contacted the Methodist minister in our town and told him about my trip and what I had said. He urged the minister to counsel me. Well, the minister tried to counsel me, but my resentment at this breach of confidence was such that I didn't want to have anything more to do with the Methodist church.

But I was determined to get some answers to my questions. I found another excursion and this time traveled all the way to Atlanta. It was a Sunday morning and I attended the service at an Episcopalian church. I listened to the minister preach, and he seemed a nice enough fellow. I approached him after the service and told him I had come a long distance to see him, but that I didn't want to give him my name or tell him where I was from. I just wanted to tell him my problem. He asked me to wait in his study. He came in and in a very nice manner asked me what I wanted to talk about. When I had finished he looked upset and said, "If I'd had any idea that you wanted to talk about that, I wouldn't have given you my time. You people that are inclined to find that kind of pleasure in life should be destroyed."

So there I was. I had sought help from two ministers: men who I was taught to believe were sources of wisdom and understanding. One man double-crossed me, and the other one totally rejected me. Where was I to turn? I had to make my own decision without any help whatsoever. From that point on I ceased to believe in churches and denominations. I figured that there was a relationship between me and God, but the churches just confused that. They had become commercial organizations bleeding the people and using them.

Rather than turn to the churches again, I came to believe that I was born like everybody else and that my life, too, had come from God. If He had not wanted me to love other men, He would not have made me this way. This became a personal creed that I carried inside me wherever I went.

I did not know it at the time, but another event in my life was to substantiate this creed. It was the year after I had finished college. My aunt had stored all of Daddy's medical books and the china and all the mementoes he had left for us, and she approached my brother and me about disposing of these things. John and I decided that we would donate the medical books to the University of Georgia Medical Library and we would dispose of the other things. The medical books were mixed in with all sorts of other books and papers packed away into dozens of big boxes. John had married and was living in Chicago at the time, so the arduous task of going through these books and papers fell to me.

I started taking those boxes out one at a time, and I came upon one box that said "Contents of Joseph's Desk." I opened the box and found among the other papers a stack of letters from a Dr. Allan Pritchard in Wilmington addressed to Father. They were love letters and they were very beautiful. The letters talked about how my father and Dr. Pritchard still had the dream of having a clinic together, so they could work side by side. And they talked of their love for each other.

Both men had married and both had families, but I'm sure they married because it was the thing to do and because it would help them in their profession. They loved their wives–had learned to love them. But their first concern was to present the proper face to the world.

So I learned that I was not alone in the world. Father, just like me, had these feelings for other men, and he also had a great deal of goodness that he passed down to me. To this day the biggest regret in my life is that I lost my family at an early age. I was never again in my life to feel that I belonged to a family of my own. Had Father lived, I am certain he would have shared his homosexuality with me, and all the struggles I experienced for self-acceptance would have been made easier. But through these letters Father had left me a most valuable inheritance–the beginnings of my self-acceptance.

Soon after I read the letters I traveled to Columbus, went to the telephone company office, and found the local directory for Wilmington. There I found a listing for Dr. Pritchard, still at the same address from which the letters were sent. I was determined that sometime soon I would take the opportunity to drive to Wilmington to see that man.

After college I had taken an interest in upholstery and interior design, and during that year after college I worked for a furniture store. Through this store I became aware of a course that was being given in Boston by a prominent interior design school. I consulted with Granddaddy, and he agreed that I should spend the summer taking this course and he would pay for tuition and expenses. So I went.

On the way to Boston I stopped in Wilmington and called Dr. Pritchard's office. I told the receptionist, "Dr. Pritchard won't know me, but if you will tell him that I'm the son of Dr. Joseph Collins, I think he will talk to me." And he did.

He arranged for me to meet him–not at his office, but in town. In retrospect, I imagine he was being cautious. He was warm and open. He said, "This is a delightful surprise. I've always wanted to meet Joseph's children." He also told me that he hoped I would grow up to be the man Father was. This man cancelled all his afternoon appointments and spent the whole afternoon with me, which was a beautiful thing to do. We drove out to a cabin he had on the lake and we had a picnic lunch and talked all afternoon.

I told Dr. Pritchard how I had come across the love letters to Father, and how I also had the problem of loving other men. I told him I hoped he might answer a lot of questions for me, that I needed his help. In a way I was taking a big risk in saying all this. But I knew that I could drive away from Wilmington that day and never see this man again. I was very frank and honest with him, just as I feel I have always been an honest person. I'm not very good at lying–but Dr. Pritchard gave me a feeling that I didn't have to be dishonest anymore. And because this was a man who had feelings like I did and still became a reputable physician and was on the staff of a medical college, I felt that he was a wonderful fellow.

Dr. Pritchard spent the afternoon telling me all about Father and all about himself. We talked about loving other men and he patiently answered my endless questions. He provided me with a great relief from all the things that were worrying me. We discussed the religious aspect and the relationship of one person to another. We covered the physical aspect as well. It was a very full afternoon, and by the end of the day my brain was just whirling all around.

When I listened to Dr. Pritchard I no longer felt like a freak. I felt that there must be many, many people in this world, both married and unmarried, who suffered with the same problem I had. I just decided that I wasn't going to be a pretender any longer, that I would try to live my life with a form of dignity and pride.

For me, this was a true "coming out" experience. To most people I imagine coming out means exposing yourself as a homosexual to others–like telling your parents or your friends that you are homosexual. But to me coming out is a matter of self-acceptance. I came out after talking with Dr. Pritchard in the sense that it was the first time I truly accepted myself as a good human being, a person with a right to love and a right to live my life in the way I see fit.

Of course, in later years there were situations where I felt I could not be totally honest with others, particularly with clients for whom I worked as an interior decorator. There was a time when I would wear a wedding ring just to fool my clients into believing I was heterosexual. This was a part of my growing-up process, I suppose. I learned with time that the deception doesn't last for long. Sooner or later the client will ask you about Mrs. Collins, or ask you to bring her over for tea. Well, you *have* no Mrs. Collins, so then you're caught in a lie or else you have to create another lie to cover the earlier ones.

Just like most people of my generation, I learned early on to live a two-faced life. We had to. I don't think the young people today have quite the problem that we had. I always felt *evil* living a double life, and I wasn't good at it because I have a poor memory and so had trouble keeping up with the deceptions. I knew that my lifestyle was not acceptable to society, but I could never understand why.

In order to understand what it was like to be a homosexual at that time, you have to know something about the social climate. For the homosexual it was a climate of total rejection. After all, you couldn't take another man to the governor's ball; so you lived a double life. You made certain to have a girlfriend. You socialized with girls, and then you took them home and went home with the boy who was double-dating with your date's girlfriend. You really wanted to be with him all along. You made it a point to be seen with your girl at concerts, picnics, and whatever social events were taking place. And your big problem was never to let the girl fall in love with you. For instance, you might be invited to dinner and told to bring your girlfriend. So you dig up some girl and take her to dinner, and she is all wild to think you are fond of her. But you're not. She is just a pawn. It's a nasty little game that fortunately young people don't have to play so often today. It was so unfair.

The meeting with Dr. Pritchard freed me up to live my life according to my needs and to relate to that great society of homosexual men that I now knew existed. Over the years I had a series of lovers, but never more than one at a time. I have never been a promiscuous person, even as a young man. Most of my sex life has centered around love involvements. On the few occasions when I had sex just for the sake of sex–because I was a man and performed the sex act simply because I had the equipment for it–I have felt very cheap. Yet when the other person is meaningful to me and I have a love for him, it is a beautiful event.

My first one-to-one relationship was with a man who owned a small store in a neighboring town. It was just a couple of years after I graduated from college, and it only lasted about a year. I was very fond of Robert, but I felt that he was too involved with his wife and children to give me the attention I needed. I was never allowed to visit him at his house; we always met on the sly, and we could only get together when Robert was able "to get away from the family." Well, I heard that excuse a bit too often, so I ended the relationship. I knew there was no future with Robert.

After that, Bruce and I were lovers for a time. Bruce is a fellow I first met at college. I had been working in Massachusetts for about four years and I received a letter from Bruce, telling me how unhappy he was teaching in a small college back home and how much he envied my life. There was an opening in the firm I worked for, so he came up to visit, applied for the job, and got it. We lived and worked together for four very happy years. But Bruce was under great pressure from his parents to marry. He was the only son, and they wanted him to marry so as to carry on the family name–the typical sort of thing. He found a girl back home, married her, and brought her up North.

Bruce insisted that I live in the house with him and Mary. On the one hand I loved him, enjoyed him, and wanted to be with him; but on the other hand I felt this was an evil thing. I did move in with them, and before long he started getting up early in the morning, before his wife awoke, and coming to my bedroom. I felt that this was leading to something very dangerous. Besides, I was very fond of Mary and she was always very good to me. She was a lovely person and I didn't want to hurt her. I'm sure she knew what was going on, but there was never any discussion of it to my knowledge. After a time I felt I could no longer stand the deception and I moved out. Actually the relationship ended very amicably, without hurt feelings on either side.

Ralph was my most recent lover. We met shortly after World War II and together built a lovely home which I decorated. The relationship lasted for over five years, and I'm sure it would have lasted longer if it had not been for Ralph's drinking. He became quite an alcoholic and I couldn't cope with that. I moved into another house a half-hour's drive away, where I still live. I needed to do that for my own sanity, even though it meant giving up a beautiful house. After all, what does a house mean? Ralph and I see each other at the Metropolitan Community Church (MCC) on Sundays, and we get together for dinner often. But his drinking has gotten steadily worse over the years, to the point where he has been disoriented and confused at times, so I find it difficult to relate to him.

By the time I left Ralph, I was in my forties. Since then I have not had what I consider to be a lover, but I have had a number of young men who attached themselves to me. I suppose you would call them protégés. Somehow, after Ralph I began to find that younger men attracted me. I was glad to have them. The relationships were sexual and very satisfying to me, although they never lasted very long. After the relationship is over we are always on friendly terms. In fact, I can't really think of any lover that I had in my life that I'm not still friendly with. Of course, some are deceased. But I never experienced a fuss or a fight when any of these relationships ended.

At this point in my life, my sex life is rather slow. I would guess that I have sex about once a month, always with a friend I've known for a while. There is no commitment, but it is enjoyable. My sex life as a younger man was much more active, but I never felt comfortable with anonymous sex or pickups. Even when I was a young man I could never bring myself to go to one of these cruising areas and pick up a stranger. Sex must be with someone I've known, someone who is a friend and not a stranger.

On occasion I have met people at a party or in a bar. If I see a man I'm attracted to and if he is alone, I might ask him if I can have a drink with him. We talk for a while and if he seems friendly I might suggest we have dinner together, and it might develop from there into a sexual relationship. I have stuck to a funny little personal code that I won't have sex with anyone the first time I meet him. If he likes me well enough to plan a return engagement and we can spend some time getting to know each other, then that's fine. I just wouldn't do it any other way. I could certainly never pay someone for sex. I'm not condemning people who do, but I know that is not my style. Although I would like to have sex more frequently, I won't cheapen myself by going out to find someone just to have sex. It isn't worth that much.

I don't go to the gay bars very often, and I'm even less likely to visit a bathhouse. In a bar situation you have greater opportunity to socialize, to get to know the other person, than you have at a bathhouse, where most of the sex is pretty casual. But there is another reason I don't like bathhouses. The only time I will go to a bathhouse is if I am in a distant town. If I were to go to a bath in town I would meet people whom I know, people I've met at church or at the gay rights organization, and if they avoided me I would feel a great sense of rejection. Out of town, on the other hand, I have no concern about whether I'm accepted or rejected. It doesn't make any difference, since I'm a stranger in town just out for a night of fun.

As I get older I find the bars and bathhouses less and less interesting. People just don't communicate with each other at an intelligent level, and I find that I'm not interested in what the men at the bar talk about. They are mostly younger men, and when they talk about what they did at the beach or how many pickups they had, I get the feeling that these sorts of concerns were so far back in my life that I can no longer relate to them.

I'm much more likely to go to a meeting of the gay rights organization. In fact, I've been a member of the local group here since it began three years ago, and I attend most of the weekly meetings. I'm well aware of the problems in that organization. Financially the group seems to be continually on the edge of collapse, and I'm sure there were several times when the group would have folded had it not been for donations from several wealthy people. There are also leadership problems because there are those who are obviously in it just to satisfy their own inflated egos. This leads to a lot of infighting and wasted energies.

Despite the problems, I'm all in favor of the gay rights organization. When a local minister organized a movement against gay people, the gay rights organization led the fight to protect our rights. And we have done a lot of other things that are less noticed but just as important. We do a lot of advocacy. There have been several cases where gay men or women have lost their jobs because of their sexual orientation; we came to their defense, got a lawyer, and raised money for their cases. We also do a lot of educational programming. For instance, at this last meeting we had a speaker on venereal disease among gay people, which is a great problem. We also send speakers out into the community. We also serve a social purpose–many people come to meetings to meet other gay people, and then there are groups that will meet there, like a group of gay alcoholics and a group of older gay people.

I have also been active in the Metropolitan Community Church almost since it was first started here. Like most people, I initially went there primarily for the social activity. But later I became more interested in the functioning of the church and in ensuring that it would survive. The church does not follow any particular denomination, and although it is under the authority of the mother church in Los Angeles, each congregation is generally conducted as the local minister sees fit. It's not a well-formulated, well-organized religion at all, and it is often difficult to keep things going because of the many different kinds of people in the congregation. The religious backgrounds vary all the way from Episcopalians to Holy Roller types, and then of course there are gay men and lesbians, blacks and whites, and people of different social classes. So there are many conflicts and disputes.

Nevertheless, MCC is a much-needed haven for so many gay people who are not welcome in their own churches because of their homosexuality. Can you imagine how much easier it would have been for me if MCC had existed when I sought help from ministers as a young man? That is why I am such a strong supporter of MCC today.

My social life revolves primarily around MCC, which sponsors a number of dinners and social events in addition to Sunday services, and with the gay rights organization. But I do have a considerable number of heterosexual friends, because many of the clients in my interior design business have become friends over the years. I have had some very interesting experiences with clients. You see, back even when I was young, if you were an interior designer you were considered to be a homosexual, whether you were or not. There were many occasions where I had to deal with the husband of a client who was interested in more than having his parlor redone. Occasions would arise where you would make your entrance into their life, usually through the wife, and the husband would indicate a desire to see the decorator to find out what he thinks about the work. And he would invariably drop by, say with an invitation to lunch, so that plans for the house could be discussed. But he really didn't have this in mind at all. It finally came down to a sort of blackmail proposition: if you wanted the business, a sexual liaison with the husband was required.

As I got older this became less of a problem, both because I became less desirable sexually and also because I learned to handle these sorts of situations. I think as you get older you learn to be more matter-of-fact about sex relationships. You learn to recognize when you are attracted to the other person; you learn to talk about it, and to lay down the law: you may be my client, but you are not my bed partner. If I'm attracted to you, I may be interested; if not, then I just say so.

I don't socialize a great deal with younger homosexual men. I have reached the point in life where there are few shared interests between me and younger people. I suppose you could say that the younger gays discriminate against me by not including me in their activities, but this is a natural sort of discrimination between the generations. Why should they invite me to the beach to play fris-bee? I don't run around throwing plastic disks, so I'd be so much excess baggage. In the same way I am not invited to the baths with younger men. That is understandable. I do get invited to the movies or to dinner, which are activities that are more appropriate to an older person.

I suppose I have more younger gay friends than most older people, probably because of my involvement with MCC and the gay rights organization. I imagine most older homosexual men think of youn-ger men as children. They don't have very much to offer socially or intellectually, but they may be very attractive sex objects.

I have known many gay men under thirty who have indicated their attraction to me. On a few occasions men in their early twen-ties have approached me for a sexual relationship, and I feel that is beautiful. There is no monetary exchange or anything of that sort. Perhaps they are seeking a certain father image; maybe it's a rela-tionship something akin to my relationship with Dr. Pritchard. They are comfortable with me and they feel they can talk openly.

The men I have known between the ages of thirty and fifty are much more conscious of the age difference. They are simply not open to the idea of a sexual relationship with a man in his seventies. After the age of fifty there is a sort of camaraderie. The thought is, "You're in my same age bracket, you've got the same problems I have, and the same urges I have. So let's see what we can do about it."

Growing older brings many changes. The worst thing about growing older is losing the ability to do the things you always took for granted. It's harder to get things out of the bottom drawer. You drop something on the floor and it's an ordeal to pick it up. You have to think about how many steps there are to get upstairs. And you lose a little bit of your mind, too. You become forgetful and a bit paranoid. You are inclined to think, "They are pushing me around because I'm old." But in reality, if you analyzed your life, you would realize that you got pushed around at thirty, forty, and fifty, and you're going to get pushed around the rest of your life if you allow it. As you age, you also lose your patience. Things seem to be routine, repetitive. You've heard that opera so many times, you don't want to hear it again.

The best thing about growing older is all the special privileges you get. Instead of being blamed, you are excused. You are offered the front seat of the car because it is easier than squeezing into the back seat–little things like that. Another advantage of age is that all the things that mattered so much when you were young don't seem so important now. You are upset less easily.

There is no difference between heterosexuals and homosexuals in adjusting to aging. It doesn't matter what your sex life has been like, everyone has to accept that we have no choice but to grow old. The process is much easier if you accept it. I think lying to yourself and to your friends about your age is about the most horrible thing people do. I think it is tragic to try to look and act fifty years younger than you are. You're clumsy at it; you can't do it. If it's time to go to bed, do it! And if you don't feel well today, admit you don't feel well and would rather not do something. Don't go out there and be miserable; it will show on your face and in your actions.

I have never understood why people hesitate to tell their age. Everyone who is younger than I am is looking forward to reaching my age. Living to the age of seventy-two and having done it well is an accomplishment.

CHAPTER 4

William

As he stepped lightly into the university office, William looked younger than his sixty-six years. The interviewer was not surprised when William revealed that he did exercises every morning in order to keep his trim figure. He had a bright glow about him. It was hard to tell whether this was due to his immaculate attire or to his happy smile. Here was a man who, in his retirement, was finally free to enjoy life.

Some of my earliest memories are memories of being poor. Although we were never really impoverished, I grew up with my cousin Chuck and his family, who were very wealthy, and in contrast our family seemed to have so little. My uncle owned a huge cattle ranch in Wyoming which he and his family used as a summer home. The place was managed by my father, and I remember there were constant squabbles between the two men. When Chuck was sent away to boarding school, my uncle offered to send me along, since Chuck and I had grown up together and were inseparable. My father could never have afforded a private boarding school for me. Chuck and I were both ten when we left. We were together in boarding school for three years, until my father and my uncle had another big fight. The result was that my father left the ranch and I was called back from boarding school. It was quite upsetting for me to have to go back to public school.

As I suppose it does for many young boys, boarding school provided an opportunity for sexual experimentation. I had never been aware of sexual feelings until my first experiences there. My first sexual experience was quite interesting. There were four of us on the bed, including Chuck. I remember putting a sheet over the penis of one of the boys and then taking it in my mouth. Later on I would get into bed with one of the other boys–he was about two years older than me–and we would "69," although I didn't know it was called that until I was fifty and first heard the term from my psychiatrist.

During the summers, Chuck and I were together on the ranch. We would fool around quite a lot–mostly masturbating each other. I guess we practiced some of the things we had learned at boarding school. Even after we grew up there was some sexual contact between me and Chuck. One time he groped me and then masturbated me in his car. When we were in college I introduced Chuck to a girl whom he married a couple of years later. After they were married I happened to be spending the night at their home on one occasion. Chuck's wife was sick then, and he used that as a excuse to sleep in the guest room with me. I didn't think he would want to do anything since he was married now, but to my surprise he did want to. He came into my bed and we fooled around. That was the last time Chuck and I had any sort of sex together.

Do I think Chuck was homosexual? Yes, I think he was; but he never admitted it, and that caused him a lot of problems. He and his wife did not have a good relationship. He took no interest at all in his son, and the poor boy was raised mostly by his wife's mother. Chuck and his wife were separated a couple of times, but Chuck's family took her under their wing. I think they knew he was having some problems. In fact, he even spent some time in a psychiatric hospital. Chuck had a lot of emotional problems and I think they were all due to the fact that he didn't admit he was homosexual.

After college I went to work for a financial investment firm, which is the career I just retired from three years ago. I met another fellow at the office who had interests similar to mine and we ended up having a affair, although we never lived together. After a couple of years this fellow left the firm and I never saw him again. Although I realize now that this was a homosexual relationship, somehow at the time I didn't think of it in those terms. I don't even know if there were gay bars or clubs back then. I didn't know other homosexuals, and I wasn't familiar with the terms. If you had asked me at the time if I was a homosexual, I think I would have quite sincerely said no.

I did not admit to myself that I was homosexual until I began seeing a psychiatrist at the age of fifty. Up until that time I had been reasonably happily married, and since my marriage I had not had any sexual experience with another man. I guess I just didn't think about it. But I knew for years that something was wrong. I was having regular sexual relations with my wife, but I was having trouble maintaining erections, and I think we were both feeling frustrated. I felt really guilty, too. I felt that life was passing me by, that I was not getting out of it what other people did. I would be driving down the road alone in my car, and I would see a couple in a car with a gang of snotty-nosed kids and I'd think, "I could never put up with being married in a situation like that. They must have something I don't have to put up with all that." I don't mean I didn't love my son; I was delighted that I had a son of my own. But something didn't feel right.

So I went to see the psychiatrist. I don't remember how long I saw him, but it was a long time. I spent $10,000 on that psychiatrist. But it was worth it. It was the psychiatric help that made me understand, finally, that I was gay, and that this wasn't any great tragedy. I really believe that if it hadn't been for the psychiatrist I would not have come out again in my middle age. Talking to the psychiatrist was like a dam bursting open; it sort of loosened me up inside and made me more relaxed so all of those feelings which I had pushed down for so many years could finally come up. It even had an effect on the sexual relationship with my wife. The evening after the very first session with the psychiatrist I had intercourse with my wife, and for the first time in quite some time I had no difficulty.

At this point I began to think more and more about being gay. Of course I read everything about homosexuality I could get my hands on. It was also at this time that I happened upon the first people I had ever met who were openly gay.

Every winter my wife and I would travel to southern California for a vacation, where we would rent a cottage near the beach. The cottage was much smaller than the home we were used to, and I would often feel like getting away from those close quarters and from my wife. I would take long walks up the beach on my own. I did that for many years. I didn't know it at the time, but one section of the beach was a sort of gay cruising area. As I walked down the beach, I noticed a man out in the water who seemed to be waving at me. Later, when I turned around and was walking back, he waved again and invited me into the water with him. When we came out, he guided me up into the bushes to a spot where he had built a sort of little hut with leaves and sticks. We went in there and he asked me to take off my trunks. We played with each other and he sucked me off. This was the first time since I'd been married–for more than twenty years–that I had been with a man. Like the experience with the psychiatrist, this too felt as if a huge dam had suddenly burst open. It was wonderful.

The next morning I could hardly wait to return to the same spot on the beach. I didn't see the man I had been with the day before, but I met another man who I had sex with. This was the first man whose semen I took into my mouth. A couple of months before this I had taken my own semen into my mouth, just to see what it was like. My psychiatrist and I talked about it. But the actual experience with another man was new. It was thrilling!

I went back to that beach many times. I learned that it was a roaring gay beach and a very good place to meet other men interested in sex. It was easy to keep all this from my wife, since I had been taking long walks on the beach for some time. One man I met on the beach told me about a gay bathhouse in a city close to our house back home. I had never heard of a gay bathhouse. Never in my wildest imagination did I even think there were such places!

When we returned home from our vacation, I drove into the city on the first weekend night and managed to find the bathhouse my friend on the beach had described. I must have acted like a little kid in a candy store. I would just talk and talk to everyone I met, and I would tell them my name and where I was from. I was just so delighted to have found this place! Finally a fellow approached me and told me not to talk so much and not to give out information about myself. Now that I'm familiar with the baths, I realize that I must have seemed very strange to the other men there. It's a place where there is little conversation. Sexual contacts are made by glancing at someone, perhaps walking up to him and touching, curtly inviting someone into your room or joining several men in an orgy room–all without discussion. It is also a very anonymous place where little is revealed and few questions are asked.

After this experience I started going to the baths every weekend. Of course I had to make up some excuse for Eileen, my wife. She knew I was seeing the psychiatrist. At first I told her I was going to a psychiatric hospital in the city on an outpatient basis for more extensive treatment. Later I told her that I had so much experience the doctors wanted me to work with other people who had problems. Eileen accepted my story without any questions. After I had met my current lover, Fred, at the baths, I would go up to his place on Saturday night instead of to the baths. Eileen never suspected anything.

After I had been seeing Fred for a while, I introduced him to Eileen as a friend I had met at work. She never suspected he had anything to do with my weekend trips into the city. After that Fred often accompanied us to church on Sundays and to dinners. The next winter vacation Eileen and I were scheduled to spend in southern California, I suggested Fred join us, and Eileen agreed. At the last minute Eileen was unable to go because of some minor health problem, so we made plans for her to join us in a few days. Fred and I stayed in a beautiful hotel on the beach. I'll never forget the first night there. There was a full moon and we could hear the lapping of the waves just outside our room. It was lovely. When Eileen arrived, Fred moved to a motel down the street.

Eileen and I had been married for almost twenty-five years, and this was the first time she was to know about my homosexuality. It happened almost by accident. I didn't plan it. When Eileen, Fred, and I would go to church back home, Fred would often hold my hand. I guess we thought it wasn't noticeable. But Eileen had noticed, even though she never said anything. Then on our vacation she again noticed Fred holding my hand when we went to dinner. We were scheduled to entertain friends that evening and Eileen wanted to talk with me. She said. "When the Donaldsons come over tonight, would you tell Fred not to hold your hand? They might misinterpret it." This was another of those times when it felt to me as if a dam had just been opened. It was the first time Eileen had said anything about my relationship with Fred. Without hesitating I told her that Fred and I were in love, that he was my lover and I was homosexual, and that from the beginning of our marriage I had been a homosexual. This was true even though I had not had sexual relations with a man for the first twenty years of our twenty-four-year marriage.

Eileen was aghast. All of this was completely new to her. She knew nothing about gay people and had never suspected the truth. When we returned home I immediately went to live with Fred in his house.

Somehow gossip began to spread in town about my relationship with Fred. Because of my wife's talking, the information got back to my firm. At this time I was about to be made a director of the office I worked in. It would have meant a higher salary and more status, and I had been counting on the promotion. But due to the talk about my homosexuality another person was given the promotion in my place. At least I was not fired; but I also was not given a raise until about six months before my retirement, which was several years later.

My son Don was twenty years old at the time. After I told Eileen about my homosexuality she must have had a talk with Don. I suppose she really felt she could confide in him. While Eileen's attitude toward my sexuality was one of repugnance, Don was supportive. He actually seemed delighted that there was a change in me. He told me that I had always appeared sort of gray and depressed. He said that now I was more alive, happier than I had ever appeared before, that I even wore different, more lively clothes. He is quite an astute young man. I think he felt that I had been held down by his mother and that now I was free to be an entirely new person.

Actually, I suppose I was surprised at how understanding Don was. I had often thought, before all this happened, that if someone knew I was a homosexual he would feel sorry for me and look down on me. Certainly Eileen did. But Don seemed genuinely pleased about the changes I was experiencing. In fact, shortly after I moved in with Fred, Don and I began to talk about Don moving in with us. Fred has a very large house and Don was to have a bedroom of his own. Plans were worked out and Don was all set to make the move. But at this time Don was engaged to be married, and apparently the girl's family knew about the upset in our family. They must have told him that, if he moved into the house with Fred and me, everyone would think he was gay, even though he had no inclination in that direction. I guess they believed, like so many people, that gays recruit young people into homosexuality. They make us out to be Svengalis. That's Anita Bryant's philosophy that she has poisoned so many minds with. Don must have been convinced, because in the end he did not make the move to Fred's house, to my great disappointment.

I wish that all heterosexuals could learn, like my son, what homosexuals are really like. All of these stereotypes of homosexuals being hairdressers, of being so anxious to lead children astray, are very harmful. I hope that what my son realized is that after you learn someone you know is gay, it doesn't change that person at all. He is the same person he was yesterday.

After three months with Fred, I discovered that he is a very domineering person. I decided to leave his house. All the while, Eileen and I saw each other regularly. I don't think she ever really accepted my homosexuality, but at least the shock had worn off. When I left Fred's house, she took me back. I continued to see Fred; Eileen was aware of this, because we lived in the same part of town. She objected but there wasn't much she could do about it, so it went on like this for six or seven years.

I was finally approaching my sixty-fifth birthday, which meant I would be retiring soon. Since Eileen and I had spent so many vacations in southern California, I guess we both assumed we would retire there. But after all that had happened I did not feel like retiring with my wife. At about this time Fred had the opportunity to buy a home in Laguna Beach. It was a beautiful spot, on a hill overlooking the ocean. Fred was interested in having me purchase the home with him. It occurred to me that this was a perfect opportunity to get away from my straight life and from my wife. I would also be getting away from Fred, since he would only come down on vacation or for short business trips. This would be ideal, since I wouldn't have to be with him all the time. I didn't want to trade a stifling marriage for a stifling relationship with a man.

Fred and I went ahead with our plans, but I never discussed any of this with Eileen or with my son, who was married by this time. Well, Eileen knew that I was due to retire soon and so she asked for a meeting with me and our son. She said that she had heard gossip to the effect that Fred and I were going into business together and that I would be moving to California. I'll never forget when she asked me, "If you're moving to California, am I moving to California?" I told her clearly that she was not. It was finally decided that when I retired later that year I would leave temporarily and live in the house in Laguna Beach. It would be a sort of trial period. The day I retired Eileen helped me pack some things in the back of my car that we thought I would need until I came back after the temporary period. But I knew it wouldn't be a temporary period–I knew that this was it, that I was leaving her. I spent that night with Fred celebrating, since this was my sixty-fifth birthday.

After I moved into the house, Fred and I hired a decorator. We shared the expenses on everything. We bought new furniture, drapes, dinnerware. We made it into a real home.

We have been here for three years now and I'm very satisfied with my current relationship with Fred. Fred is here for two to three weeks at a time several times a year. We go to the beach, we enjoy horse races and movies. When Fred is here we tend to socialize quite a bit. Fred is a gourmet cook and just loves to cook up a meal. Some of his dinners have really been quite extraordinary.

Fred is fastidious. When he is here everything in the house has to be in its place. Sometimes he gets impatient with me because I don't know all the things he does about keeping house, cooking, and entertaining friends. My answer to him is that we each have our strong points. I may not be much in the kitchen, but I know how to balance a checkbook and do an income-tax return. Fred is helpless at these tasks.

Until recently most of the friends we entertained were heterosexual. Fred is an estate lawyer and many of his clients live in this area. I also have friends from my hometown, a fellow and his wife, and several others, who visit during the winter. When our friends come here they love this place because it is so pretty. We often put guests up for the night since we have guest quarters out back of the house. Although all of these friends are heterosexual, I find them to be completely open and comfortable about my relationship with Fred.

I have a gay friend here who told me just the other night that he has nothing but gay friends. He said that it is too complicated to mix straight people with gay people. I really don't understand that, because it never seemed complicated to me.

I would say that only a few, a very few of my straight friends actually know that I'm gay. A lot of gay people think that, if their friends knew, they wouldn't want to be friends any longer. I have had just the opposite experience. My straight friends who know I'm gay have never made any advances to me or made any insinuating remarks about my lifestyle or anything of that nature. In fact, after we talked about it, it seemed they were friendlier and we were closer than ever. It's like one person's self-disclosure begets the other person's self-disclosure and everybody ends up feeling closer.

Of course most of the time my homosexuality is just not discussed. My straight friends who don't know about my sexuality are the type of people it wouldn't make any difference to anyway. It has never been discussed, but I'm sure they realize that Fred and I are lovers. They know I divorced my wife and that when I go back home I stay with Fred. In fact, they treat us like a couple. I went back home in August for Fred's birthday. My friends put on several parties that were basically for me, but we were both invited, and when we had a celebration at Fred's place these people were invited there. Fred and I are both accepted. Now I think that if you asked any of these people if we were gay, they would say, "Yes they are, but it doesn't make any difference to us."

As I said, until recently most of our guests have been heterosexual. I have met many gay men since I've been here but I never invited them over when Fred was in town. Perhaps I thought he would disapprove. But on this last visit Fred asked me if I had any friends here that I would like to invite for dinner. On two occasions we entertained two of my gay friends and we had very enjoyable times. Fred prepared elaborate meals with cocktails, hors d'oeuvres, and so on, and we were all impressed.

I don't think Fred is too happy about the fact that I go to the baths, and I've assumed he doesn't relish the thought of my having other relationships while he is gone. After we settled in our new home he learned that I was still going to the baths. Shortly after that Fred told me that he went to a bathhouse–in fact, the same one in which we had met–and he met a fellow, David, whom he has been seeing. He was quite open about it. Now I don't know if they are having a sexual relationship or just a friendship. I never mention David to him, and I don't really know what Fred does for a sexual outlet when we are apart. Fred has told me that he is satisfied with masturbation, but I find that hard to believe when I know there are so many other outlets available to him. After all, he is a very attractive man. He is much younger than I am–only forty-three–and he lives in a city where bars and bathhouses are readily available.

When Fred is not here I lead a very active gay life. I go to bars and bathhouses and have many friends. I suppressed my sexuality for twenty years for a heterosexual marriage; I am not about to repeat the same mistake for a homosexual relationship. I have a very simple understanding with my gay friends here. I tell them when Fred is going to be here and it is understood that at those times they will not call or stop by, that they won't contact me at all. Now this last time Fred met two of my gay friends, but I still prefer to avoid these friends when Fred is here.

We did recently have a disagreement. I think it revolves around the fact that I have a very active sex life with other men while Fred does not. In fact, almost all of Fred's friends are heterosexuals. After Fred's last visit I happened to discover a letter he had written to his friend David whom he met at the bathhouse. It was quite an intimate letter. Now I thought, did Fred leave this letter here on purpose just to show me that he has gay friends, too? I guess I won't know until we talk about it.

I'm pretty well satisfied with my social life except for one thing. I would like the gay people I know here to be of a higher caliber. By that I mean I would like to have more gay friends who are cultured, well educated. One of the first gay men I met after I moved here is Joel. He picked me up at a gay bar. I am not a gay bar person, but when I first came down here I was lonely and I had heard of that bar. That night Joel took me to his apartment, where we slept together. We had sex a few more times after that but now the relationship is platonic. We get together often, and in fact Joel has me over to dinner every Monday. Now I'm fond of Joel, but he is just not the caliber of person I am used to knowing. I've gotten to know a number of gay people through him and they are pretty much at the same level as Joel.

I can think of a very good example of this–a fellow Joel

introduced me to a couple of months ago. This is a man in his late forties who is very much of a "swish." He is terribly feminine. He uses his hands too much, and he walks like a woman. When we went walking past some shops he looked in each window and said, "Oh, isn't that gorgeous?" I suppose he is the sort of person heterosexuals imagine when they think of a homosexual. This fellow was really outrageous. Joel and I went back to Joel's place and later that evening we met Mr. Swish and his lover at their place. I hardly recognized him because he had on a very obvious wig. It was a man's wig, but this fellow is fairly dark and the wig was blond. It looked awful. I was embarrassed to be seen in public with him.

After that day he called me several times. One day he came up to my place unannounced. It happened to be the day Fred was due to arrive. I was furious and told him not to come back, that I was not interested in his friendship. So I haven't seen him since then.

When I am friends with a homosexual I want it to be with someone who looks like a man. I've had a wife, and I've been put to great expense to get rid of her, so I don't want to take on a man who looks like a woman.

I feel the same way about those lesbians who dress up to look like a man or who look like truck drivers. That is why I avoid going to the Metropolitan Community Church in town. I must say I truly can't stand those lesbians. They actually come to church in dirty jeans. Some of them have children who always seem poorly clothed and running out of control. There are one or two who I think are very attractive girls and I will talk to them. But the other lesbians who come to church are a pretty sorry lot. Maybe they are appealing to God for help. I hope so, but I don't like to be there with them.

I avoid the local gay rights group for the same reason. It seems like half the people who go to those meetings are lowlife. It sort of depresses me to go there. I think many of them have come to California thinking this must be some sort of paradise. They come here without jobs and then they seem to be unemployed all the time. They beg the minister at the Metropolitan Community Church for jobs; they try to find other gay people who will employ them. But they don't have any real skills and they are just down-and-outers.

I also don't go to gay bars very often. The bathhouses are much more efficient if sex is what you are after. If I'm with a friend and he suggests going to a bar, I'll go. For instance, I have a friend–he is in his early sixties–who loves the bars. He comes here about once a week and we go out for dinner and then to a bar. But I don't think I would go to a bar alone. I'm not much of a drinker, and the smoke and loud music don't particularly appeal to me. Sometimes they do have shows where men dress up as women and mimic songs from a record. That doesn't appeal to me, either. On the other hand, I can understand why my friend likes the bars. There is a certain comradeship in a gay bar. Everywhere else you go you are sort of "in hiding" because you assume everyone else is heterosexual. In a gay bar the tables are turned: everyone is assumed to be gay. This becomes very apparent when some straight people walk in by accident and gradually discover they are in the wrong place. They feel uncomfortable, just like we might in a straight bar. It's really quite amusing. It is also true that, in the bar my friend likes, the same people are there week after week. So it becomes like the neighborhood tavern: a place to meet your friends.

For me the bathhouse is also a place of comradeship. Some older gay men have said to me, "Aren't you afraid when you go there that someone you know will see you?" My answer is, "Well, that's all right because they must be there for the same reason I am." Before I retired I went to bathhouses back home regularly, as I've told you. Occasionally I would see someone I knew, but since they must be gay too I wasn't embarrassed or concerned.

I would say that while bars are not my cup of tea I am definitely a bathhouse person. I don't know, there is something about being with a man that does something to me. I feel that I'm never at the baths long enough; the time always goes too rapidly. There is one bathhouse in town that I prefer. It is always clean, unlike some of the others I have seen. You can rent a locker for six dollars where you keep your clothes. Or for a little more you can get a small room with its own key, which gives you privacy. You can spend all night there, but I usually don't, because I like a good night's sleep.

Most of the time I will have sex on a one-to-one basis with another man. We might meet in one of the corridors or in the whirlpool or the sauna and then return to my room or his. But there is also a room that looks like a dormitory with bunk beds along the walls and a king-size bed in the middle of the room. This is the orgy room. There is hardly any light in the room, so you have to stay there for a while until your eyes adjust and you can make out the figures. Things can get pretty wild in there, with quite a few men piled on the bed and another group of men just watching.

I will say without any compunctions that I enjoy the baths. You see, I have Fred, who is here for a few days or weeks at a time. When he is here I never go to the baths. When he is gone I don't want to have an ongoing relationship with another person. I would rather go to the baths and see several people than date someone. I have a friend whom I met at the baths; he is in his sixties. We have gotten into a pattern where he stays here with me overnight. I enjoy being with him and he enjoys being with me, but I keep thinking to myself that I don't like this ongoing relationship. I don't really and truly know how to explain it. I think it's because I like a variety. I often have sex with a person at the baths and then see him there again. And when I see him again, if he doesn't approach me, I won't approach him. It's like I want a different one each time. I don't really understand that part of myself.

I would say that my sex life now at the age of sixty-eight is much more active and much more satisfying than it was in my earlier years. Of course this is a result of leaving my wife and coming out as a gay person. When Fred is here we have sex on a regular basis. If he is here for a week, we will generally have relations two or three times. When Fred is gone, I go to the baths. At the baths it is hard to remember how many sexual contacts you have, but there are quite a few. I would guess that on the average I have sex about twice a week, with Fred or with others at the baths.

I limit myself to gay people who are older–in their forties and up. Sexually and emotionally I just don't relate to young people. In my experience young gays avoid the older ones. They don't want to have anything to do with us. I guess they think our sexual capacity is worn out. I can recall only one young person who has ever approached me at a bathhouse.

At my age I can appreciate the advantages and disadvantages of growing older. I think the worst thing about age is deterioration of one's health. I'm still in fairly good health, but in the last few years I've developed some medical problems that really concern me. I have to be careful to take my pills on schedule, and I have to limit my physical activity. I can't walk or swim nearly as far as I used to, and I have to accept those limitations. Another aspect of old age is loneliness. I'm pretty lucky. I have Fred, and my son, and his children. I also keep pretty busy, so I don't feel lonely very often.

The best thing about being older is that you don't have to worry about what people think. I know there are a lot of older people who worry about what other people think, but I couldn't care less. For instance, I don't care who knows about my homosexuality. What can it do to me now? I'm sure there are people around here who see men come and go from my house and probably realize that I'm gay, but it doesn't concern me. For me, age has brought with it a freedom I never had before.

Retirement is an absolute delight. I love to read, correspond with friends, listen to music, and putter in the garden. When I was working I always had to squeeze these things in during free moments. Now I do what I like to do, when I like to do it.

In adjusting to age I don't believe there is any difference between heterosexuals and homosexuals. For anyone to be happy he must find his niche in life. For me it was living as a homosexual. It is also essential to develop interests other than your job and to plan your retirement—where you will live, what you will do. I also think it helps for older people to not restrict their activities to other older people. Older people who adjust well are those who are open-minded about younger people. Some older folks I know criticize young people for their dress and habits and believe that the younger generation is carrying the country down the ragged road. That is nonsense. We older people must accept the fact that today's lifestyle is entirely different from what it was fifteen years ago, and we must accept younger people as just a different generation.

When our ideas become rigid, we are unable to adjust to the changes life throws at us. I made the biggest change of my life in my later years. I left my heterosexual life behind and began a new life as an openly gay person. And I'm delighted with the change.

CHAPTER 5

Mike

mid. 40's

Sitting in a dimly lit and deserted bar, the interviewer was aware of her attraction to Mike. Even seated, Mike struck an imposing figure: tall, bearded, with piercing green eyes. He reminded the interviewer of a burly stevedore. His rapid and articulate speech was strangely out of keeping with this setting, which was accustomed to the meaningless babble of crowds. Mike's self-assurance and articulateness made his thoughts seem particularly important. By the end of their time together, the interviewee and the interviewer felt like two friends. They hugged and kissed good-bye.

I've never discussed with other people what "coming out" means to me. To me, coming out means reaching a realization that you are gay, that you share something special with a larger group of people. To a lot of people coming out refers to your first sexual experience with a member of your own sex. But in fact there is a lot more to it. Most gay men go through a frightening and lonely period when they don't quite understand what is happening. The guy falls hopelessly in love with the boy next door and realizes that this attraction is stronger than anything he could ever feel for the head cheerleader at school. In jest he embraces another guy in the shower room, and suddenly he admits to himself that his feelings toward other guys are sexual. He may fight it, or he may yield to it. The other guys may make fun of him; he may be branded a "sissy"; rumors may be spread around school. It will be one of the most frightening experiences of his life. He will go through a period when he looks inward and thinks to himself, "My God, I'm a freak. I'm the only person that is like this on the face of the earth. There is no one else and I'm all alone." Coming out, to me, means going beyond this step and realizing that you are a brother or sister of a much larger group that has been going on before you were born and will go on after you are dead. Nothing can change this. It doesn't matter how far back into the closet you are pushed by society.

It is normal for me to be gay, just as it would be abnormal for a heterosexual to be anything but heterosexual. It's all programmed in the genes before we even start the race. On the other hand, it is possible for a gay person, if he desires it enough, to fight his homosexuality to the point where he can live a heterosexual life complete in every detail. It is simply a matter of will. My personal philosophy of life is to choose to do whatever you choose to do, whenever you choose to do it, as long as you are willing to accept the consequences of those choices. So if a homosexual man wants to be heterosexual badly enough, he can push his gayness back and bring out his heterosexual qualities. Gay people often say there is a little bit of the gay in everyone. It's also true that there is a little bit of the heterosexual in all gays. You simply develop that part that is within your heart, your mind, and your will to develop.

If you are comfortable with your role in society, you are probably in the role that best suits you. If you are uncomfortable with the role, then I think it is your duty to change your life so that it will please you, even if that means going against society's rules. Change your role! For instance, say you lived a public gay life. It is possible to relocate in another state where you know absolutely no one and start your life over as a heterosexual–if that is what you want.

I had a very close friend who made the change from a completely homosexual to a completely heterosexual life. My lover and I were best friends with this fellow and his lover. We did all the things couples normally do: theater, dinner parties, and the like. My friend had been with his lover for two years when he met and fell in love with a girl from his hometown. He moved back there and married her. Now, several years later, his rejected lover is still heartbroken and is not able to justify in his own mind how his mate could leave him for a woman. But my friend seems to be completely happy in his new life. Last time I spoke to him, he and his wife had two children and were still happily married.

Someone once asked me if it makes a difference to a gay man if he loses a lover to another man or to a woman. I don't think so. There is only as much as the difference between losing your billfold or having your pocket picked. Gone is gone.

My early family life? I was an only child. I never knew my father, really. He took his own life when I was very young. My mother boarded me with an aunt who lived in a neighboring town. This was probably the worst thing that ever happened to me. The woman was a total bitch. She ran a foster home for underprivileged children. It's a pity there wasn't a social worker to look into the situation. All the children were abused. I was family, but I was treated as badly as any of the other children. My aunt slept in one room with the girls, while my uncle slept in a separate room with the boys. My aunt died not knowing I was gay, even though her husband, the father of five children, was responsible for bringing me out at the age of ten. One night he quietly slipped out of his bed and into mine. He put his hand between my legs. Soon he began to masturbate me. I liked what he did. First I began to masturbate myself. Later I experimented with other boys. My aunt's husband slipped into my bed many times after that, but my aunt never suspected anything. Did this relationship cause my homosexuality? I don't know. But I do think of this relationship as a diving board into a larger, more satisfying pool.

I've never shared this with anyone before, but I've often thought about how my childhood experiences affected my interests later in life. Being fatherless, not living with my mother, and hating living with my aunt presented me with a set of unique circumstances. At about the age of five or so, I remember thinking that if I could find a mate for my mother then I would get to live with her and all my unhappiness would end. It was at that age that I began looking at men very carefully. I would pick out men who fit a certain father image. Now, looking back on this, I believe that rather than picking a husband for my mother, I was really picking what appealed to my taste as far as a man goes. I remember very distinctly that the face and build were important. He had to have a kind face and a sturdy, masculine build. Two other features were important. It sounds ridiculous, but they were very important then: the fingernails had to be clean and manicured, and the shoes had to shine. Now I think all of this was a prelude to my attraction to other men.

I escaped from my aunt's house at the age of nineteen by joining the military. By then I had had many sexual experiences with other men.

I had one of my earliest sexual experiences with another man when I was eleven years old. He was a total stranger. I'll never forget that it was on the Fourth of July because of the rather dramatic way it happened. We climbed up to a high hill, hid in the bushes, and both took off our clothes. I didn't know it at the time, but there was a lookout tower on that hill and fireworks were set to go off at that tower. We were having sex in the bushes when suddenly we heard an explosion of sound. Flares, sparklers, roman candles, and everything else went off. It was a fitting way to come out: with a bang!

There were other experiences. At the age of eleven I started working after school at a grocery store. I had an allowance from this job which I used to travel to the city near our town where my mother lived. Every Saturday after I visited her I would catch an afternoon movie. It must have been a place for gay men to congregate, because it always ended up with the man next to me placing his hands all over me. After that we would usually meet in the men's room and I would get a blow job or be masturbated by the other man.

I had my first lover at the age of thirteen. To me he was an older man, in his late twenties. My aunt and uncle played bingo every Saturday night at the VFW hall. For some reason I was brought along, although I wasn't permitted to play. Perhaps they thought I was too young, or that it was wrong for children to gamble. So I would go into the lounge and read old magazines. There was a man who also didn't play bingo but hung around in the lounge. We became interested in each other. Every Saturday night we met out behind the VFW hall and had sex in the bushes. I was very cautious. When we were in the lounge, I would keep one eye out for my aunt and uncle; if they approached, I pretended I didn't know the man. But to me he was my first love. The relationship lasted for over a year.

Even with all these experiences it took me a long time, perhaps four years or so, before I admitted to myself, "I am gay." There were few opportunities to find other gay men in the town where I lived, but, as I said, I made regular trips into the city where my mother lived and where I began to develop close ties with other gay men.

But I was always very guarded. I never gave out my address or phone number, and I used my first name only. Of course, this part of my life was carefully hidden from my straight friends and family. Eventually I made a lot of gay friends so that by the time I was sixteen I regularly went with gay friends to movies or dinner or to a gay bar. You had to be eighteen to enter these bars, but I look older than my years and usually managed to get in whenever I wanted to.

What was it like to come out then? These were the early post–World War II years. If you had access to a large city, like I did, there were plenty of opportunities to meet other gay men. There were cruising spots that I used: places where men would meet and then go elsewhere for sex. Railroad and bus stations were often cruising areas and good places to meet other men for quick sex. There were gay moviehouses and one or two gay bars. You did have to be careful. Several of my friends who were too obvious or who approached the wrong person were beaten up on occasion, although I never had a problem with that.

Have I ever felt attracted to a woman? There was a brief time in my life when I was involved in a romantic relationship with a woman. I was twenty years old and in the service at the time. We met through common friends and eventually we became engaged. It just seemed like the thing to do at the time, even though I remember being repulsed by her physically. She had a two-year-old daughter from an earlier marriage. I was madly in love with that child; I loved her more than I loved her mother. We had some photographs taken at a professional studio which I sent home to my mother. My mother wrote back saying this woman looked like a whore and that I should break the engagement. Thankfully, I followed my mother's advice, although to this day I don't know why she had this reaction to my engagement. In retrospect, I know that the marriage could never have worked.

As a younger man I did date women occasionally, but only when I had to. In the military especially I dated for the sake of appearance. Many of my gay friends did the same. I must admit that I feel a certain repulsion at the thought of being physical with a woman. I am a fingertip person and there is a softness to a woman that my fingertips don't respond to. I appreciate women and I appreciate how attractive they can be, but there is no sexual interest. A woman to me is a red light; a guy is a green light. That's all there is to it.

My situation is different now. I don't know if it's because I'm older or more accepting of my gayness, or if it's just the tempo of the times, but I never worry anymore about appearances. I've just started a new business, a boutique. It's located next to a gay hotel and I assume all my customers are gay. You can't own a gay business and not spend a lot of time socializing with other gay people. Right now I'd say all my friends are gay. But it's been like that for a long time. In the late 1960s I was very active in the homosexual rights movement on a national level, and so I was around groups of gay people all the time. Since then I have moved to another part of the country and am no longer involved in the movement. Now I am in the process of trying to decide in my own mind if the gay movement needs me. I have been a writer for a number of years and have written for newspapers and have published articles and short stories in national magazines. I have a talent for writing and I would like to use it to contribute to the gay movement, perhaps in the form of contributions to the newsletter of the local gay rights group. But as yet I am not involved in any gay organizations. I certainly don't want to get involved in the gay religious organizations. I have my own opinion of God, my relationship to Him and what He expects of me, but I don't believe in organized religion.

In all I'm pretty well satisfied with my social life. Of course, everyone's social life could be improved. We constantly try to make new friends. But, ironically, it seems the harder we try, the worse it turns out. When we first meet someone, we are on our best behavior. We try to impress them. We project an image of the person we would like them to believe we are, rather than letting them know who we really are. Everyone has faults. We know our own faults, and we even manage to hide them from ourselves. We would like to hide them from our friends, but we're not always successful. Occasionally we have little flare-ups, we don't feel well or are out of sorts with the world, and then our friends see the raw edges of our personality. Perhaps they decide they no longer wish to be our friends. And so relationships are always fragile. I think it's the same in both the gay and the straight worlds. I think Sigmund Freud described the essence of human relationships. People are initially attracted to each other on the basis of sexual attraction. It develops from there into a deeper, more lasting relationship, sometimes involving sex, sometimes not.

For myself, I see nothing wrong with brief relationships that are purely sexual. I do go to gay bathhouses. Often I find that time is of the essence when sexual needs arise. When I go to a bathhouse I know that I can quickly select from a large group of people who have come there specifically for sex. Now, I might not be a particular man's idea of a sexual partner for the moment, but I know that if I stay long enough, eventually I will find someone who is just as willing as I am. Beaches and gay bars are also good places for casual encounters. Actually I often find that I am not limited to homosexual settings. Several weeks ago on a Saturday morning I ran down to the supermarket to pick up a few things. The place was very busy, and as I was hastily turning the corner at the end of the aisle, my shopping cart collided with another young man's cart. Although it was my fault, we exchanged apologies. At that point our eyes met, and each of us knew in an instant that we each had a desire to be fulfilled. I went through the checkout counter sooner then he did. I waited on the other side of the counter until he had completed his shopping, and then we met outside and had a cigarette. We exchanged addresses and phone numbers and met later that day at my place, where we had a very enjoyable sexual encounter. To me it isn't really necessary to go to a place like a bathhouse that is specifically designed for sex. There are of course no gay supermarkets. Maybe one day there will be. But this was a heterosexual supermarket, and yet two gay men met there quite by accident and established a liaison.

On the other hand, I know that many heterosexuals believe that whenever gay people get together it is for the purpose of having sex. That's a lot of nonsense. Gay people socialize with others just like heterosexuals do. In fact, last month I attended a party that was held at a bathhouse. Now a bathhouse is generally a place where gay men meet for sex, and in fact there were men there who were not with the party who were engaging in the usual sort of sexual interplay that goes on at bathhouses. But the people with the party were there for a social gathering. I'm sure if anyone had wanted to join in with what was going on in the background it would have been permissible. I for one didn't join in, and I still had a very good time.

The bars and bathhouses are of course dominated by younger men. A lot of people would say that this is because younger gays reject older ones. I don't think it is that simple. I find a variety of attitudes toward older gays on the part of younger ones. There are of course the hustlers, those who have flesh for sale. They prefer older gay men because older gays are the most likely customers and they generally have more cash. They naturally gravitate toward older men out of necessity, rather than out of any sort of sexual attraction.

Gay men under thirty who are not hustlers have really bought into the idea that life is over at thirty. Many of them are desperate to find a lover before that dreadful age is reached, or before one more hair falls out or one more wrinkle appears. It is a fast life between the ages of twenty and thirty. There is a desperate search to find Prince Charming. The presence of this mythical gentleman is felt in every bar in every city across the land. Young gay men sit up past their bedtimes in bars, hoping that the next time the door opens Prince Charming will walk in. These sorts of gay men would not even consider relating to a gay man over thirty. Prince Charming never ages.

Then there are gay men under thirty who are only interested in older gays. They have a father fixation. They are looking for a kind older man who will play a father role for them. Perhaps they relate more to the personal as opposed to the physical qualities of the older man. Or perhaps the sense of security that they get with an older, more established man is the most important thing to them.

Everyone has a set of rules or mental images that determines who will be considered a potential sexual partner. We carry a sort of mental map in our heads, complete with an inventory of physical and personal characteristics. When we encounter others, we compare them to our map. If the fit is close enough, they are judged acceptable. Otherwise they are rejected. But our mental maps may change; our standards may be modified because of recent events, the way we feel at a particular moment, or a particular quality of the other person. What a lot of older gay men don't realize is that the mental maps of younger gay men are flexible. There are always exceptions to the rule, and so a younger man who never considered sexual relationships with older men may decide to be sexual with a particular older man.

I am able to attract young gay men to me by fitting into their mental maps. I overcome my age in the way I relate to them. The most important element in the ability of the older gay man to relate to younger men is the attitude of the older man. We can, as human beings, attract or repel others depending upon our own personal attitude at the moment. I relate to younger people at their own level. I approach them. I engage them in conversation around topics that are of interest to them. I find out what they are interested in, what turns them on, and I zero in on that. At a certain point they stop thinking about my physical appearance and start thinking about the union of our minds. In fact, once younger people get to know me, they are fascinated because they know that I have something to contribute to their lives that they cannot find in their peers. We develop a common ground in a way that will eventually lead to the bedroom.

It may be true that most young gay men would not choose the company of older gays. But if the older gay man has a certain essence and puts it to work for himself, he will draw people to him to such an extent that, as I do, he will have to say no to someone's request. It takes an outgoing personality and a genuine concern about the other person. And it requires patience not only with the other person but with yourself as well. It involves showing respect toward the younger man, showing him that you value his thoughts and his company.

I know that an older gay man's attitude and his approach can be even more important than good looks in attracting others to him. I have a gay friend who is ten years younger than me and very attractive. He is slim and muscular and has everything going for him. But while I'm successful at cruising, he can never seem to make out. He looks at me and says he doesn't understand, but I know that his negative attitude drives others away.

A lot of older gay men spend long hours in loneliness that is self-imposed because they repel others with this sort of negative attitude toward themselves. They will look at an attractive young man and say to themselves, "I would love to make love to him, but I know he will reject me, so I won't even try." Perhaps they have been rejected many times before and don't want to be hurt one more time. So they let the opportunity slip by. They would rather be silent and not suffer any emotional pain than venture one word in a conversation. So they don't take the risk, and thereby they fulfill their own negative image of themselves.

Older gays are less diverse in their attitudes toward younger gays than younger gays are toward older ones. Older gays are of course attracted to youth. Gay people in general place a premium on youth and attractiveness. I think heterosexuals do, too. But the older gay man may feel resentful. He is resentful because he feels left out. He is left out of social gatherings. His name is the last on the list of those to be invited. He is the one who is forgotten at Christmastime and at birthdays. In my opinion, and it is just an opinion, the average older gay man feels that he is over the hill. He doesn't really feel a part of gay life; he does not get his full share out of life. Although I can surely relate to these feelings, I must say I don't share them. I think we get out of life only what we put into it. And if we are willing to put forth an effort, to take the risk of reaching out to others, then by the law of averages we will reap something in return. I'm reminded of Kipling's poem "If." If you can keep your head when all about are losing theirs, if you can say, "I'll try one more time," you'll be ahead. Forget last night's defeat or last week's refusal or last month's rejection and say to yourself, "Today, I will have a positive attitude. I will smile at everyone I meet today and maybe that smile will attract." As an older gay man, I feel I must keep my positive attitude. If someone rejects me, that is his loss, not mine, because I had a great deal more to offer than he realized. Everyone has something to offer. It's like the old saying, "No man is so poor that he cannot be of value to others." I feel very, very strongly about this.

I consider my current sex life to be very satisfying. I have more sex now in my mid-forties than I had when I was younger. In fact, over the past six months I have turned down many offers. I would like to give you a little background to help you understand this. I don't consider myself to be very attractive physically. I am quite a bit overweight and very self-conscious about that. So, two or three years ago, I decided it would be propitious to become a john. A john is a patron to a younger person. The younger person offers his time, attention, affection, and sex; the john offers money in return. Many older gay men would consider this sort of arrangement as beyond the realm of human possibility. That is easy to understand. In order for them to be johns, they would first have to admit that they are unattractive to those who attract them. I have accepted that. I find it extremely flattering to have attention paid to me for a few dollars. I am able to have sexual relations with persons who are young and attractive and very alluring, simply by freeing myself of a few of these dollars. To me there is no difference whether you buy hyacinths for the soul in the form of a piece of jewelry or a new suit, or in the form of an attractive young person you can take into your arms and make love to.

One time as I was sitting at a bar I noticed two young men playing pool near me. After a while it became clear that they were competing for my attention. The movements of their bodies were a ballet, a special performance for my benefit. There happened to be another older gay, someone who was also known as a john, sitting at the other side of the pool table. This man decided to compete with me for the young men. I was very amused by the situation, because I knew it was now a private showing on stage for the two of us alone. To me it was sexually gratifying to see this foreplay in motion: two young men offering themselves on an auction block. The young men decided who the victors would be, and that night the other older man and I each ended up with a young man who was very nice to be with.

There are gay men who will spend a considerable amount of money entertaining a date by providing dinner, an evening at the theater, and a few drinks at the bar. Then they go home with that person and have sex. They fool themselves into believing they have not paid for the sex, but they have, just as surely as I pay for it. The difference is that I leave out the rationalizations. To me it is the same thing.

Of course the cost varies. There is a sort of market economy. The price varies depending on the hour, the weather if you are outdoors, and the quantity and quality of the competition. It depends on how many hustlers there are (the hustler being the counterpart to the john–the younger man offering himself for sale) and how many johns there are and whether you can outspend them. I have paid as little as five and as much as fifty dollars at one time.

Often the relationship continues for a time. If I find a young man who is very attractive and affectionate, I become his patron. I have at times supplied housing, usually a room in my apartment or sometimes an apartment I rent for the fellow. In the past year, on separate occasions, I have had three young men who moved into the apartment I share with my partner. In each case I had sex with them almost on a daily basis. I have also supplied food and clothing. I might take the young man shopping for shoes or slacks or whatever he might need. When we go out to a bar, I treat him to drinks.

My philosophy is that all human beings, heterosexual and homosexual, are basically selfish. We all do things because there is a payoff to us personally. Now we may lie to ourselves and say, "Look, I did that for you." But in reality we acted because it pleased us, and for no other reason.

These relationships I'm describing don't last for more than a few weeks or months, but I find them satisfying. So long as the sexual relationship remains satisfactory, it can continue regardless of the cost. As long as the services I receive match the purchase price, I'm satisfied. When the balance swings the other way, it's time to end the relationship.

Although these sexual relationships come and go, there is a relationship that has remained a constant in my life. I'm very proud and gratified that this past week my partner and I celebrated eighteen years together. Our relationship began as a lover relationship; that is, we were sexual with each other. In fact we remained true to each other sexually for the first two years. After that we both decided we would seek sexual release elsewhere. For the past ten years we have not had physical contact with each other beyond a simple touch. As far as we are concerned, our decision not to be sexual has not caused the relationship to deteriorate in the least. We are as close and as committed to each other as ever, and we have continued to share a home all these years.

I think there are two primary reasons our relationship has lasted so long. For one thing, we have mutual respect. We respect each other's feelings and each other's needs for support, as well as needs to be left alone, to be independent when necessary. The other binding force is our history together. Together we have endured all the adversity that life can throw at two people in eighteen years. We have weathered financial crises, job losses, illnesses, geographical relocations, disappointments with friends, and verbal abuse from heterosexuals who objected to our homosexuality. We have shared crushed expectations and sadness as well as laughter and joy. The relationship is strong enough and always has been strong enough to withstand the problems of each day. And as the relationship exists from day to day it stretches into months, years, and decades.

I don't think our relationship is unusual in the gay community. We have met many couples who have been together for more than ten years. I know one couple of twenty years and I have two friends who have been together for twenty-two years, although I have no idea what their sex lives are like. But this is not to say that gay relationships are not fragile. Especially when two gay men first establish a lover relationship it is easily broken. There are very good reasons for this. For one thing I think two homosexual men tend to be somewhat more promiscuous than a heterosexual couple. Physical attraction plays a greater role. So when the couple socializes there is always the opportunity and the threat that someone more attractive will come along and damage the relationship by taking one of the partners out of it. The other factor that makes gay relationships more fragile is that there are no societal restraints to keep the relationship intact. There is no marriage license; there are no religious vows, no children, no community property laws, no relatives supportive of the relationship. There are only two people who have nothing but their attraction for each other and the desire to please each other that will keep them together once they have begun this relationship.

What does the word "lover" mean to me? A lover is someone with whom I have an emotional and a sexual relationship. To say we are lovers means that I belong to him and he belongs to me, to the exclusion of all others. Although my partner of eighteen years is no longer my lover, I have had many lovers in my lifetime. I would say there have been fifteen or twenty. Each relationship ended in a somewhat different way. After all, you can't get into the number twenty without reaching variations on a theme. I can say they all ended amiably. Those past lovers who live in this area have remained good friends. There are others who are in different states, and although I've not kept in touch I still have a warm regard for them.

Let me give you an example. About ten years ago–this was during a time when I was with my present partner–I met an attractive young man. He was the father of two lovely children and his wife was pregnant. His interests were bisexual. We fell in love, and ours developed into an extremely close relationship. We did everything together. We went to the horse races, picnics with his family, drives in the country, and so on. He used to come over to my place and have dinner quite often. When he returned home he would tell his wife he wasn't hungry. I don't know if his wife ever suspected anything. Things went on like this for two years. Then he had an argument with his wife; she threw him out, and he came to live with me. But it turned out that he could never really live without a woman. Before long he met another woman. She looked remarkably like his wife and was a widow with two children. I wasn't surprised when he told me that he was in love with her. We both agreed that he should live with her. After that, I moved to another part of the country and lost track of him. Eight years later I ran into him on the street quite by accident. He was so glad to see me, he threw his arms around me and kissed me in public. He was married to the widow and living happily with her. They had a child of their own. Now he lives in the area and stops at the boutique to visit me occasionally. He brings his wife and his son with him, and right in front of them he gives me a bear hug and a big kiss. So the affection between us has lasted even though the love affair is long over.

I have had other relationships in my life that have not been sexual but that have been complete in every other way. Many heterosexuals would not believe that two gay men can share a home and not have sex, but that is a misconception. When I was in my late twenties I met a fellow to whom I related instantly. Our personalities were magnificently interwoven; we complemented each other. We became very intimate, although the idea of a sexual relationship never occurred to either one of us. We rented a house and set up housekeeping like a young married couple. We bought linens together, we bought dishes, we furnished the house from top to bottom. We lived together quite contentedly for almost three years. I mention this because I really believe in platonic relationships. I think that many older gays who are lonely don't need to be; they can be close to another person in a platonic sense and have almost all their needs met. They need never go home to an empty apartment. If finances are low, especially if they are retired, they can reduce their expenses by living together. In fact, our social security laws, which penalize married heterosexuals, do not penalize two men or two women who live together. And then all the housekeeping chores can be shared, making life easier. For instance, in my relationship with my current partner we are each responsible for those chores we like the best. I detest doing the laundry, so he does the laundry and I make up for it by doing the grocery shopping. Between the two of us, everything gets done. We are a partnership, and a very workable one.

But of course many heterosexuals don't understand that homosexuals have these sorts of relationships, or they just don't believe it. Heterosexuals can't possibly understand what homosexuals are like. The heterosexual is an outsider looking through a frosted window. He doesn't see inside very well. People like me, who have been gay for forty years and who are part of a gay community, have a totally different picture because we are inside looking at the situation as it is. I think it is very unfair the way heterosexuals stereotype gay people. They harp on their notion that gay people are interested in little else but sex. Sure, there is a lot of cruising among gay men. Some gay men are always on the hunt for sexual release. They want to dispel the loneliness they feel because they don't have a lover or children at home. But what about gay people like me? Gay people who have deep, lasting, committed relationships? One of my greatest pleasures is looking forward to the time each day when I will return home, open the door, and find my partner of eighteen years there waiting for me. And yet my experience is overlooked because we've all bought into stereotypes. They don't fit, but they don't die easily, either. We form a fixed idea of what a group of people is supposed to be like, and it's difficult to overcome that.

In the past ten years a homosexual rights movement has blossomed, and as a result there is a great deal more information available about what gay people are like. We've made a lot of progress. As I said, I was involved in the early homosexual rights movement way back in the 1960s, and since that time I have seen a lot of changes. Many people who would never before have dreamed of being open about their homosexuality have come out of the closet. Of course, many people are still very guarded. Professional people and those with responsible jobs are still afraid they will lose their positions.

Someday homosexuals will have their human rights, but that day has certainly not yet arrived. The Supreme Court of the United States has closed its doors to us. It will not hear cases concerning a state's right to discriminate against homosexuals. The judges have reduced us to second-class citizens. They have violated our human rights. Today any schoolteacher can be fired from his or her job simply for being homosexual. A landlord can throw you out of your apartment if he finds a gay magazine on your dresser when he comes in to check the plumbing. When you congregate with other gay people in a bar or club, the police can bust in, flash a light in your face, and take you in. We need first of all to be protected in our jobs, in our homes, and among our friends.

But even if the courts and the legislatures grant us equal rights, that is only the first step. Attitudes cannot be legislated. And there are still many people who fear and hate homosexuals. It is a sad truth that every society needs an underdog. It is human nature for people to find someone in life who is beneath them. Everyone needs to feel superior to someone. Various groups have played the role of underdog: blacks, foreigners, homosexuals. But homosexuals are at the very bottom. They are everyone's underdog.

At a gay pride rally I attended last month, a speaker told a story that for me illustrates this point. You know, because gay people are stigmatized and harassed by the law, they are often forced to limit their socializing to rundown and unsafe bars. This speaker told the story of a fire in such a bar in New Orleans last year. Thirty-two homosexual men lost their lives. Relatives were asked to come to the city morgue to identify the bodies. Do you know that many of the parents of these gay men refused to come down and identify the bodies of their own children? That is the very lowest point of tolerance on the human scale–to refuse to claim the remains of your own flesh and blood.

If this study does nothing else, it will be successful if it can create some understanding and acceptance of homosexuals, an understanding that we are all human beings first. The other differences among us are secondary. I feel sad in a way that it has taken so long for a study of this type. Imagine how many people it would have helped if done ten, twenty, or thirty years ago.

This study can also help gay people who are dealing with the issue of being homosexual and older. I know that many men who are gay and over forty feel left out of things. That is not surprising. As I've said, gay people do place a premium on youth and good looks. What happens to us as we grow older? We lose our hair, our figures, we become less attractive physically. We tend to withdraw from others and spend a lot of time alone. But I don't believe any of that is necessary. I'm a good example. I consider that I have spent the happiest years of my life since I turned forty.

In adjusting well to age, the most important thing is a positive attitude. The older gay man must realize that age has absolutely no bearing on his self-regard, on his social life, or on his ability to attract others. He is as old as the attitude he projects. His age cannot be adjusted. Forget about it! Tear down the calendars and throw them away if that will help. Concern with age is a hang-up, and he has got to get beyond the hang-up to what life is really all about. His main purpose in life is not to mark the years, but to reap as much happiness for himself and bring as much happiness to others as he possibly can.

The worst thing about growing older is becoming aware that time is running out. Since your days are numbered, you have to cram all the happiness and all the accomplishments that are left in fewer and fewer days. The hardest part is facing the realization that it will all end. It's like being forced to leave a party before the rest of the guests go.

The best thing about growing older is that you make fewer and fewer mistakes. You have been permitted to make most of your mistakes in life. With age you are able to reflect on those mistakes and make fewer in the future because you apply the lessons you have learned. That is the beauty of growing older.

CHAPTER 6

Arthur

47

The cramped kitchen could barely accommodate the interviewer, Arthur, and Arthur's pet parakeet, which chirped incessantly throughout the interview. Arthur was eager to talk about himself; even so, he was as stern and humorless as when he gave one of his serious speeches on police harassment at the human rights organization. This man was intensely devoted to the gay cause. Although he spent most of his free time with gay people, his loud and overtly masculine manner would have been appropriate in the locker room at a football game.

I was ten years old when I had my first sexual experience. A group of boys from the neighborhood would go swimming at a rock quarry near home. Four of us became very close, and we formed a sort of gang. Some of us had begun to explore the feelings in our genitals on our own, and I guess one day we decided to do it as a group. There was no orgasm or anything like that, but just what might be called exploration. This experience was repeated several times. Interestingly, three of the four of us are now gay. The other fellow never admitted to being gay and even got married. But I know he goes to gay bars, and I'm sure he is suppressing his sexuality.

These early experiences were important to me. When they began I had no idea what having sex was all about, but I slowly began to learn that having sex was something that gave me a sense of enjoyment and a sense of being close to another person. It also gave me a chance to compare my very strong feelings of attraction to these boys with the feelings I had toward the girls I took out on dates. With the girls the feeling was different–there was no excitement.

99

Right from the start when I began to take girls to school dances there was no desire to explore them sexually. Somehow I did get into sexual exploration with one girl, but I had no desire to repeat the experience. That was pretty easy to do because I came from a very religious background and my parents disapproved of any kind of sexual activity. So it was always easy to avoid being sexual with a girl, without calling attention to defects in your masculinity, by saying that you "respected" her too much to expect her to put out.

I first began to realize that I was attracted to other boys about a year after the first sexual encounter with my buddies. The first couple of times it was just fooling around. But after it happened three, four times, I began to realize there was something special about my relationship to my buddies. Of course we never talked about it amongst ourselves. We just stuck together in our little gang of four. Whenever you saw one of us, you saw all of us.

I didn't think about it too much; I just enjoyed being with my special group of friends. Whenever I had to go off with a different group, like on a camping trip, I didn't have a good time. When I was with *my* friends I felt comfortable. That's where I had all my highs. We stayed together as the years went by, right up until the time I went into the military at the age of seventeen.

When I went into the service I felt like I was among total strangers, but gradually I began to meet men who I somehow sensed were gay. I have always been able to sense when another person is gay, although I really don't know how. A group of us just naturally seemed to come together. It was always the same group. We never went to the dance bars like the other guys but rather to the quiet bars or what I called the "executive bars" where you weren't expected to dance with girls.

I did manage to have brief affairs with several of the men in this group, but we had to keep our guard up, because there was a constant threat hanging over us. When I did meet someone, we were limited in our activities. We couldn't exactly walk around base holding hands! Fortunately I spent most of my time in the military in Germany, where I had private quarters off base, which made it easier to have some privacy. I was also involved with a young German man who of course did not have to worry, as I did, about being courtmartialed.

In the early 1950s I was ordered back to the States, and the relative freedom I had had in Germany was over. My living quarters were on base, so it was harder to go anyplace with other gay men or to maintain a relationship. You didn't have all sorts of social and political organizations for gay people like you have today, and the very few gay bars were usually not known to military personnel. In our base area I wasn't aware of any gay bars.

When I got out of the military I came home to my town and got involved sexually with some of the boys with whom I had gone through school and who were still living in the area.

Then at some point I decided to get out of gay activities. I can't remember precisely why I made this decision, but I suppose I felt that my earlier gay activities were a part of my adolescence and that perhaps it was time to grow up and settle down. My parents, who were very traditional, expected me to marry and raise a family, and times were such that even people who didn't want to marry were pressured to do so–if not by family, then by friends or employers. This was the early 1950s, the era of Joe McCarthy and the witch-hunts, and everyone did his best not to call attention to himself.

Lela was introduced to me by a mutual friend, and we soon developed a close relationship. We dated for a year and then got married. At first it felt good. Later the relationship had an empty feeling to me. After several years I finally admitted to myself why this was: it was the fact that I was more attracted to strange men than I was to my own wife. When she discovered my gayness, she reacted violently. I still feel that if she could have accepted the fact that I was gay, we could have worked something out and stayed together. But she just couldn't cope with it.

For the first ten years of our marriage I did not have any contact with gay men, although I was becoming increasingly aware of my own feelings of attraction toward men. As my relationship with Lela deteriorated I felt the need for other men more and more, so I eventually began to venture into gay bars and restaurants in the city where we lived. I began to build up a circle of gay friends and had brief sexual relationships, all of which I hid from Lela.

I got involved with a very handsome but very troubled gay man. I think he hated himself for being gay and his hatred expressed itself in hostility toward other gay men. With me, he decided he had found a chance to get even with a gay person. He called the police, they confronted Lela, and it all came to light.

When Lela and I were married, we never discussed our previous sexual experiences or relationships. We didn't even talk about my experiences in the military. So when this event occurred, my homosexuality came as a total shock to Lela. Ours was not a good marriage. There was a lot of hostility even before this event, and I guess Lela felt tricked or betrayed. Unfortunately for me, she took the information about my sexuality and used it as a very effective weapon against me.

We had two children: Burt, five, and Laura, who was less than a year old at the time. The most painful part of all this, for me, was that because of Lela's opposition I was unable to see my own children.

After the visit from the police Lela confronted me in a rage and I admitted everything. I told her that I had been homosexual before we met and that I had had relationships with men during the marriage. She filed for divorce on the basis of cruel and unusual treatment. I guess that I was so upset over this turn of events that I allowed the wool to be pulled over my eyes. Lela's lawyer convinced me to agree to the divorce, and in return they agreed not to bring out in court the fact that I was gay. But of course they did bring out this fact in open court, and things got quite messy. The court granted the divorce, but this was just the beginning. First we got into a protracted custody battle and later there were disagreements about my visitation rights. When Lela refused to allow me to see the kids, I held up support payments and we ended up in court again.

The judge appointed a counselor to investigate me for the purpose of deciding on visitation rights. He announced in court that he would abide by the decision of the counselor, and the counselor recommended at the next court session that I be allowed visitation rights without my ex-wife's presence. I could take the children on my own for an afternoon. I didn't know it at the time, but Lela worked as a sort of executive secretary for a fraternal order of which the judge was a member. While I struggled along, she pulled strings behind the scenes. So, given all that, the judge's decision was predictable. He restricted my visitation rights to the point where it was impossible for me to visit with the children. The visitations had to be arranged at times according to her discretion; she was to be present, and I was allowed one hour. That's not visitation.

Lela was extremely hostile to me. She put every obstacle she could think of in my way. She would announce arbitrarily that I had to be there at a time when she knew I was working, and her attitude was "Be there or else." When I was with the kids she forced them to sit on the sofa and not run around or make noise. They never had to do that for other company. It got so the kids didn't look forward to my visits and were terrified of their mother's temper. I tried to tell Lela that she was making my visits unhappy for the children, but she was one person I just could not talk to. The kids were too young to understand that their mother was using them against me, and the pressure they were under was terrible. I didn't want them to grow up hating their father, so after six months of unhappy visits I made a decision that was one of the hardest I have ever had to make.

I decided to end my relationship with the children. I would just get myself scheduled for duty at work when the kids would be available and I would use this as an excuse to not visit. I have not seen my children for seven years now; I often miss them and wonder how they have changed and what they are doing. But I do think, looking back on all this, that I made the right decision. I think the kids have had it a lot easier this way.

I have always planned to have a talk with my children when the right time comes. I think around the time they graduate from high school they will be old enough to understand my lifestyle and the painful events back then. At the time they were just too young to understand what was happening. I do know that they are growing up in a part of the country where gay rights organizations are active, so I'm sure they are learning something about gay people which will pave the way for their understanding of me. In fact, I've been on national TV a couple of dozen times as part of my activism in the gay community. Whether they realize it or not, my kids must have seen me on TV sometime in these past few years.

These events, as painful as they were, were part of a very necessary coming-out process for me. The divorce and the separation from the children solidified my gay identity and forced me to realize how important it is to work for civil rights for gay people. Ever since the divorce I've been very actively working with gay rights organizations.

To me, coming out means being honest: honest with your family, your friends, people at work, everyone. It means knowing who you are and accepting that. It's the self-acceptance that is the biggest part. That is something I had to work at and think about for many years. Once I did that, being honest with people came naturally. I could say that coming out is the easiest thing in the world to do–the hardest part is thinking about it.

My one heterosexual relationship was with Lela and it was a disaster. However, I've had a number of homosexual relationships that have been much more satisfying. I met Smitty about three years before the divorce and continued a relationship with him for four years. I guess you could say this was a relationship that worked despite a lot of obstacles. Smitty worked in my office, where we met. I was in my late thirties and married and he was seventeen. We saw a lot of each other at work and also after hours. It really was a difficult situation. Since I was married and hiding my homosexuality from my wife, we had to be careful about being seen in public. We couldn't go to gay bars because Smitty was underage. We couldn't go to Smitty's place either, because he lived with his mother and she didn't know we were seeing each other. Mostly Smitty and I would meet for dinner or take in a show. Often we would sit in the car after work, listen to the radio, and talk.

It was really a very tender love affair despite all the limitations. After four years Smitty decided to attend college in a different part of the country and the distance made it impossible to keep up the relationship. At college Smitty fell in love with another fellow and when he came home to visit we both understood that our relationship was over. We parted with no animosity, but rather with a lot of caring and affection for each other. We are still the best of friends.

After Smitty, I was on my own for a while. I did have a brief relationship with a man named David, but it didn't work out. He was very excited about me and wanted us to declare a relationship right away. I don't believe in doing that until two people have been together for a period of time to demonstrate their commitment. My present lover, Bob, and I did not declare our relationship until after we had been living together for a year. A lot of people are like David–on the second date they are ready to call it a relationship. It doesn't work that way; it takes time. In retrospect, David's reactions were very typical. He rushed in with a bang and then lost his enthusiasm. But in order for a relationship to survive, two people have to work on it, and David wasn't willing to put in the work; he left it all up to me. I went to the trouble and expense of getting a larger apartment and redecorating it. David could have cared less. This was a clear signal to me that David was not truly committed, and I ended the relationship a few months later.

My current lover, Bob, and I have been together for five and a half years now. The relationship has had its ups and downs. We have times when things run very, very well and then we have our rough little hurdles. There is a big age difference. I'm forty-seven and Bob is thirty-one. That really doesn't cause too many problems. Very often when we go out in the evenings Bob will want to stay late and I will want to come home and go to bed. You see, I get up at five-thirty to go to work, and after work I spend my time working in gay community groups, so I've got to get to bed at a decent hour. So it is not unusual for me to head home while Bob will stay until the early hours of the morning. On the weekends, of course, we can both stay at the bar to dance and socialize.

Bob and I spend a lot of time working on the Gay Hotline. This is a service organization that I created. We run a crisis phone line out of the homes of volunteers and we do a lot of counseling, information and referral, and advocacy where we can. I also do a lot of panels–that is, public speaking to university classes and other groups interested in learning about gay people. Bob functions as a sort of secretary for me. He types all my notes and correspondence and corrects my grammar, since he is much better at that than I am.

We have little battles over political issues all the time. He may disagree with a position I take at a gay rights group meeting and sometimes he gets mad at me after the meeting. Politically, we are very independent of each other. Bob is a Republican and I'm a Democrat.

The biggest problem in the relationship now is that Bob has not held a job for over a year. This creates financial problems. We like to go away for vacation and to visit relatives back east, but we can't manage to do that on one salary. Bob's problem is a defeatist attitude. By contrast, I have a very positive attitude. When I go out for a job, I am very positive and very aggressive. I may know only a little bit about the job, but I'm not about to let the employer know that I don't know enough about the job to do it. I fake it if I have to. Once I get in, I work my ass off learning the ropes, and I get promoted. When I worked for a farm implement company I went from guard to unit supervisor to field operations supervisor to head of sales operations in less than two years. And I didn't have any special skills or even a college education when I started. Bob has some office skills but he doesn't know any technical trades or the like, and so he gets discouraged easily and gives up. But I tell him, "You've got to project a positive attitude. You cannot let people know you are discouraged or think you can't do the job. That way you'll stay on top." It's part of surviving in life. It's done in the straight community and in the gay community.

I think part of the reason that Bob and I have been able to overcome some of our problems is the support we get from our families. My father died when I was eleven, but I have a mother and sister who have been very supportive of my relationship with Bob. My mom in particular has made a real effort to get to know the gay community. She has been to the Metropolitan Community Church (MCC) and to the MCC ministers' conference. She understands the gay community. Both my mom and my sister attended the holy union services for me and Bob. Bob's family also knows about our relationship and has been very supportive. When we go home for visits, we are expected to visit both families, and we are always made to feel at home.

Bob and I have a relationship based on commitment, not just on physical attraction. For some people the relationship has to be almost all sex. I'm different. Sometimes I put sex completely out of the picture. In the last six months Bob and I have had sex only four times, but that is certainly all right with me, because there are lots of things more important than sex–things like building the relationship and de- voting myself to work for the gay community. When I was in the military I had much more sex than I do now, and although my desires are the same now at the age of forty-seven, it doesn't bother me to keep busy with things other than sex. As a practical matter I just don't have the time or energy. Most nights we have meetings and we don't get back until ten or eleven and that is just about time to go to bed.

The sex that I do have is not very satisfying–I suppose if I were to rate it, I would say it was rather stale most of the time. But I don't really think about how satisfied or dissatisfied I am. It's like working yourself up to an orgasm, and then that's it; it's over and it was no big deal.

Bob has sex a lot more often than I do, and he does it with other men. I allow him his freedom because he is, after all, sixteen years younger than I am, and he would get bored just being with me all the time. So once a week or so Bob goes off to the bathhouse or a bar and he usually has sex.

Now, I never go out looking for a sex partner for myself, but very rarely I do happen to meet someone and I'm not closed about it. I don't believe that two lovers have to be completely monogamous. Just a couple of months ago I was driving home in the evening and I happened to give a ride to this young kid who was hitchhiking. My only intention was to give him a ride. When I asked him where he was going, it turned out he wasn't really going anywhere, and before we had gone more than a few blocks he asked me, "How long is it going to take us to get to your house?" So then I guessed his intentions. I don't know, it was just one of those things that happen, wham! And I'm not sorry for it. If I saw the kid again, I'd pick him up and give him a ride again. It was a very enjoyable experience because the kid had such a beautiful happy attitude–no commitment, just sharing a lot of joy and affection for a little while. You don't just meet someone that way all the time. In fact, this was the only person other than Bob that I've had sex with in a couple of years.

Sure, there are lots of times when I see an attractive guy that I would like to have sex with. But there is usually a good reason not to pursue it. Bob and I socialize with a lot of young people and many of them are very attractive. But if I notice an attractive guy, it might just be that he is my friend's lover and I think, "I can't do that. I'd better leave him alone."

I talk to a lot of gay men about sex. Some of them are friends and many of them are the people who call me on the Gay Hotline. How often have I heard the same complaint: "I can't find anyone. I never have a lover. I haven't had any sex in six months, what am I going to do?" My attitude is, I'm not going to worry about it. There is no need to. It's something you have to learn to live with. I don't ever intend to let it bother me, because I know that if a sexual involvement is going to happen, it will happen, and you can't really enjoy it if you force it to happen or worry about it. Some men I know actually feel guilty if they are not having sex constantly! I know enough to be satisfied with what I have, and if I'm different from other men, that's OK. Some people are not satisfied unless they have four or five bottles of beer a night. Give me one bottle a month, and I'll be satisfied.

I know where my priorities are. The most important thing in my life is helping to build organizations that will increase understanding among gay people–organizations like the Gay Hotline. My job is the next most important thing, and after that my relationship with Bob. Next comes my leisure time, time spent with friends, and sexual enjoyment comes at the very bottom.

For the last ten years gay community organizations have been a big part of my life. I think that, as gay people, we will only win our rights if we can organize into strong and viable community organizations. The heterosexual community has its organizations, whether they are for political power or for social services. I have found that it is very hard to keep the community strong with organizations because they require a very great time commitment. Few people are willing to give up their leisure time to work for their communities. This is a very sad situation for us, because the gay community is made up of very diverse groups which pull in opposite directions. There is bitterness and misunderstanding among the sado-masochists, the drag queens, the transvestites, lesbians, the coupled versus uncoupled gays, and the various religious groups. How are we going to defend ourselves against all the bigots when we are fighting among ourselves? So I've devoted a big part of my life to helping make gay community organizations a reality by being an active member in the local gay rights group and by starting my own organization, the Gay Hotline.

There are other ways that gay people can support their own community. Whenever I go to a bar or to a restaurant, I make sure that it is a business that supports the gay community–a business that is either owned and operated by gay people or at least supportive of our rights. I'm tired of supporting the people who have been putting me down for years. Why should I support them? I patronize bars and restaurants three or four times a week and I spend my money there. Why should I patronize businesses owned by heterosexuals who oppress me? If it's a matter of driving a couple of extra miles to support my own community, I'm happy to do that.

A couple of years ago I got this idea. Have you ever heard of Duncan Hines approved restaurants? The Duncan Hines people sent out teams of experts to inspect and approve restaurants all across the country. My idea was to start a Lambda approved program similar to this. (Lambda is a Greek letter which is a symbol of gay rights.) Any bar, restaurant, or other business that serves the public could be approved if they supported gay people in their community. Even straight bars could get the approval if they were openly favorable to having gay customers and supporting gay rights. That way the gay community would know who its friends are and gay people could choose to support businesses who support gay rights. I think this program is a good idea, but I've never had the resources to organize it.

I think organizations are also important for older people. Our country is structured in such a way that when we reach the age of sixty-five we are told that we are no longer useful. We are forced to retire and we're sent off to the scrap heap. Retirement can be a very negative experience for those people who just don't want to carry on their lives. But it can be an opportunity for us to leave our paying jobs and get into areas that are really of interest to us. When I retire from a paying job, I intend to continue working, but as a volunteer.

Older people have a great store of knowledge acquired over the years. Instead of saying people are useless at sixty-five, the government ought to sponsor programs where older people in different trades and occupations would serve as advisors to young people—for advice, rehabilitation, vocational training, and the like. The way it is done now we will only pay professionals to do this training. Professionals may have read all the books in the world, but they don't have the kind of well-rounded knowledge that older people have to share. A lot of valuable crafts especially, like engraving and hand weaving, are being lost forever because we haven't given the old artisans an opportunity to pass on their skills.

All of these retirement communities are a good example of how we have made older people useless. When we put older folks into these segregated communities we are saying, "You are not needed anymore, so stay out of the way." These retired people have decent shelter, food, and clothing, but that is not enough. They need a sense of responsibility, a sense of being needed, and they can only get that if we have programs set up so older people *can* be useful to younger ones.

Another one of my ideas is to buy up seventy-five or eighty acres of land and build a retirement community for gay people. But this wouldn't be an age-segregated community like the ones we have now. In order to live in the community, an older person would have to be willing to devote time each day to teaching his knowledge to other people. There would be classes where all sorts of skills could be taught–housekeeping, cooking, financial management, trades, crafts–whatever skills people had to share. Why should all this knowledge go to waste?

Another thing that gay organizations like this can do is to unite the younger and older gay people. I don't think you can say, well, this is how young gay people feel about older ones. It's not that simple. There are probably two phases that young gay men experience. There are gay men who are very young, say sixteen to twenty-two. They have become aware of their sexuality very recently; many are still in school and dependent on parents. In a word, they are youngsters. They are out for a good time. They have no concept of what it means to be in a relationship; they don't quite understand what that involves, and I suppose they are not interested. Among men in this age group I find a great deal of hostility toward anyone who is more than five years their elder. It's like anyone older is from a different generation.

As they get into their late twenties they are less likely to reject another gay person just because that person is older. They get the first inklings that they, too, are moving up in age, and that they had better not reject the next older group because soon *they* will be there, too. They realize that if they limit their relationships to too narrow a group they may be left all alone. They start to get more serious about their friends. This is where some of the negative attitudes toward older gays begin to break down. I think that, after the late twenties, young gay people are pretty open about older ones. Really, the hostilities between gay men and women are much greater than they are between age groups.

As for how older gay people feel about younger ones, I'm sure there is a lot of diversity. There are older gays who are very uptight about having people know they are gay. These men tend to avoid the younger ones–who are much more open and upfront–like the plague. But then some of the older gay people I've met have been so closeted all their lives that they can't stand any gays who are open, even other *older* gay people. They are put off by the drag shows that younger people like. They tend to think that younger gays are flighty and immature, that they have nothing interesting to talk about.

Less-closeted older gays are much more tolerant of younger gays. They accept them as they are. They may not be into the discos, loud music, and young dress styles, but they can accept them. There is no hassle. I'm one of those older gay people who can accept younger ones. In fact, I almost prefer to be with gay people who are under thirty. I enjoy their company. They do not want to hide their gayness like many older people do. They want to be themselves, and they are willing to accept and be accepted. I value that. I haven't had any real problems as a result of associating mostly with gay people who are younger than me, because our values are the same. The only limitation I've found is that they like to stay out later than I do.

It is a shame for there to be hostility among groups within the gay community, because we certainly have enough to handle with all the hostility we experience from the straight community. When Bob and I lived back east it was much easier, but since we've moved we have found that straight people are a lot less open about gays. We never had any problems out there with landlords, neighbors, stores, or friends at work. It seems like here we've had nothing but problems.

For instance, back east I had many straight friends who socialized with my gay friends. They had no trouble accepting my gay friends. When I had a dinner party or went to a dance or a show, my gay friend would be there and there was no problem. Here I've found that my straight friends, say those I've met at work, are very uptight about gay people. So I just don't mix straight and gay anymore. Except for social events at work like the Christmas party, I always prefer to be with my gay friends. If there is a choice between the two, I always choose to go out with my gay friends.

We have also been made to feel a lot of hostility in our neighborhood. We live in a real conservative Baptist area. We don't have very much to do with our neighbors because when we have approached them they have been very hostile. We don't have our gay friends over to the house anymore because they get harassed by the neighbors. We don't have the freedom we would like to have in our own home.

But even in this conservative area there are always some people who are enlightened, and I think the experience of having an openly gay couple as neighbors has had some educational value for one or two people here. I'm thinking of our next-door neighbors, who have been pretty accepting. They have an eleven-year-old son in a parochial school, and one day when the nun was putting down gay people in front of the class this boy decided he would confront her. In front of the whole class he told her that she wasn't qualified to speak about gay people, that she didn't live near one or socialize with one like he did. We felt very good when they told us that. It just shows that a slow process of learning about what gay people are really like is taking place. It made it easier for Bob and me to stay here in this neighborhood.

When Bob and I first moved down here we had an awful time finding someone who would rent to two single men. As I said, this was quite a shock to us, because we had not had these problems back east. The first place we got was a two-room apartment we rented from a gay couple, so of course there was no problem. But it was a different story when we decided we needed more room and attempted to find another apartment. None of the landlords we spoke to would come right out and say, "I won't rent to two homosexuals." But we sure ran into a lot of hostility. Several times we literally got the door slammed in our faces. It always came down to the fact that we weren't known in the community and they didn't feel we were stable. I had been working at my job for a year and had good references. How could they say we were not stable?

It was the same story whether we applied to a complex run by Mom and Pop or to one of those large five-hundred-unit complexes. When we were turned down at one large complex, I filed a discrimination suit with the state's attorney and that at least got them scared. They offered to return our deposit, but they still wouldn't rent to us. We finally found an apartment in a small complex where we lived for a year before buying our home, but it was like hell living there.

Everyone stared at us but was afraid to be seen talking to us. Luckily, when we found this house and decided to buy it there weren't too many problems. The people we bought the house from knew we were gay and they told all our neighbors. The realtor and the people at the mortgage company must have known we were gay because our checks had both of our names on them. In fact, when the mortgage company sent an insurance man to talk to us he said, "The mortgage company told me it was a male couple who bought the house." Imagine that.

Department stores have been a problem. Bob and I have applied for charge accounts at every major department store in this area and we've been turned down every time. And the excuse is always the same. We're told that we are not "established" enough–despite the fact that I have owned my own home for two years and I've been at the same job for four years. At this point my attitude is, "If you don't want me, then you don't need my business." So that is why I try to do as much of my business as possible in places that are owned or operated by gay people.

You know, dealing with discrimination is not new for me. In the early 1950s I was dishonorably discharged from the military for my homosexuality, and I have been fighting it ever since. I can't remember how many appeals I have been through and I know I have spent thousands of dollars fighting this thing. The military is not like civilian life. In the military they don't need any *proof*; all they have to do is coerce five people into testifying against you, and they can hang you. With gay people what they do is find one guy who is willing to admit that he has had sex with another guy on base, and they scare the living daylights out of him by telling him all the terrible things they are going to do to him: throw him out of the service, make sure he can never get a job, lock him up for years. Then they tell him they will go easy, maybe even let him off the hook with an honorable discharge, if he will "cooperate." The poor guy ends up naming names, these guys are interrogated and name more names, and before you know it you have a witchhunt.

In my case I had been having a relationship with another private, and this fellow in our barracks must have overheard one of our conversations. This guy had been on my case for a long time, and when he found out this bit of information he decided to use it against me. He knew I was gay and he was looking for a chance to destroy me–he told me so himself. I might have beaten the rap, but the private I was involved with panicked when they brought him in for interrogation, and within a day he had signed a statement admitting everything.

For the next three months I went through hell on that base. Finally I came up in front of an administrative panel made up of all of these officers, most of whom were from very conservative areas of the country. In a word, they were bigots–not just against homosexuals, but against blacks and anyone else who was different from them. They decided I was to be given a dishonorable discharge, which of course means that I was booted out of the service and stripped of all my benefits, after having served five years of my life for my country.

I wrote to each one of the officers on the panel and I appealed the decision and went through several hearings with a private attorney. I never got anywhere. Today men in the military who are discovered to be homosexual are given honorable discharges, so I still have some hope after all these years that I can get at least that. But several of the officers on the administrative panel have passed away by now, which makes it very difficult.

Now, as an older man, I have had to face discrimination based on my age as well. Since I relocated to a different part of the country in my early forties, I had to face the job market again. I know, from my own experience as a personnel officer in a large company, that most businesses don't want older workers. Of course, they don't like to admit this, but most of them figure they can get the same work out of a younger person for a lower wage. They figure that an older person with more experience is not going to be satisfied with what they can pay a new kid just starting out. When I started looking for jobs here I was told again and again, "We wanted somebody younger." They never said, "We want someone with more experience or someone better qualified."

The problem with businesses today is that they are just out to make a buck. They don't realize that the older worker can offer more quality, that he will be more dedicated to the job and will work harder, and that this will help the business in the long run. I think this is why so many businesses are going to the dogs today.

Of course, you don't have to go outside the gay community to find discrimination and prejudice. I think even more important than the discrimination gay people experience in the heterosexual community is the prejudice between men and women in the gay community. We are our own worst enemies. Actually, I can understand in many ways why gay men are often offended by gay women. Some gay women are too radical, too domineering. They try to force everyone to use words like "chairperson" instead of "chairman," or "woman" instead of "girl." That's silly, because words like girl were never *intended* to be offensive. But then the women will claim, "He is sexist; he harassed me." Blacks do the same thing. Where I work, if you ever tell a black person to be quiet or to shut up, they get very offended, even though you may say this to white people all the time. I find that the majority of people who will get offended are those who see themselves as failures. The blacks who are so sensitive are the ones who maybe never got beyond the sixth grade, so they are just defensive. Of course, just because you don't have much schooling doesn't mean that others won't recognize that you may have a lot of knowledge about how to do your job. But people who see themselves as failures probably never realize this.

I say, let's get beyond this hang-up of so-called sexist language. The women want us to say "person" instead of "man" or "woman," but this is just a way to deny our identity. There are such things as *men* and *women*.

In the gay community we need to understand that men and women can get along together if we try. The men need to recognize that the women are a bit more personal about their affairs and that they need their privacy, their right to women-only meetings. And the women need to get over the idea that "men don't like us" and "men cause all our problems." We cause our own problems by refusing to communicate with the other side. We need men and women to come together. We need more bars and social outlets where *both* men and women are welcome–enough of these women's bars and men's bars. And we need for men and women to socialize together. Bob and I do such socializing all the time, especially with one lesbian couple that we spend a lot of time with. We don't want just male friends. There are women in the world, too, and they are part of us. That is the only way the gay community can survive.

And of course we also have to survive the years. The worst thing about growing older is worrying about it. I never use the phrase "growing older." To me there is no such thing. Aging means accomplishing things and acquiring knowledge. It's not growing older; it's reaching your goals, completing projects that you can look back on with a sense of satisfaction. There are two types of people. One type talks about "growing older," gives up activity at the first sign of age, and expects to be pampered and cared for. The other type is constantly seeking new experiences and new knowledge and is active all through his life. This is the person who never grows old.

CHAPTER 7

David₍ₒ

While David prepared drinks, the interviewer observed that he was the type of older man whose attire was always appropriate and yet self-consciously "mod": solid polyester slacks, white patent leather shoes, and matching belt. Everything about him was deliberate. The two men sat face to face, and yet the interviewer felt that David was peering down at him. It wasn't so much that David sometimes contradicted the interviewer's comments as a teacher might correct an errant pupil; rather, a barely perceptible noblesse oblige defined his style. Still, David was a man who, although peering from behind carefully built defenses, was ready to open his heart.

I was the first son in a very traditional Italian family and as tradition has it, as the first son, I was doted upon. I was spoiled rotten by my parents as well as by my grandparents, who lived with us until I started high school. I was a very good-looking youngster, so I received a lot of attention from adults that other children did not get. The unfortunate result of all this attention was that I was set apart from my peers and I became a conceited child. This was quite a hard thing to overcome as I grew older.

My parents would never allow me to get into rough games or associate with some of the rougher boys in the neighborhood, for fear that I would get hurt. While other boys were learning to wrestle and box, I played quietly in the yard or with little girls whose company I enjoyed. So, in addition to being conceited, I grew up to be a sissy.

As a youngster I knew I was gay, but I didn't know what "gay" was. I thought there was something wrong with *me*, because I did not realize there were others who had the same desires, the same curiosities that I had.

I suppose I was nine or ten years old when I first realized that I was different from other boys. I went through the usual adolescent routine of mutual masturbation, going out to the woods with some male friends and stripping down, the sort of things most kids do. But even at that point I did not realize that there was a whole society of men that was interested in doing these sorts of things with other men.

To understand my attitudes toward homosexuality at that time, you have to know a little bit about my family background. As I said, my family was Italian, and my mother and father were from the old country. They were very devout Catholics and extremely conservative, even backward, about any matter relating to sex. I never saw my father in the nude until I was forty years old, and my mother was one of those people who dressed and undressed under another gown–she was that modest. Any conversation relating to sex was considered completely out of line, so of course I grew up knowing little about sexual matters.

The only time I ever remember hearing about sex was as a teenager, when I heard the adults in the family having a discussion about why certain individuals never married. The consensus was that if you did not have a heterosexual existence, there was something seriously wrong with you. I recall my father saying that such people were crazy and belonged locked away in an institution.

Growing up, I did not have an easy time learning how to handle my sexual feelings. Since my early adolescence I have always been a highly sexed person. I am very easily aroused. In high school I loved to go to dances and was an excellent ballroom dancer, but I remember so well how embarrassed I would get dancing with girls. I was always afraid to get too close to them because I would automatically have an erection, and I was terribly embarrassed to have my partner or anyone else know this.

When I was eleven I remember meeting a girl about my age and going up to the hayloft in a barn where we had some mutual exploration. I was intrigued with her genitalia and how different they were from mine. We must have been a silly pair because I had no idea what I was supposed to do. I asked her which felt better for her, in front or in back. I really didn't know.

By the time I was fifteen I found myself feeling highly aroused sexually, and I began to be very interested in females as a way to satisfy my sexual urges. I did not satisfy them with males–I did not know this was allowed, and the idea was foreign to me. But I knew I could satisfy my desires with females, and so I did.

I had always been turned off by contact sports like football or basketball. I don't like perspiration, especially someone else's perspiration. I never liked the smell of a locker room. When I played a contact sport I was always afraid I would get my head in somebody's armpit, so I always went for individual sports. I became an excellent tennis player. There was a woman in our neighborhood who had a tennis court behind her house, and I would go there to play tennis with her every week. This woman and I became very close and she introduced me to heterosexual sex. Before her I did not know what intercourse was all about.

I went into the service in my late teens, where I continued to satisfy my sexual needs with women. I had many heterosexual experiences in the military, but no homosexual experiences–I didn't know they existed. Later, when I found out from others how common homosexual experiences are in the service, I thought how unfortunate I was not to be aware of this at the time.

I was the sort of person who could very easily have been broken in the military. My upbringing had made me into a complete sissy, a person afraid of rough sports and manly things. Up until my time in the service I felt set apart from my peers, different from other boys. In the military I came out of my shell and found out, for the first time in my life, that I could operate successfully in a world of my peers.

At the age of twenty-three, shortly after I left the service, I married my present wife, Sue, and before long she became pregnant. I have always been an individual with very high moral standards, and as a result I have taken my commitment to my family seriously. I was raised in the Catholic church, which does not believe in divorce. So I felt committed to my marriage, and after the children arrived I felt responsible for having brought them into this world. I had to see to it that the children had a decent home life and a decent upbringing.

Even when I married I knew that I was gay. It really didn't matter that I had not had any gay sexual experiences. I decided to marry because the culture within which I was raised said you had to marry. If you didn't marry, the eyebrows went up, and I was not man enough to handle that. I did not have my first experience with another man until I had been married for twenty years.

We had two small boys, and for a time Sue and I took in a boarder to help with expenses. It was shortly after the war and finances were extremely tight. So we shared our apartment with a fellow I had met at work. He was gay, but I was so naive at the time that I did not realize he was gay–I didn't know that such a thing existed. It's funny. I knew I was attracted to other men, but the thought that there was a whole community of men who felt the same way just didn't occur to me.

I remember one time this fellow and I went to a restaurant and suddenly he ducked behind me. He had seen another fellow whom he wanted to avoid and he said, laughing, "I was with that guy last weekend and I don't want to see him again." Being naive, I didn't realize he was talking about an old flame.

On another occasion, when Sue had gone off to her mother's house with the children, this fellow came over to my bed completely naked and asked me if I would massage his back. I agreed, but as I began to massage his back I developed an erection and I had to stop. The fact that I was really unaware at the time of what this fellow wanted will give you an idea of how naive I was.

My marriage was not a happy one. I think Sue and I were mismatched. She is very obedient and docile on the surface, but she gets her way by encouraging me to walk all over her and then making me feel guilty. I have a hard time relating to people who make me feel guilty. Still, I have never considered divorce. I made a solemn vow to carry through with my responsibilities and I will fulfill that vow. I am concerned not about my promise to my wife, but rather about my promise to God. Staying with my marriage is, for me, fulfilling a promise between me and my God.

So divorce is out of the picture. But separation is not. Even when the boys were small I often thought, "Once they are grown up and on their own I will separate from my wife and I'll be free." After the children were away at college I began to have my first homosexual experiences. We lived in a small town at the time, but it was close to Boston, which had a variety of gay bars and bathhouses and some parks where men cruised. I learned how to use these places to make contact with other men and soon I was leading a very active gay sex life, having sex sometimes two or three times a week. Most of the sex was pretty anonymous, but there were several fellows who I saw regularly.

I have always kept my gay life separate from my heterosexual life. Neither my two boys nor my wife know about my homosexuality and I don't intend for them to find out. Now I know some men would not be able to handle a double life, and they should not try to. But I feel that I have handled the situation in a way that is best for *me* and my family.

Leading a double life does have a cost. I can't say that I am proud of hiding from my family, but on the other hand I can't say I should not have done it. As far as I can see, it would have been extremely selfish for me to have done it any other way. You see, I can handle my homosexuality, but my family could not. Sure, I could have gotten a divorce when the boys were young and I realized that I really wanted to be with men, when the relationship began to be very hard. Men do this all the time. The marriage gets tough, so they pull out. But then what do they end up with? A broken home, a broken family. I think this is the sort of thing that contributes to a lot of society's problems today. I think it is not fair, not so much for the man and wife, but for the children, who have had no choice whatsoever about who their parents will be. I think it is absolutely dreadful the way people put the welfare of their children completely aside for their own selfish motives. I could not live that way.

I'm sure my sons, both of whom are married, would never suspect anything. My wife is a different story. It is really quite difficult to lead an active gay life and absolutely never give yourself away to someone who has shared your life for over thirty years. When I first began to have homosexual relations, I very foolishly gave my phone number to a fellow who I had seen for a while but who I was no longer interested in. This was very unwise, of course, because the man was quite effeminate. In response to Sue's questions I told her that this was someone from work, but I'm not certain she believed me. She must have suspected what was going on.

Just the other night I learned something that makes me think even more strongly that my wife may suspect that I am homosexual. I went to an outdoor concert with some gay friends, and in the course of the conversation I noticed two of them watching me and laughing. It turns out that they were amused because I was cruising, that is, looking at other men. This really made me angry because I didn't realize my behavior was so obvious. I checked it out with a friend, and he agreed that it was often perfectly obvious that I was cruising, even though I was not aware of it. Well, this made me realize that not only my gay friends but also my wife may have noticed me looking at men. I have noticed in recent years that when my wife and I go to a restaurant she has kept a very close eye on me, especially when there were male waiters. So perhaps she does suspect.

On the other hand, as I said, I'm sure that neither of my boys suspects. In fact, my older son has talked to me about some of his gay friends and he has sometimes said derogatory things about gay people, so I assume he is not gay himself. Although I don't like to hear him put gay people down, I am able to deal with his statements without any problem. I have had to maintain a split personality for so many years that it really no longer makes a difference. I don't join in his criticism of gays, but by the same token I don't say that he is right. I stay neutral.

Last year my younger son left home, and an opportunity became available for me to take a position with the downtown office of my company. Since we lived in the far suburbs, it would have meant a long commute every day. When this opportunity presented itself, I thought that here at long last was my chance to get away from my wife, to lead a completely free life now, at the age of sixty. Sue had no desire to relocate to an apartment in the city, and she has always known that I dislike commuting–you see, I am not a very good driver, and I get anxious when I drive on the freeway. Besides, all of Sue's friends are other housewives who live in our neighborhood. One thing I must say for my wife: she has always been supportive of my decisions, and this one was no exception. Her attitude was, "If that's what you want, do it." So I transferred to the downtown office, found an apartment nearby, and moved in.

The experience of living on my own has had a tremendous positive influence on me. I had never really been on my own before, and my needs had always been subordinated to the needs of others: first to my parents, and later to my wife and children. For the past thirty-seven years my entire life has revolved around my wife. All of our friends were our friends, not my friends. My new gay life has helped me to shed all that. Now that I am on my own I have found out, much to my surprise, that people like me for me. They don't like me for my wife or for my family; they like me for me. Sometimes I think, "Here I am, sixty years old, and imagine what I have been missing all these years!"

Some of my friends have suggested that I leave my wife. But never having been married, or having been married only a short time, they can't really understand where I'm coming from. I owe my wife a lot. There are a lot of memories, and we've been through hell and high water together. Now, Sue and I have talked about the future, and we both realize that we can't predict what will happen. Who knows what the future will bring?

I don't know if I want to stay married. I feel ambivalent about this now that I have found my true life, the gay life. This is where I'm happy; I was not happy in the heterosexual life. But I also realize that this is the selfish way of looking at it–because I'm thinking only of taking care of me. What about my wife and the years we have shared?

Another selfish way of looking at it is that, as you grow older, how do you know you are not going to become an invalid? You don't know. So staying married is a kind of insurance–an insurance that there will be someone there when you are in need. I don't feel as secure in gay life as I do in the other one. It is no great mystery that I am putting on age–I no longer try to hide it by dying my hair or trying to dress like a young man. And gay society is, after all, a very youth-oriented society; so there is always the possibility, even the likelihood, that I will be rejected as an "old man." To me, heterosexual life means security: a home and a wife I can always go back to. The gay life is much more satisfying to me right now, but there is no security in it.

It is really a choice between security and freedom: security in my heterosexual life, and freedom in my gay life. Right now I have chosen freedom, but I haven't given up my security. I remain married. I see my wife every weekend, and when I am with her I play the heterosexual role completely. During the week I have my own apartment, my own set of gay friends she knows nothing about, and the freedom to meet other gay people in bars, bathhouses, and so on.

One result of this arrangement is that I have been able to make comparisons between the two lifestyles, and I realize why it is that I feel so much freer in my gay life. In my straight life I have to maintain a secret self, a hidden personality that I must never let out for fear of retribution. I have the feeling that out of nowhere someone is going to jump on me, put me down. What if some old flame somehow gets my phone number and threatens to reveal me to my wife? What if I let something slip out of my mouth while I'm asleep? I feel that I can't open up to other people, I can't level with them.

In my gay life it's different. One of the things I really enjoy about gay life is that I can let myself go. I'm not so naive as to think that everybody in gay life is going to keep everything I say a guarded secret. But I do know that there is no part of me that I am afraid to reveal to other gay people–there are no potentially disastrous secrets lurking in the wings. So I have a lot more freedom to be myself. I can let myself go. Now that I am on my own here in the city, for the first time in my life I am thoroughly enjoying myself.

I have a wide circle of gay friends here and we go out quite often. I am in gay company quite a lot, so naturally there are many opportunities to meet other gay men. I suppose I am like most people in that the thing that attracts me to men first is their physical appearance–the way they look, the way they dress, and how they move. But I'm not the sort of person who will just rush in. I weigh the other person's pros and cons and I consider what kind of reaction I will elicit. I'm sure I miss out on a lot of tricks that way, but I prefer to talk to men and meet them on an intellectual level first. It starts off with an intellectual exchange, and if there is a compatibility the relationship deepens. If you feel that you can trust the other person and that you are trusted, then you can get to what I would call the ultimate plane: the nitty gritty of having sex with another person.

To me, sex is not limited to a sex act. Sex is all around. Sex is in color to me; it is in painting, in books, in the theater. The sex act is just a small portion of it. At this point in my life I am having sex with men about two to three times a week. As I said, I am a highly sexed individual, and so I find a need to satisfy my sexual desires.

Yes, I would prefer to relate to men first on an intellectual level, and I try to do this. But the fact is that if I limited myself to this approach I would not be averaging two to three tricks a week. I don't have a lover and I feel I'm not ready for a lover, so I do need to go out to satisfy my needs. I go to the bars regularly and it is not uncommon for me to pick up a quick trick there. I will see somebody in a bar who particularly turns me on for that moment, so I go after him. I try to strike up a conversation, and if I am successful I will either bring that person back to my apartment or I will go to his home.

If I fail at the bars, I will go to the baths. The bars are better for getting to know people–there is more opportunity for conversation. But the baths are failsafe. I can always find sexual release at a bathhouse. I will find the need to visit a bathhouse two or three times a month–it depends on whether I get what I need in the bars. If I don't get it in the bars, I go to the baths. It's that simple. I suppose you might say that it is almost mathematical.

I must say that my move to the downtown area has opened up all sorts of opportunities. Since I began having sex with men, I have become a devotee of cruising areas. Living downtown is ideal for easy accessibility. There is the lakefront park, the warehouse district, the concourse–I run the gamut. It's funny. Most people think of the lakefront park as a good family park, and most of it is. But there is a section on the south side that is very cruisy at certain hours. There are also two male theaters where pornographic films are shown, and it is quite easy to make a contact sitting in the theater or visiting the bathroom. I almost always take a friend along when I'm cruising. With one fellow in particular I often drive out to the park, park the car, and cruise around in the evening. I think we both feel that if we find someone, that's great; if not, that is OK, too. We still have each other's company.

This particular fellow and I have become very close friends and we see each other several times a week. We have never had sex, and yet I consider our relationship to be erotic. I think a lot of people would have trouble understanding this. You see, I enjoy people. To me it is just as erotic to sit down and talk with someone on an intellectual level as it is to go to bed. It is just as erotic to go to bed and love and fondle without committing a sex act. It's just as erotic to me. I don't have to go the whole route to enjoy a gay person's company. There are plenty of gay persons that I have known are gay, and I have no desire to go to bed with them. But they are pleasant to be around. My friend is one of these people. I do not have a desire for his body, but that doesn't mean we will never have sex. For now, we relate as two close friends. We have the same likes and dislikes in music, clothing, literature, and even in the types of people with whom we like to associate. So consequently it is a pleasure to be around him.

As I said, this fellow and I often go cruising together. I have been pretty successful at cruising: I would say that when I go out I find a sexual contact more often than not. Of course, cruising does take a certain amount of skill and a certain amount of guts. That's funny because I don't think of myself as a gutsy person. I am not at all aggressive when I go cruising. All of my friends would agree that basically I am a shy person. I have an inferiority complex that just won't quit. So when I am in a cruising situation I much prefer to be cruised than to be the cruiser. Still, I have learned how to strike up a conversation. But I am never aggressive like some other people I see. I take a casual, roundabout approach; I try to find out what the other person is like. Sometimes I wish I were more aggressive, but it's just not in me. I'm sure that is because of the age hang-up: I have the fear that someone will say, "Get out of here, old man. Nobody needs *you*."

I use the same approach in a bar situation. I never force my attentions on anyone or get physical in any way, until it is clear that there is a mutual interest. I might sit next to someone at the bar for thirty minutes, never saying a word to the person. I hesitate. As I said, I weigh the pros and cons. But after a while something is bound to happen–they will be looking for a match, or I will offer to share my ashtray–and that allows me to strike up a conversation. I find the process difficult, so I am always looking for a crutch or anything to help me along.

I do try to use my appearance to attract people to me. Like Mae West said, "I'd rather be looked over than overlooked." I'm very conscious of my body and of the way I dress. I try not to overdress: I don't want to look like an old man trying to be a youngster. But I don't want to look like a ninety-year-old, either, so I try to dress somewhere in the middle. I think this helps me when I go out to meet new people.

I know what I am looking for in a sex partner. I don't go home with every Tom, Dick, and Harry, and I am very careful to avoid anyone who gives the slightest indication of being violent. I don't want to be caught in a situation where there may be violence. Forget this leather jazz–I'm not interested in that. I had one fellow who wanted me to beat him with a whip–he went out the door fast. I don't like pinching or biting or any of that. It turns me off, just like dirt turns me off and body odor turns me off. I also find myself repulsed by obesity–I am sorry to say it, but fat people turn me off. Age makes no difference. I've been with men older and younger than me and I've enjoyed both age groups.

The important thing is not age but the other person's style. To me sex should be free, giving, easy, and loving. I want a man who is man enough to be gentle. I find that a man, if he is not trying to be overly macho, is a lot more tender than any female.

There is a problem that I have in meeting other gay men, and this is that I do not give the impression of being gay. To others, I come across as a heterosexual. Many gay men who have met me in a gay bar or a gay organization have told me that if they had seen me in any other setting they would not have known I was gay. Even a lot of people I meet who I know are gay are surprised to find out that I am gay, too. I don't know why this is.

Not being obviously gay is, of course, an advantage in heterosexual society. I have never been discriminated against, never lost a job promotion or any other opportunity because of my homosexuality. I'm sure this is because the other people didn't know I was gay. I like the idea that straight people cannot spot me. I can relax and don't have to consciously act butch.

But in the gay world my straight appearance has been a handicap. When other gay men tell me they never would have suspected, I feel put down. I would like to be able to be recognized by other gay men for what I am. I would like for them to recognize what I am without going out of my way to be obvious, without being flamboyant, which makes me uncomfortable. I'm no good at it. So what happens very often is the other gay person sort of pussyfoots around, checks me out to find out what I am. How much simpler it would be if we just had some way of knowing instantly who we were–a way that was easily understandable to us, but meaningless to straight people.

But of course there is a lot more to being gay than trying to attract other gay men. I don't spend all of my time cruising. In fact, I'm sure I spend much more time at the Metropolitan Community Church (MCC) and at the gay rights organization. I spend enough time at the gay rights organization that people down there assume I am a member. But I refuse to join this group, just as I refuse to join MCC–on principle.

I refuse to join these organizations because they espouse the philosophy that because you are gay you must act in certain ways. The people in these groups believe that if you are gay it is a cop-out if you don't declare yourself as gay to the whole world. I don't believe in that. So I do what I can to help these organizations–I go to church services, I make my devotions, I help with mailings, but I won't be part of them formally. I won't be told that I am wrong because I made a decision to protect my family from knowledge about my lifestyle. I feel very strongly about this.

I also feel that I want to limit my involvement in these organizations because of the constant bickering. A great number of people are attracted to these groups for ego reasons. Everyone wants to be a big leader, and everyone wants to have his way. I don't need that crap.

Spending time with these organizations has allowed me to get to know quite a few younger gays. I would say that most of the younger gays don't have a very high opinion of older gays; there are some who are so hung up on age that they reject older gays outright. They stick with gays their own age. Their sex drives are strong, and all they are interested in is finding attractive men to have sex with. They have no time for older gays. But these younger gays are a minority. I find that with most younger gays, once you get to talking with them, once you open up a line of communication, age is no longer a barrier. It is simply a matter of getting over that first hurdle.

I am often surprised at how receptive some younger gays are toward older ones. There was a time about twenty years ago when I was in my forties that I used dye to color my gray hair. I was afraid I would be rejected for having gray hair. It was quite a surprise to me to find out that a lot of young gays groove on gray hair; they are drawn to older gays. For some I suppose it is a father fixation, but for most of these men it is a genuine interest in relating to an older person.

Now there is one type of younger person that is drawn to older men for an entirely different reason. I'm talking about the hustler–the one who is out to make a buck. Every hustler goes after gray hair, so if you are older you can bet your boots you are going to be approached by hustlers. I have no problem with this because I am up front with them. I let them know from the start that I am not interested, so if money is what they want, they had better flake off.

So, other than the hustlers, I find that I relate very well to younger gays. A lot of older gay people that I have talked with don't feel the same way I do. They have said to me, "How can you have anything in common with a younger person? They don't have any background; they don't have anything to offer. What do you talk about?" I think they are making a mistake in thinking that all younger gays have nothing to offer. It is true that there are younger gays who are very adept at talking in words of one syllable. I'm not interested in them. But there are also a great many very serious-minded young gays who know the arts, theater, literature. They are interested in politics, in history, in what is happening in the world today. I find that I have a lot in common with these younger gays and we can communicate on an equal level.

What it boils down to is that the type of person and his interests are a whole lot more important than age when two people want to relate to each other. When a younger gay man has a sexual relationship with an older gay, there is a recognition that some things are important besides sexual release. A lot of younger gay men would agree with me that when you go with someone, you have sex for perhaps a couple of hours. But after that, what do you talk about? So, for a meaningful relationship there has to be some common interest beyond the purely sexual, and this is something that is independent of the age of the two people. I would guess that about half my friends are in their twenties and thirties and half are my age or older, and I find interesting people and dull people in both age groups.

What turns me off in young people is flightiness. I can't stand gays in their twenties, say, who believe everything they hear and take it up as gospel just because they heard it from someone else. But there are just as many young gays who have some experience behind them, who have thought things out and know where they stand. I find these young gays are easy to relate to.

Unfortunately, there are times when an older gay man like myself does not get a chance to relate to younger gays because of discrimination. It is a sad commentary on the gay community that we discriminate against older people right here in our own community. Just look at any gay publication that advertises gay bathhouses and you will see ads that say, "Free membership 18 to 24." I used to belong to one of the bathhouses in town, but it happened that some of the younger gays felt that a few of the older ones were pushy. I can see where they might have an argument, but what they did in response was unfair. They restricted certain days to gays under a certain age; older gays were not allowed on those days. This really offended me so I stopped going altogether, even on those days that were open for the older people.

I don't feel the bathhouse had any right to exclude a whole group of people. Every patron should have the right to use the facilities and to choose for himself who he wants to be with. If a young one doesn't want to fool with an older one, why he can just choose not to. And that works the other way around, too.

As long as I retain my good health I really cannot see any great disadvantage to growing older. The best thing about growing older is being able to handle problems as they come up on a day-to-day basis because you've had experiences you can draw on to help you. Almost every day I recall experiences I had when I was a teenager, or in my twenties, thirties, or forties—as I am faced with a situation today, I remember a similar situation back then, and something clicks. It all makes sense. I think a lot of older people get into trouble because they dwell too much on past experiences. I don't dwell on the past, but I do try to use it as a resource. I also try not to worry about the future. As I get older, I feel that I am entitled to think about what will make me happy today, right now—like moving into an apartment on my own after more than thirty years of married life.

Growing older brings with it a certain amount of satisfaction, too, because younger people look to you as someone who has been through it all, someone who has useful advice. It is very satisfying to play this role.

I think I would be very frustrated if I were perpetually young. It would be boring to stay the same, just as it would be boring if it were summer all the time. People thrive on change. Age is just one form of change. Really, people tend to make more out of it than there is.

I feel that the most important part of adjusting well to age is a sense of belonging. This is very difficult in our society—both heterosexual and homosexual—because we are a youth-oriented society. When older people feel they are left out, it may in fact be the case that they are ignored by younger people. For me, being able to communicate with all ages has made growing older easier. It opens up a whole new vista that you were not aware existed. Older people are likely to develop something of an inferiority complex because of our society's attitude about age. But when you do open up these vistas with younger people, you find out that a lot of your fears are not really justified. And you also find out that relating to younger people keeps your mind open and active.

Another result of our society's negative attitudes about age is that a lot of older people try to interfere with the aging process. Look at all the effort that is devoted to camouflaging the signs of age: hairpieces, working out in the gym, facials, permanents. The truth is that older people who try to hide their age end up looking like fools. When an individual grows older, he is expected to become a little more portly, to develop some character in his face, to become gray. Growing older is so much easier when you learn to accept these changes rather than fighting them.

What I have learned, above all else, is that old age is a time for me to be myself.

CHAPTER 8

Scott

The interviewer noticed a tremor in Scott's hand as he motioned for her to sit on the living room couch. This home was in a fashionable part of town, and the well-appointed interior reflected that fact. But the comfort and safety of the place did not alter the air of vulnerability that Scott wore–like an unnoticed cloak thrown by a caring friend over his shoulders. He was content, but his was a contentment born of resignation. His almost naive openness made him seem like a child who had, through some aberration of nature, grown old.

When I was young, being homosexual didn't seem like much of a problem. This was true even though I was born shortly after the turn of the century in a small Texas city. I was always a big boy for my age, so I guess I got a lot of experience early on. My first sexual experience was with a cousin. I was about six, and he was just a couple of years older. He taught me how to masturbate.

When I grew up we lived next door to my grandparents' house. One summer after I had just turned eight, all four of my male cousins were staying at my grandparents' house. I remember that grandma had a cow–that was back in the days when you could have a cow, living as we did on the edge of town. We had these big feed sacks for the cow which we used to build tents under the huge oak trees out in the side yard. My cousins and I would sleep out there at night and all five of us practiced sodomy. Grandma would have had a fit if she had known. After those little summer vacation things I always seemed to find some little friend my own age who would fool around. I never thought about it–it just happened.

I really didn't think of these things as homosexual. It seems a lot of kids go through that. To me, my first real homosexual experience happened when I was thirteen. In fact, I still remember it was on a lovely June night, on my thirteenth birthday. My mother and stepfather had gone to Oklahoma to my uncle's funeral. I took my meals at my grandparents' house but was at home nights.

Now on this particular night I was sitting out on the wall in front of the house, watching the world go by. This nice-looking fellow–about twenty years old–came by and started talking. I don't know whose idea it was, but we went in the house and put on some records. We were listening to dance music, and since I was studying dancing at the time I sort of put on a little show for him–doing this step, then that. The next thing I knew we were up in the bedroom with no clothes on and he was doing me. He's the one who brought me out.

When did I first realize I was attracted to other boys? Well, I guess that came very early. In fact I can't remember a time when I was not attracted to my own sex. Even though I dated girls, like everybody else did, I was very naive where girls were concerned. A funny thing seemed to happen. It turned out that the girls I dated at school were the ones that anybody could date and lay. But I didn't know that. We would go to a show, a dance, or something like that and I never made any passes at them. They never made passes at me. They were probably glad to get some guy to keep them company who didn't paw at them and want everything. I was really naive about the situation until some fellows finally told me, "Say, aren't you and so and so making out every night?" But we weren't! I never touched them. Now there were a couple of times when I got tangled up with girls and had to go to bed with them, but both times I was so drunk it was almost a farce.

I can't remember admitting to myself I was homosexual, but I never remember a time when I wasn't called "sissy" at school and in the neighborhood. It was all made worse by a bicycle accident I had when I was six. My knee was busted up so bad that I couldn't play baseball or run around with the other kids. I don't think I was any more effeminate than the other boys, but because of my knee I couldn't enter into sports and be with the guys. So I would play with girls.

Somehow I got to meet other kids, and later men, who were also homosexual. It wasn't a deliberate sort of thing. I would meet them through other people–like that first guy who brought me out. Through him I met another kid my own age. You get into a little circle of people and the circle gradually grows. I don't remember ever discussing it with anybody. I'd meet people and make love. Later on there is a sense of recognition gay people have for each other. You go to a theater or out shopping, and contact is made. After talking to a person for a few minutes, I can usually tell–from a mannerism, a glance, a certain movement. But today I have found it harder to do this, what with all the truck drivers and football players who are coming out.

I don't know whether I was just brazen or what, but being gay as a kid didn't faze me. It just seemed that so many of the people around me were gay. For instance, I was quite active in the young people's group at church, not because I was religious, but because I enjoyed it. I liked to be with people. I was very good at organizing plays to raise money for the church. Well, there were two or three other gays in that group, and we had our own thing going. Nobody else knew we were gay. Maybe if I were back there now I would have a different outlook, being closer to it. But outside of the fact that some people would call me "sissy," being gay never bothered me.

I recall one time when being called a sissy did really bother me. It was around the time I was twenty. No one in my family ever made any remarks to me about being different–but this one cousin who was four years my senior. He was always calling me a sissy, throwing it up at me. None of the other cousins said anything, but this one was real mean. One day at my grandparents' house he made a remark in front of my grandmother. I hauled off and hit him. Even though he was twice my size he fell right over. Where the strength came from I don't know, but from that day on he never said another word to me about it.

Something happened when I was sixteen that made my parents realize, in a dramatic way, that I was homosexual. My mother's older sister lived in the mountains near Denver, and every summer mother would take me and my sister to spend a month there. The last summer we were there I went into Denver to see a movie. I met this young lawyer–I can't remember exactly how we met–but I fell madly in love with him. For the rest of the summer, whenever I

could get away I would go in to the movies to see him. It was hard
to do. Finally it was time to return to Texas.

We started corresponding. Our letters were very passionate, and
when Christmas came I sent him a nice gift and he sent me a book.
It was Whitman's *Leaves of Grass*. It seems foolish now, but I was
terribly disappointed because I had expected some fabulous gift. I
was heartbroken. Unfortunately, I was too young to realize how
appropriate that book was.

On Christmas Day my stepfather told me, when I left the house
that morning, "Now you be home for dinner at six o'clock, because
I want the family to be together for Christmas dinner." I said "Yes,
sir." Well, my stepfather was a strict disciplinarian, and I knew I
would catch hell if I didn't follow his order. I went into town to
meet some of my gay friends, and I guess I had such fun that I lost
track of time. We were ensconced in a private dining room in a
Chinese restaurant at nine-thirty when I suddenly remembered I
should have been home at six.

At the streetcar station I spotted my violin teacher in the crowd.
The streetcar line went in a circle. There were two cars; one went
one way, passing my house first, and one went the other way,
passing my violin teacher's house first. I explained the situation to
him. I said, "If the porch light is on at my house, that means the
family has gone to sleep and I'll have to wake them to get in." I was
terribly frightened. My teacher offered to take the streetcar that
passed my house first, and if the porch light was on I could spend
the night with him. That is what happened, and the next morning I
was more frightened than ever.

Although my stepfather was very strict, he was also generous. He
gave me a good allowance every week but insisted I put most of it in
the bank, so I had a hefty little savings account. I also had a $50
check he had just given me for Christmas. So I went to the bank,
cashed the check, emptied my savings account, and went on a shopping trip to the department store where we had an account. There I
bought an extra suit, some extra shirts, underwear, and a few other
clothes, as well as a suitcase to pack them in. I went to the railroad
station, bought a ticket to Denver, and boarded the train. I was
desperate to see my friend, hoping that perhaps he could take me in.

When I arrived I phoned my friend's office. I learned that he was away for the holidays but was due back the next week. Since I didn't dare go out to my aunt's place, I stayed at a hotel in town. The following day I left word at his office to call. He never did. I called him at home that night and his sister said he had stepped out.

The next day was Sunday, and this time I managed to get him on the phone. I didn't recognize his voice at first, but he must have recognized mine, because he tried to change his voice to fool me. He said, "John's gone to church." But I was determined, and so the next morning I waited for him in the lobby of the building where he worked. As he walked in he spotted me. I had never seen a more frightened person in my life.

He told me, "I know what's happened. I got a telegram from your mother. She says you've run away from home, and she thinks you might have come up to me." You see, my mother had been reading my mail behind my back. So she had known about my crush on John all along. John continued, "I can't do a thing. You must understand my hands are tied because I would get in serious trouble if I tried to do anything." He refused to take me home with him, but he told me to look up this dancer he had introduced me to last summer, a fellow just a couple of years older than me. I could stay with him. But I refused, and we said good-bye.

That night I found myself wandering around the art museum, and who should I run into but this dancer. He was surprised to see me in Denver, but when he learned I was staying at a hotel he invited me to stay at his house since his parents were away for the holidays. I guess I was lucky because I was just about running out of money. A few days later, while my friend was out working, I decided to visit a department store downtown. As luck would have it, I ran into my aunt. She was very upset. "We know where you are. Your grandfather is on his way up here to pick you up, and I think it would be better all around if he picked you up at my place." So I went back out to my friend's house, packed up, and returned to my aunt's house.

My grandfather brought me back to Texas and put me in a reformatory—a boys' reform school. Can you imagine putting a sixteen-year-old boy who is a homosexual in reform school to try to break him? How naive can people be? My mother was a very understanding person and I don't think she wanted to send me away. But my grandfather pushed her and she finally went along with it. At that time people didn't understand that you should not put a young boy who is homosexual into an all-male boarding school and expect him to become a heterosexual.

I was in reform school for a year. Of course, it was not a happy time, but it is a year out of my life that I do not regret. I got along with everybody: the teachers and the pupils. They only taught up to the tenth grade and I was well beyond that, so they put me to work in the storeroom. I was better educated than the other kids there, so much so that when one of the teachers was sick or absent I substituted for that teacher. One time I taught the first and second grades for a month.

A lot of the kids were not there because they had gotten into trouble; they were put there because they had no families. The students were divided into companies because they had military training. I started out in the lowest company, C Company, where we had to sleep in the barracks. It was just a big open room full of beds. But I soon was promoted to B Company and then to A Company, where we had individual rooms and a lot more privacy. Each company had a dean in charge. The dean of athletics was the dean of A Company and was as gay as they come. He looked after me, so I didn't have any trouble there. But it was an experience.

When I came home after a year at reform school, everyone in the family knew what had happened, but no one, including my mother, ever mentioned a word of it again. In the years that followed Mother learned to adjust to my homosexuality. The only time she would ever make any remark about one of my friends was if the fellow were a swish. She wouldn't say anything while they were at the house, but when they left she would always say, "I'd as soon you wouldn't have that person in my home anymore." I don't think she ever truly accepted that I was homosexual. Every time she saw that I was getting serious about someone she would try to break it up.

When I was younger she was very successful in doing this–until I met George. We met in Galveston, where I had moved with my mother. As I became more involved with George, Mother became more upset. She pleaded with me to drop him and she even threatened to write his father in Ohio. But it was just a threat. I was sure she would never do it, and she never did. Ironically, she and George became the best of friends and she grew quite fond of him. When I went into the service a couple of years later, George would take her out to dinner, to the theater, and to the park. I'm sure they would still be good friends if Mother were alive today.

At any rate, I was thirty when I met George, and we were lovers for five years. We lived together down here during the winter, and in the summer we returned to his home in Ohio, where I would spend my vacations. One day out of the clear blue sky he said to me, "I think you had better pack your things and go back to Galveston. You're not happy with me. You're not happy with one person. You want to get around, have a good time with everybody." Now that wasn't true. I had never given him any reason to make a statement like that. There is one thing I can say about myself: I am true and loyal to anyone I commit myself to. I have always been. And I have never been the one to break off a relationship. Whether he had just grown tried of me I don't know, but I had no choice. So I left.

That next winter when he was in Galveston I did not see him, but the following year we ran into each other and eventually became friends. We even lived in the same apartment building. We shared everything. We're still the best of friends and see each other regularly. But we never became lovers again.

I didn't have a lover again until I was forty-seven years old. I had moved up to San Francisco to take a job as a bookkeeper, and when I got settled into my own apartment I brought Mother up to live with me. That didn't work out because I met David at about the same time. As usual, she tried to break things up. Since David did not have his own place at the time, we needed to use my apartment, and that was quite a hassle with Mother around. So I sent her back to Texas.

David had an elderly aunt who was really more like a mother to him because she had raised him. She lived in a lovely twenty-four-room mansion on the Oregon coast. Well, this old aunt gave David the property for the small mortgage that was on it, and he moved up there and soon found a job in a nearby town. He didn't know it at the time, but this old aunt had cancer. She knew it, but she hadn't told anyone. She had the doctor in one day; he told David that is what it was, and that she would have to go to the hospital. But she refused. She said that if she was going to die she was going to do it in her own home. And she did. But she lingered for a very long time, and David had to quit his job and stay home to care for her. He grew bored. Finally he figured, "Well, I've got to stay home and cook for her and me, so I might as well make it pay." So he decided to turn the place into a fancy boarding home for retired people, and he invited me to help.

When I got there, the place was like Tobacco Road: it had been neglected for years. We worked our hearts out and managed to restore the place to its original elegance. We began advertising, and soon the place filled up. I hate to use the word "elegant," but the boarding home was a lovely place. The residents were older folks with independent means.

David and I were together in that place for over twenty years. He was manager and I was assistant manager and we both doubled as handymen. We were completely faithful to each other in that time, but after all those years David began running around and I couldn't tolerate it. One of our residents became ill and her daughter came down from Seattle to visit. The second night she was there, she and David slept together. Every time she came down that would happen. After a while I told him it was all off as far as anything personal between us. He eventually married her.

I was in a terrible position. I had worked all those years to build this place into a successful business, but I had nothing on paper. Everything was in his name. If I had left, I would have lost everything. So I muzzled my pride and stayed on, even though we were no longer lovers. When he sold the place a couple of years later, I did finally get a little. But David couldn't handle money. For instance, he would get loans to have work done on the place, then use the money for something else. So when he sold the home there was not much left. I got less than half of what I should have gotten—and was happy to get that.

I used the money to help me retire down here. Between that and my social security check I manage to get by. I have to say that I am comfortable in my retirement. I share this rather spacious house with Bob, who is four years older than I and who has a lot of health problems. The arrangement is that I do the cooking and look after Bob and in exchange I get a rebate on the rent.

I would say that my biggest problem is that I would like to have more to do to keep me occupied, and I would like to get out more often. Since I don't drive I am totally dependent on Bob, and he usually doesn't want to go out at all. So I have taken up pottery and rug-braiding at the local school here, and that helps.

As I said, I don't get out as often as I would like, but I do attend services at the Metropolitan Community Church (MCC) most Sundays and I am also involved in the gay Alcoholics Anonymous. These are important organizations. The church is there for people who want to be with their own kind and still worship God. I hadn't been to church for years until I came down here and started going to MCC about four years ago. And I enjoy it.

I'm not politically minded, so I don't go in for the human rights organization. I have mixed feelings about that group. Sometimes I think they are doing a good job, and other times I think it would be better if they left things alone. Why? Because they make an issue out of being gay, and in the process some of them are getting hurt. By not keeping quiet about it they are stirring up witchhunts. Older people like me got through all of their lives, stayed in jobs, and were successful without ever making an issue of it. And I'm sure people knew I was gay. I could tell from the remarks they made, some teasingly, some seriously, but I just overlooked them. I went about my business as if nothing had happened, and eventually it calmed down. Now perhaps I am being too hard on the younger gays. After all, it's easy for me to talk because my life is practically all behind me, and I realize that the human rights organization is good in many ways for the younger ones who are just coming out now.

It is very rare that I ever get to a gay bar. Before I stopped drinking I patronized bars, but now that I don't drink I don't feel too comfortable there. Then there is the transportation problem. Bob has a terrible problem with alcohol and he is afraid that, if he gets around people who are drinking, he will drink, too. So he doesn't go and I have to stay home, too, since I don't have my own transportation. Now there is a gay bar on Fifth Street which has a dining room in the back, separated from the bar itself. A group of us from MCC will go there for Sunday night dinner after services. But that is the only bar I have been to since I moved here four years ago.

I never go to the gay beaches or bathhouses. I went to a beach once and I was turned off because it was only a bunch of teenagers and kids in their twenties. I won't have sex with anyone where it isn't reciprocated, and that is all these young kids are interested in. Young kids have never attracted me anyway.

Now I know that a lot of older gays prefer gays under thirty or even younger than that–they think younger gays are sexually attractive. Not me. Throughout my life I always preferred men who were older than me. Then, as I got into my forties, I liked men who were a bit younger as well. Now that I am in my seventies I would say that I like men who are thirty-five all the way up to their sixties. I have never been interested in real young people as sexual partners, or even as friends, for that matter.

The truth is, young gays could care less about us older ones. They're not the least bit interested. Many of them seem to think that a person who is old is over the hill, that there is no fire left or anything. And yet, some of the people I have met who are between forty-five and sixty-five have a lot more fire than these young ones.

Young gays don't quite understand the older person, and this is just as true in the heterosexual world. Young people think you're no longer any good, especially for sex. That isn't true. Doctors tell people every day that it's all in your mind: if you figure you're through, you're through. But if you take a positive attitude you can do anything. Look at all the men today up in their seventies and eighties who are having children. I enjoy sex now as much, if not more, than when I was younger, because now I know more about it. I know more about how to give pleasure to the other person as well as how to make myself receptive to him. So I have gotten to the point where, if someone younger rejects me, I don't let it faze me. If I see someone younger than me whom I might be interested in, I will get friendly, and I don't worry too much about being rejected. If they're not interested I can tell, so I just back off.

Actually, I'm not the sort of person who makes the first move anyway. If I'm interested I act friendly or try to let the other person know, but I never make the first approach. I guess that is a hang-up I have. Usually the other person will approach me, we'll get to know each other, and if something happens, fine. If not, that's fine too. I suppose if I were more aggressive I would do a whole lot better. The truth is, I don't have sex as often as I would like. That is frustrating. I have one friend whom I have known for years and we have sex maybe once or twice a month. And I masturbate a couple of times a week, but that is the extent of my sex life right now. I just haven't met anyone who is interested in me. That is certainly one thing about growing older which you have to learn to accept.

There are a lot of adjustments that you have to make when you get older. For the older person I guess the worst part of aging is living with the negative attitudes of younger people–both gay and straight. We're just not valued. And then there is the struggle of trying to keep yourself occupied–if you don't, you quickly sink into a lot of negative feelings. But the funny thing is, I don't think of myself as growing older. I'm seventy-one now and I don't feel any different now from when I was fifty-one, or even thirty-one. My life now doesn't seem to be that much different. When my thirtieth birthday was coming up I would say, "Gosh, this is the end of the road," and after my fortieth birthday I began to say, "Well, I guess it's how you look at it." If you want to grow old gracefully, intelligently, you can do that; or you can decide to grow old and become a sack of bones and not be interesting to anyone. It's all in your power.

The key is in your ability to adapt to new situations, new demands. If you can do that, you will have no problem in growing older. I am one of those fortunate people who have been able to adjust to any climate or society. Through the years I have taught myself to adjust to anything that came up, and so I think I have not had too much trouble adapting to growing older.

As we get older we have to learn to get out of the spotlight, because other, younger people come to take our place. We just won't be in demand forever. We have to realize that we are not beautiful forever, not on the outside at any rate. So in order to attract others we must make ourselves beautiful on the inside. We have to go easy on ourselves, make allowances for things we can no longer do as quickly or as well. And we have to keep occupied, keep planning for our future so we do not get stuck in our past.

What has been the least satisfying aspect of my life? I suppose it was the time when I was drinking too much. Looking back on it, I was fortunate that I had friends who realized what was happening and took me to an Alcoholics Anonymous meeting. They could see

I had a problem which I was not admitting to myself. For several months, every time they invited me to a meeting I made an excuse. I would say I was meeting someone at the movies when I knew full well that I was going to head for the nearest bar as soon as I left my friends. Finally I convinced myself that I could live without alcohol. I went a month without a drink. Then, one night, I ran into someone who drank; we spent the night together and I slipped right back down. After that I finally agreed to go to my first AA meeting. That was twelve years ago, and I haven't had a drink since then. So what was the least satisfying aspect of my life became, in a sense, a very satisfying accomplishment. I was able to turn it around.

One of the least satisfying experiences in my life, which I was not able to turn around, was what happened to me in the military. I served my country for four years but have nothing to show for it. The irony is that I didn't even do anything while in service. Two weeks before I was due to be discharged these two fellows from headquarters came into our company and asked the captain to call me. They placed me in a small room and began interrogating me. Well, it happened that I had had sex with these two sailors before I went into the service. Evidently these sailors had gotten caught and, under interrogation, turned my name in. Unfortunately, I am one of these crazy people who is just too honest for his own good. When I was confronted with this I should have just kept my mouth shut, but instead I admitted what I had done. I was a damn fool. By the time I realized that, it was too late.

That same day they took me over to the hospital where I stayed for a month to be analyzed. But they didn't do anything. I just sat around and read, and finally I got a dishonorable discharge. Two weeks before my time was up, I was discharged, and there was nothing I could do about it.

Later that year I was working in a restaurant, and by coincidence the fellow who had been my company captain came in. He told me something which has made me regret my confession to this very day. He said, "You are the biggest fool I ever saw. Why did you talk to those guys? You should have come to me. We would have shut it up right away and none of this would have happened." You see, I thought he knew why headquarters was interrogating me, but in fact he didn't. And he told me that he was gay, too. It was really a surprise, because he looked like an Arkansas farmer. I would have never known. But it was too late to do me any good.

My most important accomplishment in life? This is a difficult question to answer, since I believe my life has been a series of missed opportunities. When I was a young man I was fortunate to have many talents. I studied voice, and I was an accomplished violinist. My parents had arranged to finance my violin studies and I was all set to live in New York and become a concert violinist. Then the Depression came. My dreams were shattered and I had to go to work. That summer I worked as recreational director at a resort, and while there I met a woman who was looking for a young artist to sponsor. She was a concert pianist and we put on a couple of recitals together that summer. She liked my playing so well that she offered to take me to Boston, where she would have me play for the director of the symphony orchestra, whom she knew. If he liked what he heard, she would sponsor me. She would pay for my studies, room and board–everything, until I was ready for my debut. Just the fall before she had finished doing this for another fellow, and I was to be next. At the end of the summer we made arrangements to meet shortly thereafter in Boston. But when I returned home I received a letter saying she had died.

I rationalized. Perhaps I was not meant to be a violinist. But this was a sort of turning point, because since then I have never accomplished anything great in my life. I have coasted along and made the best of everything that I could. I dropped the violin and voice. And now, at the age of seventy-one, my hands are too stiff to even hold the violin. At my age, nothing works quite like it used to. My most important accomplishment is that I have been able to accept that, gracefully.

PART II: THE QUESTIONNAIRE STUDY

CHAPTER 9

Method

A number of years ago I would have been embarrassed by the questions you have posed to me. I could not have been honest talking about my homosexuality, for fear of retribution. I don't feel that way today. One of the things I like about gay life is that I feel free to open up to others.

I requested the questionnaire for a friend. It pained him deeply even to read the questions because they brought pointedly to mind all the issues he is trying so hard to forget.

THE QUESTIONNAIRE

In developing the questionnaire, we relied heavily on our review of the literature on the social and psychological adjustment of homosexuals, on stereotypes of aging among homosexual men, and on the relationship of occupation to concealment of sexual orientation. Where possible, we used questionnaire items developed and tested for reliability and validity by other investigators. In some instances we modified previously developed items or developed new ones to fit our study of the older homosexual.

In order to encourage completion of the questionnaire, we had to assure our respondents of complete anonymity. Everyone in the gay community is aware that information about an individual's sexual orientation can lead to serious problems with friends, family, and employers. This awareness is particularly acute among some older homosexuals, since most of their experience predates the current relative openness about homosexual lifestyles.

Clearly, respondents' anonymity was an essential prerequisite for this research. However, it was also necessary for us to obtain *informed consent* from each participant. Our funding source required that we demonstrate that each respondent was aware of the nature of the study, its potential negative impact on him, and his right to withdraw his participation at any time. Typically, informed consent is obtained by securing the respondent's signature on a standardized form.

In order to satisfy the requirements of both anonymity and informed consent, we designed a two-page fact sheet which was attached to the front of each questionnaire. (The fact sheet and questionnaire are reproduced in Appendix C.) The first page described, in simple language, essential information about the study's purpose, sponsorship, potential respondents, and the voluntary nature of participation. The respondent was asked not to sign his name but to check the bottom of the page to indicate that he had read the questionnaire. Our funding source also required that the respondent be able to identify his questionnaire after handing it in. To accomplish this, he was to devise a four-digit number to be placed on the questionnaire, and to retain a copy of the number.

A preliminary draft of the questionnaire was pretested on ten respondents from a local gay rights organization; their comments were used to reword several items for increased clarity and ease of responding. The final revised questionnaire contained sixty-two items and took about twenty-five minutes to complete.

A group of items elicited demographic information such as age, occupation, living situation, marital status, and level of education. Remaining items measured psychological and social adaptation. With slight modifications we used questions measuring self-acceptance, depression, and degree of passing (concealment) from Weinberg and Williams (1975); respondents were asked to indicate agreement or disagreement on a five-point scale from "strongly agree" to "strongly disagree." An example of an item measuring self-acceptance was "I take a positive attitude toward myself."

We used additional items from Weinberg and Williams (1975): a set of three items to measure integration into the homosexual community, and a set of fifteen items to measure frequency of psychosomatic symptoms. Life satisfaction was measured with a thirteen-item index devised and validated by Wood, Wylie, and Sheafor (1969).

Other items were designed to measure the following:

• Present and past professional counseling experience
• Perceived health status
• Extent of socializing with younger people

- Anticipation of negative reaction from younger homosexuals (for example, the respondent would indicate agreement or disagreement with the statement "Most young gays think that older gays are pretty dull")
- Willingness to associate with known homosexuals
- Extent to which the respondent is known to others as homosexual
- Level of participation in homosexual institutions such as bars, clubs, and organizations
- Past or present exclusive relationship
- Current frequency of sexual activity
- Number of sex partners
- Level of satisfaction with current sex life

We defined an eligible respondent as any self-identified homosexual, male or female, forty years of age or older. (Due to the limited number of female respondents recruited, we subsequently limited the study to males.)

In recruiting respondents for the questionnaire, our goal was to obtain older homosexuals from as diverse a cross-section of the community as possible. Therefore we used a variety of methods to reach potential respondents. We spread the word about the study by talking to individuals and leaders in the local gay community, placing advertisements and articles in local gay publications such as weekly news pamphlets, and advertising in publications distributed to local gay bars and clubs. Appendix A contains one such advertisement, as well as a copy of a brief descriptive article which appeared in local gay publications. In each case we asked the reader to fill out a questionnaire or to participate in an interview. A name and phone number were provided, and readers over forty were encouraged to call.

Concurrent with these activities, we appeared at a number of meetings of local gay organizations. We explained the purpose of the study and described the potential benefits to the gay community in terms of more knowledge about a hitherto ignored group. We distributed questionnaires, pencils, and stamped return envelopes to older individuals at these meetings.

We were aware that many older homosexuals do not frequent the social and political gatherings at which we appeared. In order to locate these respondents, we enlisted the help of about a half-dozen older respondents who had extensive friendship networks. Each of these individuals received a packet of questionnaires and stamped return envelopes to distribute to his or her friends. By marking these questionnaires, we were able to determine how many were returned from each source. We fed this information back to the individuals, who in turn contacted those who had not yet responded. In this way we were able to include many older gays who would otherwise have been inaccessible.

THE SAMPLE

The lack of representative sampling has been perhaps the most troublesome criticism of research on homosexuals. Unrepresentative sampling certainly characterized many earlier studies; often these were limited to groups of disturbed homosexuals who had sought treatment (e.g., Bieber et al., 1962). More recent studies have had to grapple with the issue of representativeness, since constraints on time, money, and accessibility of potential study subjects have inevitably produced samples which are not strictly representative of the hypothetical populations from which they were drawn; i.e., the selected respondents do not mirror the actual population on the variables under study.

Much of the research on homosexuality, for instance, is based on samples which are biased in favor of white respondents who are relatively well educated and affluent. Two of four major recent studies of homosexuals have included only very small numbers (about 1 to 5 percent) of racial minorities (Weinberg and Williams, 1975; Masters and Johnson, 1979). One of these four studies (Saghir and Robins, 1973) did not report the racial background of the sample.

Another sample bias favors those who participate in some aspect of the public gay community: a bar, club, bathhouse, or organization. With the exception of a number of fieldwork studies (Warren, 1977), most researchers on homosexuality have been forced to rely on these outlets for recruitment. We do not know how many homosexuals never or infrequently participate in the public gay community, or how these individuals differ from those who do participate. Therefore it is difficult to judge the importance of this bias. In research on older homosexuals, who are known to participate less frequently in the public gay community, this may be a difficult problem.

A particularly thorny sampling issue concerns the researcher's definition of "homosexual." The pioneering research of Kinsey and his associates established that sexual orientation can only be described on a continuum, so that where one draws the line is arbitrary. The Masters and Johnson (1979) study, for instance, has been criticized for including in the clinical sample individuals who are not truly homosexual (Suppe, 1982a). A complicating factor, as illustrated in the case histories in this book, is that individuals may assume exclusive heterosexual or homosexual patterns at different points in their lives.

Some major research studies have been criticized for limiting their samples to one or a few highly unrepresentative geographical locales–most notably the Bell and Weinberg (1978) study, which dealt with respondents in San Francisco, a highly atypical community. That study has also been criticized for being outdated (Suppe, 1982b). With the very rapid and dramatic changes in the visibility and militancy of the gay community over the past decade, and the effects of these changes on the lives of gay people, many data can be considered old after only five or ten years.

Recently a noted researcher in the area of homosexuality has argued that sample representativeness is required only for certain types of research, and that the charge of unrepresentativeness has not been applied in a meaningful way to much of the research on homosexuality.

> If the focus of one's study is demographic [inferring population characteristics on the basis of sample characteristics], sample representativeness is crucial to the adequacy of the study. If the focus is to explore diversity, sample representativeness is not particularly relevant, provided that the sample is sufficiently diverse as to represent the main variations or diversity in the parent population. . . . If the focus of one's study is to refute general claims about a population, highly nonrepresentative samples from a biased subpopulation are adequate to refute, although they have virtually no potential for establishing general theses about the total population. (Suppe, 1982b: note 2)

The sample of older homosexual men for *Gay and Gray* is biased in some of the same ways as were the samples for the other studies cited. It does not purport to represent all older gay men, and the results presented here do not provide a statistical profile of this group. Despite some serious drawbacks, such as the inability to recruit racial minorities (discussed in the next chapter), we believe that our sample is adequate for the uses to which it is put. To the extent that *Gay and Gray* purports to refute stereotypes and to explore the diversity of older gay men, the sample is sufficiently diverse. This was indeed one of our major purposes.

The other major intent was to identify factors which predict successful adaptation to aging for homosexual men. These findings, described in Chapter 11, should not be interpreted as universals. For example, while integration into the homosexual community may be a valid predictor of adaptation for older white men, the scarcity of community resources specifically for gay racial minorities may make this factor irrelevant for an older black homosexual. Nevertheless, these findings are valid for the types of respondents studied and at least suggest general relationships which may be widely applicable. As is always the case in new areas, further research to extend the findings is necessary, and this study can suggest directions for that research.

In defense of the diversity of our sample, we can make several observations. Although all respondents were white, the sample does include a wide range of age groups, levels of education and income, occupational statuses, retirement statuses, and religious preferences. (These findings are reviewed in the next chapter.) We made special efforts to include older men who were not accessible through gay community institutions. While we conducted the study in one locale, respondents came from a four-county area, encompassing urban, suburban, and semi-rural environments. In addition, since the locale was popular as a retirement community, many of our respondents had moved there from throughout the country. In defense of the appropriateness of the sample, nearly all respondents were strongly self-identified as homosexual. Finally, the data were collected in 1978, by which time the gay liberation movement of the 1970s had had its major impact.

CHAPTER 10

What Are Older Homosexual Men Like?

Heterosexuals can't possibly understand what homosexuals are like. The heterosexual is an outsider looking through a frosted window. He doesn't see inside very well. People like me, who have been gay for forty years and who are part of a gay community, have a totally different picture because we are inside looking at the situation as it is.

My sister has gone through three husbands and I have gone through three lovers. The difference is that I have remained good friends with all my ex-lovers.

In the gay world my straight appearance has been a handicap. . . . I would like to be able to be recognized by other gay men for what I am. . . . What happens very often is the other gay person sort of pussyfoots around, checks me out to find out what I am. How much simpler it would be if we just had some way that was easily understandable to us, but meaningless to straight people.

Perhaps the most notable characteristic of those who completed our questionnaire is that they were overwhelmingly male and all white. This was of particular concern, because we had hoped to study both older men and women and to include a reasonable cross-section of the community. After several efforts to interest more women in the study, we finally decided to limit our focus to males. We simply had not heard from enough women to be able to write intelligently about them.

The absence of females and minority-group members from the present study merits discussion. We made many efforts to secure respondents from both of these groups. In our presentations to community groups and discussions with respondents, we made special appeals for help in locating minority and female respondents. We secured interviews with eight women and questionnaires from eighteen women; no minority respondents were recruited. Although this limits our scope, it illustrates a characteristic of the gay community.

Homosexual individuals appear in equal proportions among every age cohort and every social, racial, and ethnic group, although the incidence of homosexuality among females is lower than among males (Kinsey, Pomeroy, and Martin, 1948; Kinsey, Pomeroy, Martin, and Gebhard, 1953). There was every reason to expect minority participants and at least a substantial proportion of female respondents. However, the "public" gay community, as represented by the bars, social clubs, and civic and political organizations, is overwhelmingly dominated by white males. There is currently some controversy as to whether this is due to the inhospitality, racism, or sexism of the established gay community, or whether it is due to a lack of interest on the part of women and minorities. No doubt both factors play a role. Although we were successful in recruiting older men through social networks, our initial contacts for these networks were made among the predominantly male clubs and civic organizations. So, although this networking helped us to recruit a more representative sample of men, it provided us with few additional female respondents.

AGE

The findings reported here are based on the responses of 112 males who completed the questionnaire. All were forty or older. Why did we select forty as our cut-off point? In our discussions with gay men and women, we found that forty represented a sort of benchmark. While forty was not considered by most to be the beginning of "old age," it did definitely mark one as no longer young. Many individuals in their thirties are still in school or unsettled in career or vocational choices. By forty they are expected to be more settled. For many, the forties bring clear physical signs of aging: the first gray hairs, facial wrinkles, and so on. Popular notions have been that homosexual men age prematurely and are over the hill at thirty. Hooker (1965: 100) suggested that, after the age of thirty-five, homosexual men were no longer considered acceptable sex partners. Minnigerode (1976) asked ninety-five homosexual men between the ages of twenty-five and sixty-eight to classify themselves as young, middle aged, or old. Most men in their twenties and thirties described themselves as young, while three-fourths of those in their forties and all of those over fifty described themselves as middle aged. Minnigerode's findings confirm our own.

In our study the youngest respondent was forty-one and the oldest seventy-seven years old. Table 10.1 summarizes the age distribution of all 112 respondents. Almost two-thirds were in their fifties and sixties; one-fourth were in their forties, and 11 percent were in their seventies. Our respondents represent a group which has been called the "young old." The very old (i.e., those seventy-five and above) are not well represented. However, the major impact of aging on homosexual men will clearly have been felt by our respondents.

SEXUAL ORIENTATION

How did the men in this study rate themselves on a continuum from exclusively homosexual to exclusively heterosexual? Kinsey was the first researcher to show that very few individuals can be described as completely homosexual or completely heterosexual.

TABLE 10.1. Age of Respondents: Percentage Distribution

	Age categories			
Gay and Gray	*40-49*	*50-59*	*60-69*	*70-79*
N = 112	25.9	43.8	19.6	10.7
Weinberg and Williams (1975) [a]	*Under 26*	*26-35*	*36-45*	*Over 45*
N = 1,057	18	30	28	24

[a] In this and all subsequent tables, data from Weinberg and Williams (1975) refer to the United States sample only.

Kinsey, Pomeroy, and Martin (1948) devised a seven-point scale for classifying individuals on a sexual orientation continuum. The ratings took account of overt sexual behavior as well as of ideas, feelings, and fantasies. We adapted this seven-point scale, although, because we recruited only men who identified themselves as homosexual, we expected our ratings to be skewed in that direction.

It should be noted that, unlike the Kinsey ratings, which were made by trained raters based on extensive interview material, our ratings were *self*-ratings. The respondent was asked to select the description which most accurately reflected the way he perceived himself. He had to distinguish between descriptors such as "primarily homosexual, only slightly heterosexual," and "primarily homosexual, but more than slightly heterosexual." These distinctions do not necessarily reflect differences in actual sexual contacts. Behavior that is "more than slightly heterosexual" (say, one or two opposite-sex encounters) for one man may be "only slightly heterosexual" for another. Although we should keep the fact of self-rating in mind, our primary concern here is with the way our respondents perceived themselves. Interpretations of the data should reflect this concern.

Responses pertaining to self-rated sexual orientation are summarized in Table 10.2. All of our respondents rated themselves as at least primarily homosexual: 87 percent rated themselves as "exclusively homosexual," 12 percent as "primarily homosexual, only slightly heterosexual," and only two respondents said they were "more than slightly heterosexual." In light of the fact that 29 percent of our respondents had been married, these responses are more heavily skewed toward the homosexual end of the continuum than might be expected, even in a group of self-identified homosexual men. In the Weinberg and Williams (1975) study of homosexual men of all ages, respondents were much less likely to rate themselves toward the exclusively homosexual end of the continuum. (For example, only 51 percent rated themselves as exclusively homosexual. These data are also summarized in Table 10.2.)

It appears that older homosexual men are more likely to perceive themselves as exclusively or primarily homosexual. This difference may be due to chance variation; that is, more men who view themselves as exclusively homosexual may have happened to respond to our survey. This explanation is not likely, however, given the large

TABLE 10.2. Self-Rated Sexual Orientation

	Gay and Gray (N = 112)	Weinberg and Williams[a] (N = 1,057)
Exclusively homosexual	86.6%	50.6%
Primarily homosexual, only slightly heterosexual	11.6	29.8
Primarily homosexual, but more than slightly heterosexual	1.8	13.1
Equally homosexual and heterosexual	0	4.4
Primarily heterosexual, but more than slightly homosexual	0	2.1
Primarily heterosexual, only slightly homosexual	0	0
Exclusively heterosexual	0	0

[a] Wording of categories was slightly different in Weinberg and Williams (1975).

difference in self-ratings between our older respondents and those in the Weinberg and Williams study.

It may be that, as men grow older, they tend to become more constricted or exclusive in their sexual orientation. This may be part of a pattern which explains Bell and Weinberg's (1978:107) finding that older homosexual men have more restricted sexual repertoires. If men do in fact become more exclusive with age, then homosexual men with heterosexual interests and experiences may relinquish their heterosexual interests as they grow older. Or they may abandon homosexuality entirely and fail to be included in studies of self-identified homosexual men.

The more exclusive sexual orientation self-ratings among older men may be due to differences in the value systems of the younger and older age cohorts. Our older respondents were part of a generation which believed in exclusive sexual orientation categories to a greater extent than does the younger generation. That is, individuals were believed to be either exclusively heterosexual or exclusively homosexual, with little tolerance for the shades of bisexuality that have come to be accepted since the 1960s. It was this tendency to "divide the world into goats and sheep" that Kinsey railed against in the 1940s. Today the popularity of unisex clothing, the opening up of traditionally male sports and occupations to women, and the prevalence of sexual experimentation all attest to a greater willingness at least to consider (if not to accept) sexual ambiguity. The young man of today, faced with homosexual feelings or a homosexual identity, is less likely to adopt an exclusively homosexual orientation.

Another factor accounting for the more exclusive self-ratings of older homosexuals may be a positive association between the length of time an individual is identified (to self and others) as homosexual, and the likelihood of that individual viewing himself as exclusively homosexual. Older homosexuals who have been "out" longer are more likely to think of themselves as exclusively homosexual precisely because of their lengthy experience in this role.

LIVING SITUATION

For the homosexual man, determining with whom to live is a very significant decision. This is true for the heterosexual man as well, but for him the path is clearly laid out–all he need do is follow. There seem to be two major patterns for the heterosexual: he may move directly from his parents' home into a living situation with a wife or other female partner, or he may spend time in an intermediary "bachelor pad."

For the homosexual man there are no such clear paths. How long should he remain with his parents? When he does leave their home, should he live alone? With roommates? With a lover? Do roommates turn into lovers or lovers into roommates, and how is this all handled?

Perhaps the most important consideration for the homosexual man is that his living situation can solve a range of practical and social problems or needs. Sharing a home with another person does, of course, lighten the financial burden of housing. It also provides companionship. This is particularly important for a homosexual man who has few gay friends or who lives in a rural area distant from an accessible gay community. A gay roommate, in particular, meets many social and emotional needs. Within the apartment or house, a value system is in force which provides an alternative to the harsh antihomosexual value system of the outside world. The home becomes a sort of protective haven from the larger world, just as the gay bar or social club may serve as an alternative "subsociety." The subsociety or home functions with a set of values which validates and supports a homosexual lifestyle. The home is a place where the homosexual man can let his defenses down, where he can be himself.

For the older homosexual man who is likely to frequent public gay institutions (bars, clubs, and other social/sexual outlets) less frequently, the home is an especially important source of social and emotional support. The popular stereotype of the older gay man tells us that his company is unacceptable to others; therefore he lives alone in social isolation. None of the men in the interview study fit this stereotype, which was further refuted by our questionnaire respondents. (See Table 10.3.) Only 39 percent reported living alone. Forty-three percent lived with a lover, and the remainder resided with roommates or family members. Four men lived with both a lover and one or more roommates, and eight men with a roommate or roommates only. It is not unusual for two gay men to live together as lovers and later as roommates, or vice versa. Another arrangement is for two lovers to maintain separate living situations. The image of the solitary older gay man is inaccurate. There are a variety of options available to him, and most decide not to live alone.

MARRIAGE AND LOVE

Kinsey, Pomeroy, and Martin (1948) found that, as we look at older groups of unmarried men, the incidence of homosexuality

TABLE 10.3. Living Situation of Respondents ($N = 111$)

Alone	38.7%
With lover only	39.6
With lover and roommate(s)	3.6
With roommate(s) only	7.2
With family only (spouse, children, relatives)	5.4
Other	5.4

increases. Apparently there is some truth to the notion that a man who has not married by the age of thirty or forty is more likely to be homosexual. Seventy-one percent of our respondents said they had never married heterosexually. However, equally interesting is the fact that the other 29 percent *had* been married. (See Table 10.4.) Many of these men said that pressures from family and society led them to marry. These men reached marriageable age in the 1930s, 1940s, and 1950s, when social pressures to marry were much greater than they are today. Marriage ended constant questions from family, who continually badgered the individual to "settle down." Marriage also facilitated socializing with age peers who themselves were marrying, creating a "couples society." It lessened suspicion that the individual was "different," and it often made employment and career advancement easier.

Perhaps the most tragic, but certainly a very frequent reason for marriage was the man's belief that his homosexuality would "go away" once he was happily married to a woman. Unfortunately for both partners, it never worked. The belief in marriage as a cure for homosexuality is a heterosexually inspired myth. The heterosexual man, for whom sex with a woman is already a powerful attraction, erroneously believes that homosexuality is caused by fear of or lack of opportunity with women. In fact, there is consensus today among counselors that sexual orientation is very stable and not easily changed (Tripp, 1975).

The unrealistic expectations of the homosexual man who married with the hope of changing led to frustration for both partners. Since most of these men did not discuss their feelings openly with their wives, both often experienced confusion, self-recrimination, and anger. The relationship may have lasted only briefly, although

TABLE 10.4. Marital Status of Respondents (*N* = 111)

Never married	71.2%
Married	3.6
Divorced	17.1
Separated	3.6
Widowed	4.5

sometimes it continued unhappily for many years, especially when there were children or strong religious beliefs against divorce.

Today there are fewer pressures for the homosexual man to marry. The single lifestyle has earned such widespread acceptance that heterosexual and homosexual blend easily into that new lifestyle. Even the gay man who has been attached to a male lover for many years can take advantage of his "bachelor" image to gain acceptance from family and friends. After all, so many people are single these days that one's marital status hardly seems to matter. It is becoming less accurate to label as homosexual an older person who never married or who has remained unmarried for most of his life. Future cohorts of older gay men are likely to include even more who are unmarried.

Not all homosexual men who marry heterosexually have unsuccessful marriages. Although it is a rare man who can maintain a homosexual identity and a successful marriage, we did meet several such men in the course of this study. Invariably the wife and children are unaware of Dad's interest in the homosexual world. The marriage and the gay world are scrupulously separated, each existing in a hermetically sealed environment. While a traditional home and family life are maintained, the man ventures into the gay community, often on a regular basis. He may have a group of gay friends, or his contacts with the gay community may be limited to brief sexual contacts in anonymous settings. (For a description of this type of lifestyle, see Humphreys, 1970.) Usually the man will not consider "coming out" to his wife and children; he has spent too many years carefully constructing two separate worlds which will never meet. In some cases, however, the husband will finally leave a marriage of many years to join a male lover or assume a homosexual lifestyle.

Most of the men in our study never married heterosexually. What kinds of love relationships did they have with other men? Again, popular stereotypes were found to be inaccurate. For years polemicists have pointed to homosexuals' presumed inability to sustain relationships. However, a casual visit with a group of homosexuals will usually turn up several men who have formed primary relationships. The partner is usually referred to as a "lover," although this term is somewhat inaccurate in that it implies a relationship limited to sexual contact. In fact, the lover relationship is one in which two individuals share all of the sexual, social, and emotional ties that characterize a heterosexual relationship, although the societal and familial supports are usually absent. The relationship may or may not allow for outside sexual contacts, although such contacts are probably more prevalent in homosexual than in heterosexual relationships.

Collecting information about homosexual love relationships presents some unique problems. Among heterosexuals, marriage is a simple, legally based, and commonly understood criterion of a relationship; among homosexuals, on the other hand, no one criterion fills the bill. The lover relationship comes closest to approximating heterosexual marriage, but we must be careful to avoid imposing a heterosexual framework in a study of homosexuals. In addition, although there is some agreement among homosexuals on the meaning of the term "lover," there is also some ambiguity. This definitional problem is compounded by the use of other terms such as "friend," "mate," and "partner." In order to circumvent this problem we needed a questionnaire item which would be interpreted consistently by all respondents and which would, at the same time, provide us with a minimum estimate of the prevalence of committed relationships. We asked respondents to report relationships *in which the partners limited their sexual relations primarily to each other.* Findings are summarized in Table 10.5, along with comparison data from Weinberg and Williams (1975).

Over half of our respondents had, at some time in their lives, experienced such a relationship of more than a year's duration, and almost a third were involved in such a relationship at the time of the study. These data certainly refute the myth that the older gay man is unable to sustain a lasting relationship. Given the definitional problems described above, these data may in one sense underestimate the number of men who had "lovers." In the course of the study we met many couples who considered themselves to be lovers and did in fact share a deep emotional commitment to one another; however, the sexual aspect of the relationship had diminished, and for some couples sexual gratification was sought outside the relationship, though in all other aspects their lives were shared. It should be

TABLE 10.5. Respondents' Exclusive Relationships

	Gay and Gray	Weinberg and Williams (1975)
	(N = 110)	(N = 1,057)
	At the *present* time, are another gay/lesbian person and yourself limiting your sexual relationships primarily to each other?	
No	64.5%	66.5%
Yes, for less than a month	0.0	2.5
Yes, for 1-6 months	2.7	4.9
Yes, for 6 months-1 year	0.9	3.3
Yes, for more than a year	31.8	22.9
	At some time *in the past,* did another gay/lesbian person and yourself limit your sexual relationships primarily to each other? (Referring to a different relationship from above.)	
No	30.0%	30.8%
Yes, for less than a month	1.8	6.4
Yes, for 1-6 months	10.0	16.5
Yes, for 6 months-1 year	6.4	9.5
Yes, for more than a year	51.8	36.9

noted that this pattern is certainly not unheard of among heterosexual couples as well.

Although only 30 percent of our respondents had never had a primary sexual relationship with another man, 65 percent did not have such a relationship at the time of the study. Despite this situation, most of these men were living with others (see Table 10.3), so they did have steady sources of companionship and support.

Comparison data from the Weinberg and Williams study are strikingly similar to ours. Among both younger and older gay men, about one-fourth to one-third were currently in relationships of over one year's duration; about two-thirds did not have a current lover, and about 30 percent had never had such a relationship. The older men were more likely to have had a relationship of over one year's duration–which is to be expected, since they have had more years in which to experience such a relationship.

SOCIOECONOMIC STATUS

In general, respondents were highly educated (Table 10.6). Seventy-six percent had at least some college, 24 percent were college graduates, and 22 percent had graduate degrees. Only five respondents had not completed high school. These levels of education are higher than would be expected in a random sample of this age cohort. It is likely that better-educated individuals are more responsive to a research project, better able to read a lengthy questionnaire, and therefore more likely to be included in the sample. By comparison, the Weinberg and Williams respondents had somewhat higher levels of education, with 82 percent completing at least some college. This is due to a commonly observed intergenerational difference: younger cohorts, such as those in the Weinberg and Williams study, have had greater opportunities for education.

Occupations listed by respondents were categorized into low, medium, and high status, based on a scale developed by Weinberg and Williams (1975). Respondents who were retired (25 percent) listed their most recent fulltime occupation; it was believed that this

TABLE 10.6. Education of Respondents

	What is the highest level of education you have completed? (N = 110)[a]
Grade school	4.5%
High school	19.1
Some college	30.9
College graduate	23.6
Master's degree	11.8
PhD, MD, or other advanced degree	10.0

[a] In Weinberg and Williams (1975) 82 percent had at least some college education.

would indicate the highest occupational level achieved. The respondent was asked to describe his occupation in some detail, stating the name of his job and describing what he actually did. Utilizing the Weinberg and Williams definitions of low-, medium-, and high-status occupations, and a series of examples, my assistant and I rated each respondent independently. Inter-rater agreement on occupational status was 82 percent. For disagreements, reference to the definition was used to assign a final rating.

Occupational status is presented in Table 10.7. Twenty-two percent of respondents held high-status occupations such as physician, lawyer, or business executive. Sixty-six percent held medium-status occupations such as salesclerk, technician, schoolteacher, or small business owner. Twelve percent held low-status occupations such as unskilled laborer or machine operator.

One-fourth of respondents were fully retired, one-eighth were partially retired, and the remainder had not yet retired. Of the respondents who were fully or partially retired, the great majority (80 percent) said they enjoyed being retired. Fifteen percent would prefer not being retired; the remainder had no feelings one way or the other (Table 10.8). These responses are consistent with research studies on retirement in the general population. Most older people have positive attitudes toward retirement, and retirement itself is not associated with poor morale or low life satisfaction. (See Atchley, 1977 for a review of these studies.)

The income levels reported by respondents were high. (See Table 10.9.) Fifty-six percent had annual incomes of over $15,000 in 1978, and only 11 percent had incomes below $6,000.

The political preferences of respondents were ascertained. Almost half described themselves as somewhat or very liberal. Thirty-

TABLE 10.7. Occupational Status of Respondents ($N = 106$)

Low status (e.g., machine operator, unskilled laborer)	12.3%
Medium status (e.g., administrator, small business owner, clerical worker)	66.0
High status (e.g., business executive, professional)	21.7

TABLE 10.8. Retirement Status of Respondents

	Current status (N = 110)
Fully retired	24.5%
Partially retired	12.7
Not retired	62.7
	For those who are retired: How do you feel about your retirement? (N = 40)
Enjoy it	80%
No feelings one way or the other	5
Would prefer not to be retired	15

two percent were "moderates," and the remainder were conservatives (Table 10.10).

Thirty-seven percent of respondents were Protestant, 11 percent Roman Catholic, 14 percent Jewish, and 13 percent "other." Twenty-six percent reported that they were atheists, agnostics, or had no religious preference (Table 10.11).

Eighty-six percent of respondents described their health as "good" or "excellent" (Table 10.12).

PSYCHOLOGICAL AND SOCIAL ADAPTATION

Since the monumental studies of homosexuality by Kinsey and his colleagues (1948, 1953) there has been a great deal of research on the phenomenon of homosexuality and on the psychological and social status of homosexuals. Most of this research has taken one of two approaches. One involves comparing groups of homosexuals and heterosexuals. For instance, in the first study to suggest that homosexual men may be psychologically "normal," Hooker (1957) compared the personality structure and adjustment of groups of homosexuals and heterosexuals matched for age, education, and

TABLE 10.9. Annual Income: Percentage Distribution (*N* = 110)

Less than $3,000	1.8%
$3,000-$5,999	9.1
$6,000-$8,999	7.2
$9,000-$11,999	10.9
$12,000-$14,999	14.5
$15,000-$18,000	20.9
Over $18,000	35.5

Note: Data were collected in 1978.

TABLE 10.10. Political Preference: Percentage Distribution (*N* = 111)

	How would you describe your political views?
Very liberal or radical	18.0%
Somewhat liberal	30.6
Moderate	31.5
Somewhat conservative	17.1
Very conservative	2.7

IQ. Trained clinicians were unable to distinguish homosexuals from heterosexuals on the basis of the results of projective tests, attitude scales, and life-history interview material. More recent studies, such as those of Saghir and Robins (1973), Weinberg and Williams (1975), and Bell and Weinberg (1978), have also compared homosexuals with heterosexuals.

The second approach was directed toward finding out why certain individuals become homosexuals–that is, identifying causative factors. Most of this research assumed that homosexuality was an emotional disorder. Researchers examined life-history material to identify unique aspects of the homosexual's background that led to development of a homosexual identity. For example, Bieber et al. (1962) identified early childhood experiences in the lives of patients who had entered into psychiatric treatment. According to Bieber,

TABLE 10.11. Religion

What is your present religious preference?

	Gay and Gray	Weinberg and Williams (1975)
	(N = 111)	(N = 1,057)
Protestant	36.9%	53%
Roman Catholic	10.8	29
Jewish	13.5	9
No preference, atheist, or agnostic	26.1	_ _a
Other	12.6	10

a This category was not included in Weinberg and Williams (1975).

TABLE 10.12. Perceived Health Status (N = 111)

	At the present time, how is your health?
Excellent	41.4%
Good	45.0
Fair	12.6
Poor	0.9

homosexual patients were more likely to have experienced exposure to some forms of family pathology, such as a close and overbearing mother.

Gay and Gray takes an approach quite different from these studies in that it does not attempt to make heterosexual-homosexual comparisons. These sorts of comparisons were more appropriate to earlier studies, when homosexuality had just been "rediscovered." There was what now seems to us to be a naive curiosity about how "those people" were different from "normal folks." Now that we know that homosexual feelings and behavior occur among most people, the old comparisons seem less meaningful. Here we look at the older homosexual man in his own right, without reaching for comparisons with some presumed but illusory norm.

The research described here has also avoided the "causality trap"–an overzealous attempt to find out *why* something has happened, to the point of failing to observe *what* is happening. For years certain investigators have been so obsessed with identifying causal factors for homosexuality that we wonder if their energy isn't really directed toward assuring "normal folks" that homosexuals really *are* different from them. The picture emerging from more recent research, however, reveals that homosexuals are not cut from a different mold. A more realistic approach to the question of causation would involve examining the processes which determine sexual orientation for everyone. Once we understand the path that leads to heterosexuality, we will understand the path to homosexuality as well.

It is possible and important to study social phenomena without examining causation. This is the approach taken here. Given that these men are homosexual, and given that they are aging, what are they like? How have they adapted to their lifestyles? What factors lead older gay men to adapt well to their situations?

Another important way in which *Gay and Gray* differs from many earlier studies of homosexuality is that it does not make *a priori* judgments about the value of homosexuality. In the medical field these judgments have taken the form of diagnoses of emotional disorder. For instance, until recently the American Psychiatric Association classified homosexuality as a pathological emotional disturbance. In the religious field these judgments have taken the form of condemnation of homosexuality as sinful and immoral. While we eschew both of these positions, we also avoid advocating homosexuality. Our purpose is to take an objective look at the older homosexual man and to describe him as he is, noting both his strengths and his weaknesses.

Finally, in examining the older homosexual's psychological and social adaptation we have used the most *direct* measures possible. Some of the early research on the adaptation of homosexuals relied on projective tests such as the Rorschach test and the Thematic Apperception Test. These projective tests measure rather abstract inferential constructs that may have only limited relevance to actual behavior and feelings (Mischel, 1968). Instead, we have relied on a number of measures which asked the respondent to report on his own activities, attitudes, and beliefs about himself. The following scales (series of questionnaire items) were used as indexes of psychological and social adaptation and are described below. (Several scales were adopted from the Weinberg and Williams study.)

Self-acceptance
Depression
Psychosomatic symptoms
Life satisfaction
Fears and anxieties
Counseling experience
Passing (concealment)
Relationship to younger age cohort
Relationship to homosexual community
Attitude toward retirement
Sex life

Where applicable, half the items measuring a particular attribute are stated so that agreement indicates a high level of the attribute; the remaining items are stated so that agreement indicates a low level of the attribute. For instance, the self-acceptance scale contains both types of items; i.e., "I take a positive attitude toward myself," and "At times I think I am no good at all." Scales are typically constructed this way, in order to account for the tendency of some respondents to agree with (or disagree with) all items. Scoring is reversed on negatively worded items so that a high score indicates a high level of the attribute and a low score indicates a low level. Tables 10.13 through 10.27 summarize responses to the scales measuring psychological and social adaptation.

Older Gay Men: How Well Adjusted?

Examples of items from the self-acceptance scale were given above. Depression was measured by asking the respondent to agree or disagree with items such as "I often feel downcast and dejected" and "I get a lot of fun out of life." The level of psychosomatic symptoms was ascertained by asking the respondent how often he experienced a number of symptoms typically associated with anxiety, e.g., insomnia, nervousness, headaches, and shortness of breath. Results for these measures are indicated in Tables 10.13 through 10.15. Our respondents tended to score well on the "healthy" side of these variables. These results do not differ substantially from those obtained from the age-diverse Weinberg and Williams sample. Total scores were computed for each of these scales. For self-acceptance 82.1 percent of respondents scored high, 10.7 percent medium, and only 7.1 percent low. For depression 78.6 percent scored low, 8.9 percent medium, and 12.5 percent high. For psycho-

TABLE 10.13. Percentage of Responses to Self-Acceptance Items

	Strongly agree	Agree	?	Disagree	Strongly disagree
I wish I could have more respect for myself[a]	6.3	13.5	6.3	31.5	42.3
I feel that I'm a person of worth, at least on an equal plane with others	59.8	37.5	1.8	0.9	0.0
All in all, I am inclined to feel that I am a failure	3.6	2.7	4.5	27.7	61.7
On the whole, I am satisfied with myself	28.6	51.8	7.1	10.7	1.8
I take a positive attitude toward myself	33.9	50.0	5.4	8.9	1.8
I certainly feel useless at times	5.4	21.4	6.3	33.9	33.0
I feel that I have a number of good qualities	45.5	53.6	0.0	0.9	0.0
At times I think I am no good at all	0.9	8.0	1.8	32.1	57.1
I am able to do things as well as most other people[a]	36.0	56.8	3.6	2.7	0.9
I feel I do not have much to be proud of	0.9	6.3	3.6	30.4	58.9

Note: N = 112 except as indicated. Source of self-acceptance scale: Weinberg and Williams (1975).

[a] N = 111

TABLE 10.14. Percentage of Responses to Depression Items

	Strongly agree	Agree	?	Disagree	Strongly disagree
I am not as happy as others seem to be	2.7	16.1	8.0	32.1	41.1
I get a lot of fun out of life	38.4	41.1	8.0	11.6	0.9
On the whole, I think I am quite a happy person	31.3	46.4	9.8	10.7	1.8
In general, I feel in low spirits most of the time	0.9	7.1	3.6	36.7	51.8
I often feel downcast and dejected	1.8	12.5	3.6	38.4	43.8

	Very happy	Pretty happy	Not too happy	Very unhappy
Taking all things together, how would you say things are these days? Would you say you are . . .	24.1	59.8	14.3	1.8

Note: N = 112. Source of depression scale: Weinberg and Williams (1975).

somatic symptoms 76.8 percent reported a low level of symptoms and 23.2 percent reported a medium level; no respondent reported a high level of symptoms.

Respondents in Weinberg and Williams (1975) and in our study were asked, "Taking all things together, how would you say things are these days? Would you say you are very happy, pretty happy, not too happy, or very unhappy?" Our results are summarized in Table 10.14. About 60 percent of respondents in both studies reported that they were "pretty happy." A greater proportion of our respondents (24.1 percent) described themselves as "very happy" compared to the Weinberg and Williams study (16.9 percent).

Various instruments have been developed for measuring aspects of the subjective well-being of older adults (Larson, 1978). One of the most widely used measures is a life-satisfaction scale originally developed by Neugarten, Havighurst, and Tobin (1961). Our study utilized a version of the Neugarten scale (the LSI-Z Scale) developed by Wood, Wylie, and Sheafor (1969). This scale asks the respondent to agree or disagree with a number of statements such as, "As I grow older things seem better than I thought they would be," and "This is the dreariest time of my life." Results are reported in Table 10.16. Both Neugarten, Havighurst, and Tobin and Wood, Wylie, and Sheafor reported life-satisfaction scores for several hundred individuals from fifty to ninety-two years of age. These data provide a convenient benchmark against which to compare the scores of our sample of older homosexual men. Converting all scores to percentages, life-satisfaction scores for our sample compared favorably with these scores for the general older population. Over half of our respondents scored 80 percent or higher, with a mean score of 74.5 percent (SD = 5.8). Neugarten, Havighurst, and Tobin reported a mean score of 62.0 percent (SD = 4.4) and Wood, Wylie, and Sheafor a mean score of 58.0 percent (SD = 4.4). Almost three-quarters of our respondents reported a high level of life satisfaction (Table 10.16).

Our society seems to place a premium on achieving happiness or some sense of satisfaction in old age. The message that is sent to us indirectly is that if we live good, productive lives, we will be rewarded with happiness in our later years. Thus we are advised to work hard, accumulate a nest egg, and take care of ourselves. More germane to the issue of sexuality, we are told that if we raise a family our children will bring us support and happiness in our old age. Many people have begun to challenge the validity of these ideas. Too often "good" behavior is "rewarded" only with the disadvantages of old age in a society that does not treat its elders well: financial deprivation, poor health care, loneliness, and abandonment by geographically and economically mobile children. It is actually surprising that life-satisfaction levels in the general elderly population are as high as they are.

The threat of unhappiness in old age is a constant accompaniment of arguments against a homosexual lifestyle. The homosexual is led to believe that he will be isolated, lonely, and unhappy in his old age. Our data show that this is not necessarily the case. Older homosexual men report levels of life satisfaction as high as or higher than those of older men and women in the general population.

TABLE 10.15. Percentage of Responses to Psychosomatic Symptom Items

	Nearly all the time	Pretty often	Not very much	Never
Do you ever have any trouble getting to sleep or staying asleep?	6.3	15.2	60.7	17.9
Have you ever been bothered by nervousness, feeling fidgety and tense?	1.8	26.0	59.8	12.5
Are you ever troubled by headaches or pains in the head?	0.9	5.4	46.4	47.3
Do you have loss of appetite?	0.0	3.6	29.5	67.0
How often are you bothered by having an upset stomach?	0.9	10.8	58.0	30.4
Do you find it difficult to get up in the morning? [a]	5.4	6.3	48.6	39.6

	Many times	Sometimes	Hardly ever	Never
Have you ever been bothered by shortness of breath when you were not exercising or working hard?	2.7	17.0	25.9	54.5
Have you ever been bothered by your heart beating hard?	2.7	20.5	29.5	47.3
Do you ever drink more than you should?	15.2	26.8	22.3	35.7
Have you ever had spells of dizziness?	0.0	18.8	27.7	53.6
Are you ever bothered by nightmares?	0.9	9.8	31.3	58.0
Do you tend to lose weight when you have something important bothering you? [a]	1.8	9.0	17.1	72.1
Do your hands ever tremble enough to bother you?	0.9	6.3	13.4	79.5
Are you troubled by your hands sweating so that you feel damp and clammy?	0.9	9.8	13.4	75.9
Have there ever been times when you couldn't take care of things because you just couldn't get going? [a]	4.5	13.5	33.3	48.6

Note: N = 112. Source of psychosomatic symptoms scale: Weinberg and Williams (1975).
[a] *N* = 111

TABLE 10.16. Percentage of Subjects Who Scored Low, Medium, and High on Life Satisfaction

	Low	Medium	High	N
	5.4	22.5	72.1	111

Note: Life satisfaction scale developed by Wood, Wylie, and Sheafor (1969).

Are Older Gays Fearful and Anxious?

Most gay men have been ashamed of their sexual feelings at some time in their lives. This may seem odd to the heterosexual observer, who is likely to think of the gay person as a sexual libertine. But the heterosexual must remember that we are all, heterosexual and homosexual, raised in a culture which looks upon same-sex love as shocking and "dirty." Perhaps the best way for the heterosexual to understand this is to imagine how it would feel to suddenly develop homosexual feelings. Although compelled by the idea of physical contact, he or she would at the same time be repulsed by the mental image of that contact. Most homosexuals experience this contradiction, often in adolescence. Our research shows that most homosexual men overcome their initial feelings of shame and revulsion.

Weinberg and Williams (1975) asked gay men of all ages, "Does knowing that you are homosexual 'weigh on your mind' (make you feel guilty, depressed, anxious, or ashamed)?" Over three-fourths said they rarely felt this way. We asked our older gay men this question and found that over 85 percent never or infrequently experienced such feelings of guilt or shame (Table 10.17).

Perhaps the acid test of a gay man's acceptance of his sexual orientation is his feeling about sexual relations. Sixty-six percent of the men in the Weinberg and Williams study, and 77 percent of the men in our study, said they never felt shame, guilt, or anxiety after having sex with another man (Table 10.17).

Older gay men seem to be less "uptight" than their younger counterparts—a finding that certainly contradicts our notions about the sexual liberation of the "now" generation. However, there are a

TABLE 10.17. Percentage of Responses to Items Measuring Anxiety Regarding Homosexuality

	A great deal	Somewhat	Not very much	Not at all
Does knowing that you are homosexual "weigh on your mind" (make you feel guilty, depressed, anxious, or ashamed)?	0.9 (7.6)	11.7 (15.0)	21.6 (30.4)	65.8 (47.1)

	Nearly always	Pretty often	Not very much	Never
At the present time do you ever experience shame, guilt, or anxiety after having sexual (homosexual) relations?	1.8 (3.6)	3.6 (5.2)	18.0 (25.1)	76.6 (66.2)

Note: N = 111. Source of anxiety items: Weinberg and Williams (1975). Comparison data from Weinberg and Williams are indicated in parentheses.

number of very good reasons for gay men to be less anxious about their homosexuality as they grow older.

For most younger gay men, the hardest part of coming out is dealing with the rejection (actual or potential) of parents. The older gay is less likely to need the approval or acceptance of Mom and Dad. Parents may no longer be living; even if one or the other parent is still alive, the parent-child relationship has likely undergone a change, with the parent more likely to be dependent on the child. Relationships with other close relatives follow the same pattern. The older gay man is also more likely to be financially secure, or at least settled into a stable career or occupation. He is less likely than a younger man to be kicked out of the office because the boss disapproves of his lifestyle.

Closely related to this is our culturally induced bias against thinking about sexuality in relation to older people. Think about the last time you heard someone discuss the issue of a gay person being discriminated against. What was your mental image of that gay person? Most likely he was in his twenties or thirties. Older people in general seem to be insulated from intimations of sexual nonconformity, and the older gay man, unless he is sexually aggressive, is able to cash in on this "reward" of aging.

Yet another prerogative comes with age. When a teenage healthfood devotee tries to convince Grandpa to change his eating habits, Grandpa is likely to respond, "I've lived to this ripe old age doing things my way, so I'm not about to change." We recognize that the experience of age entitles the bearer to be the best judge of his own behavior. An older gay may have experienced intense doubt and anxiety about his sexual behavior in the past, but by the age of forty or fifty it is clear that the nature of things will not change. Shame and guilt no longer have the force they possessed in earlier years.

And then there is the inevitable passage of time that comes with increased age and experience. While early sexual encounters may provoke feelings of anxiety, with time a desensitization process occurs. The pleasurable feelings of sexual release increasingly replace the negative emotions.

Another source of anxiety for the older gay man is fear associated with the process of aging and the inevitability of death. We found that most older gay men do sometimes think about growing older and about dying, which is certainly to be expected in any group of people in their forties and above. About one-half worried at least sometimes about growing older, although very few said they actually worried about dying. (See Table 10.18.)

Although we did not compare older gay men with older heterosexual men, these findings do not show any unusual preoccupation with aging and death. While most of us do ponder these issues as we become aware of our own aging, only a few of us become so preoccupied that we devote a majority of our time to worry or anxiety. The findings in Table 10.18 are significant in that they contradict the popular belief that fears of aging and death obsess gay men. If we examine these erroneous beliefs, we find that several of their supporting assumptions are incorrect.

It is popularly assumed that the older gay man's lack of progeny leads to a number of problems. If he becomes ill in his old age, he will have no one to care for him and look after his interests. He will fear death because there will be no one to carry on the family name.

TABLE 10.18. Percentage of Responses to Items Measuring Fear of Aging and Death (N = 111)

	Never	Very infrequently	Sometimes	Often	Constantly
Does the thought of growing old occur to you?	7.2	14.4	57.7	18.0	2.7
Do you worry about growing old?	20.7	28.8	41.4	9.0	0.0
Does the thought of dying occur to you?	10.8	22.5	56.8	9.0	0.9
Do you worry about dying?	45.0	35.1	18.0	1.8	0.0

He will be tormented by his inability to achieve immortality through his children. Finally, when he goes there will be no one to mourn his passing. All of these assumptions are faulty. Today older people, with and without surviving family members, have fewer people available to care for them and their interests when they become ill or die. Modern industrial society has effectively broken up the kinship system, so that even children of aging parents are no longer required to assume financial responsibility for their parents' care (Comptroller General, 1979). Of course, emotional supports *are* important; they are as necessary for homosexuals as for heterosexuals. There are a number of support options available to most older gay men. Within the immediate family there may be strong ties to siblings, who may or may not be homosexual themselves. There are also family options in addition to the traditional parental role, such as the role of "indulgent uncle." But most frequently the older homosexual can look outside the family, to friends who form support networks just as effective as those available to men who have taken the traditional vows of matrimony.

The fact is that worries about adequate emotional, social, and financial support are a reasonable response to the reality of old age in America today. This reality is essentially the same for gays and for heterosexuals. The stereotype of the older man shunned by others and isolated in a lonely world is no more true for the homosexual than for the heterosexual. Age, not sexuality, relegates us to the scrap heap when we are no longer considered "useful" to society. The older gay man may have difficulty coming to terms with wrinkles and gray hair, but the older heterosexual suffers through the same ordeal. We *all* must contend with the idea that "only young is beautiful."

In one respect, the older gay man has less to fear in growing older. For heterosexuals, the loss of a spouse is usually a major catastrophe. The problem is compounded by cultural and biological factors: husbands are generally somewhat older than their wives and live seven fewer years on the average. Because homosexual men tend to break away from the family and acquire an independence from traditional supports, they are often better able to recover from the loss of a partner. (Over two-fifths of our older gay men currently lived with a lover.) Although there are no data on age disparities among gay couples, gay relationships are not inherently subject to the male-female divergence in life expectancy which today contributes to the social problem of widowhood.

Do Older Gay Men Seek Counseling?

We asked whether the respondent had ever received counseling for his homosexuality from a professional such as a psychiatrist, psychologist, or social worker. We also asked if the respondent was currently receiving professional counseling for his homosexuality, if he would like to receive such counseling, and if he had ever received counseling for reasons other than his homosexuality. (See Table 10.19.)

These questions certainly tell us something about how older homosexual men view professional mental health services. One might presume that a high incidence of mental health intervention within a particular group is an indicator of poor psychological health, if one believes that groups that are more ill or unhappy would seek counseling more frequently. A number of psychiatrists (e.g., Bergler, 1958; Bieber et al., 1962; Socarides, 1968) have written widely on their own homosexual clients, creating the impression that there are indeed a great many homosexuals in therapy. The bulk of this literature has centered around the "unhappy homosexual"–i.e., one who wants to alter his sexual orientation. In fact, many have criticized this literature for drawing broad conclusions about *all* homo-

TABLE 10.19. Percentage of Respondents with Various Types of Counseling Experience

Regarding your homosexuality:

	Yes	No	N
In the past have you ever received counseling from a mental health professional such as a psychiatrist, psychologist, social worker, or counselor?	28.9	71.2	111
Are you presently receiving such counseling?	1.8	98.2	111
If you are not presently receiving such counseling, would you like to obtain such counseling regarding your homosexuality?	9.4	90.6	106
Have you ever had (or are you presently receiving) counseling for reasons *other than* your homosexuality?	12.0	88.0	108

Note: Items modified and adapted from Weinberg and Williams (1975).

sexuals based only on evidence from homosexuals in therapy, who are more likely to be in distress (e.g., Halleck, 1971; Siegelman, 1972; Weinberg, 1973; Tripp, 1975).

We are unaware of any study that has determined whether the number of homosexuals in therapy is *greater than would be expected, based on their proportional representation in society.* Of course, such research would be fraught with difficulties, not the least of which is the absence of a workable definition for "homosexual." And even if homosexuals were found to seek counseling more frequently than heterosexuals, this evidence has little bearing on the ultimate question of the relationship between homosexuality and psychological health, for it can always be argued that the homosexual's unhappiness and his presence in therapy are results of societal oppression, rather than of pathology inherent in his sexual orientation.

There are other reasons why data on homosexual men's presence in counseling are poor indicators of psychological health, even if we discard the question of whether unhappiness is due to sexual orientation or societal oppression. There is no clear relationship between an individual's seeking out counseling and his psychological health. In fact, many professional counselors would agree that the most disturbed individuals are the *least* likely to seek counseling. In addition, socioeconomic status (SES) is directly related to presence in counseling. Low SES individuals are less likely to receive counseling than are middle and high SES individuals. They are less likely to perceive counseling as a viable resource to help in resolving personal troubles, to have the skills and orientation necessary to verbalize the kinds of material expected in counseling, and to have sufficient time, resources, and access to mental health services.

Let us assume, for a moment, that homosexuals are more troubled than heterosexuals. This situation still might not be reflected in the number of homosexuals who seek professional counseling, simply because the counseling professions are mistrusted by many homosexuals. There is good reason for this mistrust. Oppression of homosexuals by professional mental health providers has been a major concern of homosexual rights groups and has been discussed widely in professional and lay circles (e.g., Blair, 1975; Davison, 1974; DeCrescenzo and McGill, 1978; Garfinkle and Morin, 1978; Gochros, 1972; Halleck, 1971; Kameny, 1971). Traditionally, mental health providers have defined homosexuality as a mental illness. The psychiatric profession led the way in defining homosexuality as a symptom of severe disturbance, using an interpretation of Freudian theory to justify this position. Led by the prestige and authority of psychiatry, the other counseling professions followed suit. Until recently a homosexual entering therapy for any reason could expect that the treatment would focus on changing his sexual orientation. Given the lack of effective treatment procedures, the resilience of the homosexual orientation, and the disruption that this sort of therapy causes in the client's personal relationships, this approach is doomed to failure (Tripp, 1975).

Our study and others have shown that the vast majority of homosexuals do not want to change their sexual orientation. Since most homosexuals have known that counselors would attempt to bring about this change, they have been reluctant to seek professional help. Even counseling for nonsexual issues was problematic. For one thing, it is very difficult for the homosexual client to hide his sexual orientation from the counselor; furthermore, even if he could do this successfully, it would certainly diminish the open and trusting relationship that has been found to be a necessary ingredient in successful counseling (Truax and Carkhuff, 1967).

Table 10.19 summarizes responses to the questions on counseling experience. While almost 30 percent of our respondents had received professional counseling for their homosexuality, only two men were currently in counseling for that reason, and only 9.4 percent wanted to receive such counseling.

We were interested in our respondents' reactions to any professional counseling experience. Unlike Weinberg and Williams, who asked similar questions, we did not limit our questions to treatment by psychiatrists, since the majority of mental health counseling is carried out by social workers, psychologists, guidance counselors, etc. Despite the fact that Weinberg and Williams limited their questions to psychiatric treatment, their respondents answered "yes" more frequently to each of the questions. Although their respondents were younger, and therefore had fewer years in which to experience the need for treatment, one-third had received treatment for homosexuality, 8 percent were currently in treatment, 14 percent would have wanted such treatment, and 18 percent had seen a psychiatrist for other reasons.

Our older respondents were less likely to desire treatment for their homosexuality. Younger men in the Weinberg and Williams study may not fully have come to terms with their sexuality. Age usually brings with it a greater acceptance of self; there is a recognition that the longer we follow a certain road, the more difficult it becomes to switch routes.

Lower utilization of professional counseling services by our respondents reflects the generally lower utilization of mental health services by older persons (Simon, 1968). Attitudes toward mental health services differ between generations. Today's older people were raised in an era that stressed self-reliance. Particularly for men, a premium was placed on keeping a "stiff upper lip" and resolving one's own difficulties. Mental health services are, after all, a relatively recent phenomenon (Szasz, 1970). Many older people still believe that only "sick" people see professional counselors; when they experienced their early life crises, fewer professional counseling services were available, and problems were kept within the family, or if necessary a clergyman was consulted. The mental health professional has also contributed to lower utilization of his or her services by older people. Most mental health providers prefer to work with younger clients, and many more positions are available in work with families and youth than with the elderly (Berger and Kelly, 1981). Some professionals believe that change is more difficult with older persons; others may have the attitude that the elderly are less important than other clients.

The data from our study and from Weinberg and Williams (1975), taken together, verify the crucial role of sexual orientation in the psychological and social adaptation of homosexual men. Almost one-third of men in both studies were sufficiently troubled or confused by their sexuality to consult a professional counselor, and in both studies concern about sexual orientation was the most frequently mentioned reason for seeking professional counseling.

Do Older Gay Men Hide Their Homosexuality?

Goffman (1963), in a provocative book entitled *Stigma*, noted that groups of individuals with certain deviant characteristics are singled out by society for special treatment. Stigmatizing characteristics such as a physical handicap or minority racial status are clearly visible and, as such, affect all of the individual's relationships. Other characteristics, such as a criminal past or homosexuality, are generally hidden stigmas. Since these characteristics are not immediately apparent, they may or may not color the individual's relationships. Individuals with hidden stigmas, however, are faced with the unique task of managing information about their identities. They must perpetually remain on guard against the possibility that private information will become public and "ruin" their socially acceptable identities.

Goffman's theory provides insight into passing, a phenomenon which is widespread in the homosexual community. Passing is the homosexual's method of managing his identity so that it is not "spoiled" by discrediting information. It refers to the process of playing the heterosexual role, much like a former criminal might play the role of the upright citizen. The assumed heterosexual role may be played with family, close friends, work associates, or in a combination of social spheres. The tenacity of this social fiction can

extend so far that men who engage in overt homosexual sex relations can maintain their heterosexual role with their male sex partners, providing they limit their sexual activities in certain socially
defined ways, for example, consenting to be fellated, but never
reciprocating (Reiss, 1967). More typically, a homosexual man may
be "in the closet" with family members and work associates but
"open" with a select group of friends; or he may assume some
other combination of roles.

For a long time it was assumed that all homosexual men engage
in passing in at least some spheres. The popular image of the homosexual is of a person who lives in two distinct worlds. He has a
straight life at work, with his family, and with one group of friends;
he has another, entirely separate life with his gay friends. He takes
elaborate precautions to ensure that the two worlds do not collide.
Members of the two worlds are never allowed to meet, and pseud-
onyms and other devices are used to control the potentially disastrous leak of information about his identity to the straight world.
Although this image may have been true of most homosexuals in
the past, today many more homosexuals are choosing to be "up
front" about their sexuality. This was well illustrated in the interview study, where only one of the ten men could be described as
living in two separate worlds. The gay liberation movement which
began in the late 1960s has had an enormous impact, both in encouraging homosexuals to "come out of the closet" and in increasing public acceptance of openly gay lifestyles.

Weinberg and Williams (1975) suggest that passing is necessitated
by two distinct psychological components: worry about exposure
and anticipated sanctions. Worry about exposure centers around
"freefloating" anxieties that relationships with friends, family, and
work associates will be ruined. The individual will be shamed by
others' discovery of his homosexuality. Worry about anticipated sanctions centers around more objective concerns: Will the individual be
fired from his job, lose his family, or get into trouble with the law?
Given societal disapproval of homosexuality, there is a realistic basis
for such worries. For instance, a recent study of societal attitudes
toward homosexuality found that negative attitudes toward homosexuals were prevalent among American adults. A majority believed that
homosexuals should not be permitted to be judges, schoolteachers,

ministers, physicians, or government officials (Levitt and Klassen, 1974). A number of studies have documented instances of employment discrimination against individuals who became known as homosexual (e.g., Figliulo, Shively, and McEnroe, 1978; Liljestrand, Petersen, and Zellers, 1978; Oregon Task Force, 1977).

The phenomenon of passing is important in this study because passing has profound effects on the psychological and social adaptation of homosexual men. Passing brings with it the need to hide. The hider must learn to cope with an undercurrent of worry and tension, for he may be discovered at any moment. For some, these tensions lead to extreme emotional distortions. An analogy can be made to the situation of Jews in hiding during World War II. Some Jews responded by identifying with their oppressors (agreeing with the Nazi ideology) or by voluntarily giving themselves up to the authorities. Analogously, the homosexual who can no longer bear the tension of concealment may come to agree with anti-homosexual psychological theories and "give himself up" to psychotherapy directed at changing his orientation. Another analogy can be made to the Jew who denounced other Jews in order to save his own skin. Many homosexuals who pass "protect" themselves by denouncing others as homosexual, or by verbalizing "fag" jokes and other anti-homosexual put-downs. This places the accuser "above suspicion." Kinsey himself commented that it was clear from his own research that many of the judges, newspapermen, and others who publicly condemned homosexuals were themselves homosexual (Kinsey, Pomeroy, and Martin, 1948). Homosexuals who have subsequently "come out" have talked about their earlier public condemnation of homosexuals (e.g., Miller, 1971). It is difficult to believe that these conflicts between feelings and behavior can avoid leaving some emotional scars.

Passing affects psychological and social adaptation in other ways as well. Cognitive dissonance theory predicts that individuals who repeatedly engage in a particular behavior come to develop attitudes or beliefs in line with the behavior (Festinger, 1957). Homosexuals who pass are repeatedly acting in ways that indicate that their homosexuality is bad; they may come to believe that, indeed, *they* are bad. The concealer may become locked in a vicious circle. Since he has a constant need to conceal, he cannot tolerate the company of non-concealers (Leznoff and Westley, 1967). By limiting his contacts to other concealers, he cuts himself off from persons who could serve as role models for a self-affirming, open lifestyle. Some homosexuals who pass are so concerned with avoiding exposure that their only interaction with other homosexuals occurs in anonymous settings where contact is limited to a purely sexual exchange (e.g., Humphreys, 1970). Their homosexuality must always remain a dark and taboo aspect of themselves. Support and validation from other homosexuals is simply impossible.

Passing does not always result in severe emotional problems. Most homosexuals who pass manage to maintain reasonable social and emotional stability in their lives; extreme consequences such as severe emotional illness are infrequent. More likely, passing leads to more subtle emotional repercussions. For instance, Weinberg and Williams found that passing was associated with depression, interpersonal awkwardness, and anxiety. These researchers believed that these problems were the result of worry about exposure and anticipated discrimination. (The next chapter will discuss our own findings on that subject.)

We examined the issue of passing among our respondents by assessing both attitudes and behavior. To ascertain attitudes toward concealment, we asked the respondent to agree or disagree with statements such as "I do not care who knows about my homosexuality." In order to measure the actual presence of passing, we also asked each respondent to estimate how many of various groups of people (relatives, work associates, heterosexuals, and other homosexuals) were aware of his homosexuality. Results for these items are presented in Tables 10.20 and 10.21.

Eighteen percent of our older respondents and 29 percent of the Weinberg and Williams sample would not like to associate with a known homosexual. Thirty-seven percent of our respondents but only 20 percent of the Weinberg and Williams sample do not care who knows about their homosexuality. Sixty-five percent of our respondents but only 57 percent of Weinberg and Williams's sample would not mind being seen in public with a known homosexual (Table 10.20). These results are consistent with Weinberg and Williams's findings that older homosexual males worry less about exposure of their sexual orientation.

TABLE 10.20. Percentage of Responses to Concealment Items

	Strongly agree	Agree	?	Disagree	Strongly disagree
I do not like to associate socially with a person who has a reputation (among heterosexuals) of being homosexual	7.2 (6.9)	10.8 (22.5)	9.9 (11.8)	43.2 (42.7)	28.8 (16.1)
I do not care who knows about my homosexuality	12.6 (5.5)	24.3 (14.2)	10.8 (8.6)	30.6 (40.0)	21.6 (32.2)
I would not mind being seen in public with a person who has the reputation (among heterosexuals) of being homosexual	17.1 (11.3)	47.7 (45.4)	8.1 (12.3)	16.2 (23.7)	10.8 (7.4)

Note: N = 111. Source of concealment scale: Weinberg and Williams (1975). Comparison data from Weinberg and Williams are indicated in parentheses.

Table 10.21 summarizes the extent to which the respondent's homosexuality is known to others. Comparison with similar questions in Weinberg and Williams (1975) reveals that the older men were known as homosexual to a greater proportion of friends, relatives, work associates, and other homosexuals. For heterosexual acquaintances "all" or "most" percentages were 13.2 for the younger and 31.3 for the older sample. For work associates, the corresponding percentages were 11.8 for the younger and 29.3 for the older sample. For other homosexuals, the percentages were 41.0 for the younger and 78.3 for the older sample. Not only are older homosexual males apparently less worried about exposure of their homosexuality, but they are more likely to be known as homosexual to the various people in their personal and work lives. Although others' awareness of an individual's homosexuality may pose certain disadvantages, it would appear at least to alleviate some of the concerns about concealment.

There are several reasons why an older homosexual may be less concerned with exposure. These are essentially the same reasons

TABLE 10.21. Percentage of Various Categories of Others Who Suspect or Know of Respondent's Homosexuality

	All	Most	More than half	About half	Less than half	Only a few	None	Not appli-cable	N
Straight people whom you know	3.6 (3.3)	27.7 (9.9)	6.3 (5.5)	8.9 (8.3)	6.3 (9.9)	41.1 (52.0)	3.6 (11.3)	2.7	112
Relatives (spouse, parents, siblings, children, etc.)	17.3	12.7	2.7	6.4	4.5	24.5	27.3	4.5	110
Work associates	14.2 (6.1)	15.1 (5.7)	4.7 (4.1)	8.5 (6.3)	5.7 (3.8)	30.2 (34.1)	16.0 (39.0)	5.7	106
People whom *you* know are gay/lesbian[a]	61.3 (12.0)	17.0 (29.0)	6.6 (9.0)	4.7 (8.0)	1.9 (9.3)	4.7 (28.0)	0.0 (4.9)	3.8	106

Note: Items modified and adapted from Weinberg and Williams (1975). Comparison data from Weinberg and Williams are indicated in parentheses.
[a] The Weinberg and Williams item was worded "People whom *you* suspect or know are homosexual."

why older homosexual men are less likely to feel anxiety or guilt about their sexuality: it is less important if family members find out, and older men have fewer worries about employment discrimination since they are more firmly established in their careers and less likely to be accused of sexual deviance. In addition, older gay men have the benefit of years of experience in successfully managing their identities, which in itself may lessen their worries about exposure.

Do Older Gay Men Relate to Younger Gays?

One of the most prevalent popular notions about aging and homosexuality is that younger gay men have an aversion to older gays. Indeed, half of the older gay men we interviewed believed this to be the case. There are said to be a number of reasons for this aversion. Because gay men in general are assumed to be interested in little more than sex, the idea of gay men associating for companionship, business, or emotional support may never occur to many people. Since older men are said to be unattractive as potential sex partners, young gay men presumably have little time for them. Younger gays are also said to avoid their elders because older gays are painful reminders of what their own future is likely to bring. Gay men supposedly become "odd" and extremely effeminate as they age, repulsing the people around them. Finally, older gay men are said to have desperate unfulfilled sexual needs which are satisfied by preying on the young. One observer has described younger gays' perceptions of their older counterparts: "We develop a restricted impression of what it is like to be an older gay person. We come to believe, all too often, that to be gay and sixty is to be miserable and pathetic. We think of older gay people as vampires, out to prey on our youth, obsessed with recapturing their own youth through sexual domination of a younger person" (Rogers, 1978: 21).

We asked respondents to estimate how many of their friends were age peers or elders and how many were younger. An age peer was defined as any individual within ten years of the respondent's age or older. A younger person was defined as anyone twenty or more years younger than the respondent. The results are presented in Table 10.22. As in the interview study, there was a marked preference for socializing with age peers. Over three-fourths of our older respondents said they spent at least half of their socializing time with peers or elders. Most respondents had only a few younger friends, and only a handful had a majority of younger friends.

Negative attitudes toward younger gays may underlie this preference for age peers. The prevalence of such attitudes is suggested by our interview study, which found that half of the interviewees believed that most older gay men did hold such attitudes. The inclusion of questionnaire items to assess older gay men's attitudes toward younger gays would have been useful; in the absence of such data, we can only speculate that avoidance of younger gays and negative attitudes toward them reinforce each other.

In response to the age segregation which is evident in most aspects of our culture, it is often assumed that the younger person avoids the older and chooses not to associate with him. However, it is just as likely that the older person chooses to avoid the younger one. For instance, several of the men interviewed felt that younger gays have little to offer because they lack experience and common interests. Most likely negative attitudes on the part of both young

TABLE 10.22. Percentage of Responses to Items Measuring Association with the Young and Association with Homosexuals

	All	Most	About half	Only a small amount	None
What proportion of your leisure-time socializing is with people (homosexual or heterosexual) who are within ten years of your age or older? (*N* = 112)	5.4	42.0	32.1	20.5	0.0

	none-1/5	1/5-2/5	2/5-3/5	3/5-4/5	4/5-all
Proportion of friends who are more than 20 years younger than yourself (*N* = 106)	54.7	21.7	17.0	3.8	2.8
Proportion of friends who are homosexual (*N* = 108)	4.6	7.4	17.6	33.3	37.0

and old are at work. For whatever reasons, our data show that older gay men are most likely to relate to age peers.

A primary reason for the older homosexual's avoidance of younger homosexuals is the elder's belief that the younger looks upon him with derision and scorn. Our respondents were asked to agree or disagree with items such as "Most young homosexuals think that older homosexuals are pretty dull," and "Young people in the homosexual community are often eager to make friends with older homosexuals." Responses are summarized in Table 10.23. Many older homosexuals believed that young people have negative reactions to them. For example, 43 percent of our respondents agreed that "In the gay/lesbian community most young people do not want to make friends with an older person." When all six items were combined into a single score measuring anticipation of a negative reaction from younger gays, 33 percent scored high on this variable; 58 percent scored at a medium level, and only 9 percent scored low.

These data indicate that, to a great extent, older homosexual men do not associate with younger homosexuals, and they believe that younger homosexuals will react negatively to them. Whether youn-

TABLE 10.23. Percentage of Responses to Items Measuring Anticipated Negative Reaction of the Young

	Strongly agree	Agree	?	Disagree	Strongly disagree
In the gay/lesbian community young people sometimes take advantage of older people. (*N* = 108)	8.3	53.7	25.0	11.1	1.9
In gay/lesbian bars, clubs, and bathhouses older patrons are just as welcome as younger ones. (*N* = 112)	1.8	33.9	21.4	33.0	9.8
Most young homosexuals would like to associate with older homosexuals. (*N* = 111)	0.0	10.8	28.8	47.7	12.6
Young people in the homosexual community are often eager to make friends with older homosexuals. (*N* = 111)	2.7	27.9	28.8	29.7	10.8
In the gay/lesbian community most young people do not want to make friends with an older person. (*N* = 111)	1.8	41.4	26.1	28.8	1.8
Most young homosexuals think that older homosexuals are pretty dull. (*N* = 112)	2.7	32.1	30.4	32.1	2.7

ger homosexuals do in fact have such negative attitudes is unclear. Given the misconceptions about aging that characterize most groups in society, it would not be surprising if younger homosexuals do indeed have such negative feelings. A vicious circle perpetuates each generation's preconceived attitudes toward the other. Negative attitudes on the part of both generations lead to mutual avoidance; avoidance, in turn, precludes the possibility of exposure to new beliefs and attitudes toward the other side; and so on. The results of this process are all too evident in the gay community. While public gay institutions such as bars and clubs are frequented mostly by younger gays, older gays rely on social networks (sometimes one or two friends), dinner parties, and other "private" mechanisms for social contact with other gays. In larger communities special clubs or organizations may be available for older gays. (See Chapter 12 for a discussion of several such organizations.) Homosexual rights groups and other civic organizations fail to attract many older gays, and those who do participate rarely occupy leadership positions. As a result the gay community is deprived of the knowledge, sense of history, and leadership of older gays.

Do Older Gay Men Relate to Other Gays?

Older gay men are often pictured as lonely and isolated. Their company is said to be unacceptable even to other homosexuals. In the course of this research we had the opportunity to talk informally with well over a hundred older gay men about their social networks; we found no older homosexual man who fit the stereotype. Most were well integrated into homosexual friendship cliques, and many had been involved in gay community organizations and frequented gay bars, clubs, and other social outlets. Questionnaire data supported this view. Although regular participation in the "public" segments of the gay community (such as the bar) was limited to a minority, the great majority socialized with other gay people and felt that they participated in homosexual social networks. These data are presented in Tables 10.22, 10.24, and 10.25.

The majority of our older homosexual respondents reported that most of their friends are homosexual, most of their leisure-time socializing is with homosexuals, and that they are well accepted in homosexual circles. (In the interview study, all ten men socialized exclusively or primarily with other homosexuals.) Frequency of participation in various institutions in the gay community was relatively low, indicating our success in recruiting respondents outside of the most visible parts of the gay community, as well as the lower social involvement and activity level of the older homosexual male (Weinberg and Williams, 1975). Over one-third attended a meeting or activity of a gay political or social service organization at least once a month. Of all gay community institutions, the bar and/or bathhouse was the most popular among older men, although a sizable minority (18 percent) never frequented these places. Homosexual religious groups such as the Metropolitan Community

TABLE 10.24. Percentage of Responses to Items Measuring Integration into the Homosexual Community

Which category best describes your
social situation among gay people?

Very popular socially	9.8
Popular socially	18.8
Well accepted	43.8
Not really a part of the group	23.3
Not really known among gay people	4.5

	All	Most	About half	Only a few/Small amount	None
Of all your *current friends,* how many are (to your knowledge) gay/lesbian?	7.1	48.2	35.7	8.0	0.9
What proportion of your leisure-time socializing is with gay/lesbian people?	8.9	52.7	28.6	9.8	0.0

Note: N = 112. Items adapted from Weinberg and Williams (1975).

Church and homosexual social or dinner clubs attracted a substantial minority of older men.

What Kind of Sex Life Do Older Gay Men Have?

Respondents' answers to questions concerning their sexual activity are summarized in Tables 10.26 and 10.27. The older homosexual certainly has not abandoned interest or participation in sexual activity. More than likely, the individual with a pattern of consistent sexual activity in earlier life carries this pattern into later years.

As in the interview study, the reported level of sexual activity was quite high. In the six months prior to answering the questionnaire, over 60 percent of respondents engaged in same-sex relations about once a week or more often. Most respondents limited their activity to one partner (challenging the idea that older homosexual men are incapable of sustaining relationships), although a substan-

TABLE 10.25. Percentage of Respondents Who Participated with Various Frequencies in Homosexual Institutions

	More than once a week	About once a week	About once every other week	About once a month	About once every few months	Never
Political/social service organizations (N = 108)	10.2	13.0	9.3	4.6	13.0	50.0
Homosexual bars and/or bathhouses (N = 107)	19.6	18.7	9.3	11.2	23.4	17.8
Homosexual religious organizations: MCC, MCS, Dignity, Integrity, Lutherans Concerned, etc. (N = 106)	11.3	8.5	2.8	8.5	10.4	58.5
Homosexual social clubs or dinner clubs (N = 107)	8.4	13.1	6.5	8.4	21.5	42.1

tial minority (24 percent) reported three or more partners in the six-month period. Very few had had relations with a woman.

It is instructive to compare these data on sexual activity with recent studies of male homosexual samples of a wider age range. The frequency of same-sex relations among our older homosexuals was similar to that found in studies of age-diverse samples by Weinberg and Williams (1975: 144) and Bell and Weinberg (1978: 298). While in our sample 61.2 percent reported having sexual relations about once a week or more often, comparable incidences in Weinberg and Williams (over the past six months) and Bell and Weinberg (over the past year) were 58.9 percent and 69 percent respectively. (With the exception of 4 percent of the Weinberg and Williams sample, these figures are based on samples of white homosexual males only.) It appears that the great majority of white male homosexuals have sex regularly, and that the frequency of sexual activity does not diminish after age forty.

TABLE 10.26. Percentage of Respondents Reporting Various Levels of Sexual Activity and Number of Sex Partners

Over the past six months:	Never	Once a month or less	More than once but less than four times a month	About once a week	More than once, up to twice a week	Three times or more a week
Average frequency of same-sex relations (N = 111)	6.3	14.4	18.0	14.4	27.9	18.9
Average frequency of opposite-sex relations (N = 112)	91.1	5.4	1.8	0.0	1.8	0.0

	Have not had relations	Only one	Two	Three	More than three
Number of same-sex partners (N = 112)	6.3	57.1	12.5	4.5	19.7
Number of opposite-sex partners (N = 111)	91.0	5.4	0.0	1.8	1.8

Our data do, however, reveal a striking difference in the number of partners when compared to studies of age-diverse samples. Eighty-nine percent of the white homosexual males in the Bell and Weinberg (1978: 312) study reported having three or more sexual partners in the year preceding their interview; a majority of the male respondents in the Saghir and Robins (1973: 63) study reported more than one partner in the preceding month. (Saghir and Robins did not report on the race of their respondents.) In our older sample, on the other hand, well over half of the respondents limited their sexual relations to one partner, and fewer than one-fourth reported having three or more partners over the preceding six months. This decrease in the number of sex partners finds confirmation in the Bell and Weinberg study, which also found that older white homosexuals had fewer sex partners.

TABLE 10.27. Percentage of Respondents with Varying Levels of Satisfaction with Current Sex Life

	Very unsatisfied	Unsatisfied	Somewhat satisfied	Satisfied	Very satisfied
Overall, how satisfied are you with your sex life *over the last six months?* (N = 112)	10.7	16.1	25.9	25.9	21.4

Although factors other than age may be responsible for these differences, the findings do suggest that after gay men reach forty they maintain their level of sexual activity, but with fewer partners. Given the hostility of many public gay institutions to older men, it is not surprising that their level of participation in the gay community is lower. This, in turn, leads to fewer opportunities to meet new partners and a greater reliance on familiar partners. The stigma which characterizes older gay men as unsuitable sex partners may exacerbate this situation.

Limiting oneself to only one or two familiar partners may be related to the more general phenomenon of cautiousness. A number of research studies of older people have shown that they are less likely to choose a course of action which, if successful, would result in a very favorable outcome, but if not successful would result in a loss (e.g., Wallach and Kogan, 1961). Approaching a new person who may or may not be willing to become a partner involves this type of risk-taking. Data from Bell and Weinberg (1978) also indicate that older gay men not only have fewer sex partners, but also employ a smaller variety of sexual techniques than younger gay men. Both of these phenomena may be expressions of increased cautiousness.

Another pervasive assumption about older homosexuals is that they have very unsatisfactory sex lives. Table 10.27 shows that, in fact, only 26.8 percent of the older men in this study were unsatisfied with their sex lives; the remainder (73.2 percent) were somewhat or very satisfied. (Six out of ten men in the interview study reported satisfaction with their sex lives.)

One problem with stereotypes about the older homosexual man is that they fail to take into account the diversity within this group. In terms of these data on sexual activity, only one characteristic applied to almost all of these men: very few had had recent sexual relations with a woman. On the other hand, many engaged in sexual activity several times a week, and many others did so only a few times a year or less. While most had only one partner, some had two, three, or more partners in the six-month period prior to completing the questionnaire. This diversity should do more than anything else to dispel inaccurate stereotypes about older homosexual men.

CHAPTER 11

I am not religious because religion condemns me for being homosexual. My God knows I am gay, so I won't go to church and ask for forgiveness for being the only thing I can be.

What Leads to Psychological and Social Adjustment?

It is a fast life between the ages of twenty and thirty. There is a desperate search to find Prince Charming. The presence of this mythical gentleman is felt in every bar in every city across the land. Young gay men sit up past their bedtimes in bars, hoping that the next time the door opens Prince Charming will walk in.

We get out of life only what we put into it. If we are willing to reach out to others, we will reap something in return.

THE SOCIETAL REACTION PERSPECTIVE

Historically, a number of models have described the phenomenon of homosexuality. Going back to the earliest written references, we find religious condemnation; the Old Testament views homosexual behavior as a sin, as immoral subjugation to evil. This view predominated until the earlier part of this century and the rise of psychoanalytic theory, when homosexuality began to be defined as a medical rather than a moral problem. Theorists sought to find its "causes" in the relationships between parents and their young children. Homosexuality was attributed to over-identification with mother, a domineering and protective mother coupled with an inadequate father, and unsuccessful resolution of early childhood conflict (e.g., Bieber et al., 1962; Marmor, 1965).

In recent years others have presented an alternative point of view (e.g., Berger, 1977b). This view was first recognized in the pioneering work of Evelyn Hooker, whose research showed that trained psychiatrists were unable to differentiate between heterosexuals and homosexuals on the basis of interview protocols. Hooker suggested for the first time that "homosexuality may be a deviation in sexual pattern that is within the normal rage, psychologically" (Hooker, 1957: 30).

For *Gay and Gray* we attempted to study the older male homosexual by recording his behaviors, experiences, thoughts, and feelings without making any prior assumptions about the morality or pathology of homosexuality. More specifically, we employed a sociologically based perspective known as *societal reaction theory*. This theory emphasizes current experiences of the individual and those around him as causative factors explaining his current behavior. Homosexuality as a social construct is determined by the valuations of others; homosexuality is therefore deviant only according to those who judge the homosexual actor. This view has been perhaps best expressed by Howard Becker: "Deviance is not a quality of the act the person commits, but rather a consequence of the application by others of rules and sanctions to the 'offender.' The deviant is one to whom that label has been successfully applied; deviant behavior is behavior that people so label" (Becker, 1963: 9).

This labeling process has profound implications for the form that the deviant behavior will assume. For instance, the congregation of individuals who have been labeled as deviant in isolated community institutions such as the bar, the friendship clique, the social club, and the neighborhood may form a "subsociety." Thus homosexuals, like other deviants, can become part of a society within a society. This subsociety has rules and values of its own, encouraging homosexual behavior and justifying homosexuality by presenting an alternative ideology which views this behavior as legitimate.

The concept of the "looking-glass self" is an extension of the societal reaction perspective which is germane to the present study. According to this view, the individual's beliefs regarding how others perceive and evaluate him determine his self-evaluation, and it is *beliefs* regarding others' evaluations that are crucial, regardless of the true nature of those evaluations (Kelly, 1980; Weinberg and Williams, 1975). Since the homosexual often experiences negative evaluations from others regarding his homosexual behavior, we might expect him to have a poor image of himself. On the other hand, contact with people who *positively* value homosexuality, which he might expect to experience in the homosexual subsociety, ought to reinforce a positive self-image. In any case, the evaluations of others and the homosexual's resulting self-image play a large role in determining his psychological adjustment.

We measured psychological adjustment on the basis of questionnaire responses to a number of items as described in this chapter: self-acceptance, depression, psychosomatic symptoms, life satisfaction, anxiety regarding homosexuality, fear of aging and death, and professional counseling experience. From a societal reaction theory perspective, we predicted the following relationships between respondent characteristics and psychological adjustment.

Measures of the degree to which the individual is integrated into the homosexual community should be positively correlated with good psychological adjustment, since an individual who is highly integrated into that community is more likely to be exposed to positive evaluations from others. Similarly, an individual who is highly committed to his homosexuality (unwilling to change) is more likely to be well adjusted. Such an individual is probably integrated into the homosexual community, where positive evaluations from others are more plentiful. We also predicted that a respondent who now or previously had an exclusive homosexual relationship would more likely be exposed to positive valuations of himself, and therefore would show better personal adjustment. Additional hypotheses not related to societal reaction theory were that satisfaction with one's sex life, a positive attitude toward retirement (for those who were retired), and perceived good health would be related to good adjustment.

We expected concealment of one's homosexuality to be inversely related to personal adjustment. An individual who conceals is less likely to experience positive evaluations from the homosexual community and more likely to be exposed to negative evaluations from heterosexuals. Individuals who are low in acceptance of their own homosexuality may also be more apt to conceal.

Since young people devalue the attributes of old age, we expected that associating with much younger individuals would be related to poor adjustment. In particular, the respondent's belief that younger individuals will react negatively to him should be related to poor adjustment. We would not expect that the age of the respondent or his retirement status would be related to psychological adjustment.

RELATIONSHIP OF RESPONDENT CHARACTERISTICS TO PSYCHOLOGICAL ADJUSTMENT

The correlations in Tables 11.1-11.3 summarize findings on the relationship of respondent characteristics to psychological adjustment.

Concealment

We measured the respondent's concealment of his homosexuality by asking him to agree or disagree with statements such as "I would not mind being seen in public with a person who has the reputation (among heterosexuals) of being homosexual." We expected individuals who scored high on this variable to be exposed to fewer positive valuations from others, and therefore to have poorer self-acceptance. Table 11.1 indicates that this was not the case. However, as predicted, high concealers were more likely to display anxiety about their homosexuality and fears of aging and death.

Many people, both within and outside the gay community, believe that old age is a difficult period unless there are children, a relative, or friends to look after one. This perception is particularly strong among homosexual men, who typically have no children and who are often estranged from their families. Our findings suggest that concealment of the older homosexual's orientation is closely associated with fears of growing old. If the homosexual who conceals is less able to maintain the close relationships which serve as supports, he may indeed fear old age.

We also asked the respondent to indicate how many of his friends, relatives, and work associates are actually aware of or suspect his homosexuality. This variable was not related to any measured aspect of psychological adjustment. Interestingly, the respondent's *attitudes* toward concealment were *more important* in determining psychological adjustment than the extent to which he was actually known to others as homosexual. This is consistent with our observation that the homosexual who is highly concerned with concealment often has an unrealistically catastrophic picture of the actual consequences of being known as a homosexual. Our findings indicate that the adjustment of the older homosexual male is not adversely affected by others' awareness of his homosexuality.

Weinberg and Williams, in their study of homosexual men of diverse ages, found that concealment was related to higher levels of depression, interpersonal awkwardness, and anxiety about one's homosexuality (1975: 250). An advantage of aging for some is that concealment is no longer as important. With old age the man may reach a level of financial security and independence from family which diminishes the issue. Weinberg and Williams, for instance, found that older homosexuals were less concerned about exposure than younger men (1975: 311); Bell and Weinberg, however, found that age was *not* related to concealment from the family, friends, and employers of white homosexual men (1979: 68). Some older men are highly concerned with concealment, often as a result of ties to family or employer, where revelation would indeed have negative consequences.

Relationship to Younger Age Cohort

Many observers have commented on the negative attitudes of the young toward older persons (e.g., National Council on Aging, 1975). If such attitudes are indeed prevalent, we would expect an older individual who associates with the young to be adversely affected and to therefore score low on measures of self-acceptance. In the gay community, association between young and old may be more common than in the heterosexual community, for two reasons. First, the homosexual is usually dependent on the public gay institutions for meeting and interacting with others. Invariably these institutions (clubs, discos, political organizations, etc.) are dominated by those under forty. Second, the common interest in an alternative lifestyle draws together individuals of diverse age groups who might not otherwise interact. Therefore the older homosexual may find the impact of socializing with the young to be particularly significant.

Our data did not confirm the hypothesized negative impact of socializing with the young. The respondent's answer to the question "What proportion of your leisure-time socializing is with people (homosexual or heterosexual) who are within ten years of your age or older?" (Table 11.1) was not related to any aspect of psychological adjustment. Contrary to our predictions, the proportion of the respondent's friendship group that was more than twenty years younger was *positively* related to three aspects of adjustment. In fact, respondents who had many younger friends were less likely to report psychosomatic symptoms (e.g., headaches, insomnia) and were significantly less likely to be anxious about their homosexuality or to have fears about aging or death. These findings are consistent with the observations of some of our interview respondents. When asked about the best way to adjust to growing older, some interviewees talked about the need to "stay young" by socializing with young people and keeping up with new ideas.

Although we expected association with the young to have a negative effect on the older homosexual (through transmittal of negative valuations of age by the young), it seemed instead to have a neutral or possibly a positive effect. Perhaps younger homosexuals are now growing up in a time when unconventional sexual lifestyles are becoming more acceptable, when being a homosexual is more a fact of life than a secret tragedy. These more positive attitudes may be absorbed by the older homosexual who "keeps up with the young." Therefore the older man who has many younger friends may also be less anxious about his homosexuality.

Another possibility is that complaints about physical symptoms and anxiety are less acceptable in a younger age group, and that these attitudes are adopted and reflected in questionnaire responses by the older homosexual with many younger friends.

In addition to measures of actual contact with younger people, we also looked at the extent to which our older respondents believed that younger homosexuals would react negatively to them. The respondent was asked to agree or disagree with a number of statements such as "Young people in the homosexual community are often eager to make friends with older homosexuals." Contrary to expectation, anticipated negative reaction of the young was not related to self-acceptance. However, anticipating a negative reaction from young homosexuals was significantly related to poor life satisfaction (measured by asking respondents to agree or disagree with a number of statements, such as "I've gotten pretty much what I expected out of life"). Although we predicted this relationship on

TABLE 11.1. Correlations of Respondent Characteristics with Indexes of Psychological Adjustment

Respondent characteristics	Indexes of psychological adjustment [a]					
	Self-acceptance	Depression	Psycho-somatic symptoms	Life satis-faction	Anxiety about homosex-uality	Fear of aging and death
Concealment	−.082	−.013	.066	−.046	.266**	.291**
Known to others as homosexual	−.088	.023	−.034	−.138	.147	.113
Proportion of socializing with age peers	.045	.000	−.074	.123	−.034	−.088
Proportion of younger friends	.147	−.009	−.237*	.108	−.222*	−.262**
Anticipated negative reaction of the young	−.166	.114	.049	−.253**	.079	.114
Integration into homosexual community	.273**	−.241*	−.120	.305**	−.236*	−.246**
Participation in homosexual institutions	−.027	.016	−.004	.098	.128	−.133
Retirement status	−.115	.120	.081	−.129	−.045	.006
Attitude toward retirement	−.269	.217	.058	−.254	.227	−.070
Sexual activity	.078	−.030	.059	.113	−.190*	−.094
Number of sex partners	.081	−.071	−.077	.073	−.118	.054

TABLE 11.1 (continued)

Respondent characteristics	Indexes of psychological adjustment [a]					
	Self-acceptance	Depression	Psycho-somatic symptoms	Life satis-faction	Anxiety about homosex-uality	Fear of aging and death
Satisfaction with sex life	.244**	−.215*	−.155	.287**	−.257**	−.196*
Commitment to homosexuality	.296**	−.305**	−.250**	.323**	−.520**	−.224*
Perceived health status	.146	−.092	−.310**	.231*	−.222*	−.218*
Current exclusive relationship	.116	−.172	−.131	.230*	−.171	.054
Age	.184 [b]	−.196*	−.342**	.155	−.042	−.031

[a]* $p < .05$
** $p < .01$
[b] $p = .052$

the basis of societal reaction theory, according to that theory, the lower life satisfaction of respondents who anticipate a negative reaction should come about through the effects of this reaction on self-acceptance. Table 11.1 shows that this was not the case.

Both anticipated negative reaction and life satisfaction may be components of a more global characteristic related to level of expectation. Individuals with unrealistically high expectations may be disappointed with reality and therefore may report low life satisfaction. Those same individuals may also experience disappointment in their interactions with the young, and thereby may report greater anticipated negative reactions of the young. However, the reasons for the relationship of anticipated negative reaction to poor life satisfaction are far from clear.

Relationship to Homosexual Community

We measured integration into the homosexual community by asking questions such as "Of all your *current friends,* how many are (to your knowledge) gay/lesbian?" As expected, this variable was significantly related to all measures of psychological adjustment (with the exception of psychosomatic symptoms). Respondents who were well integrated into the homosexual community showed higher levels of self-acceptance, lower levels of depression, greater life satisfaction, less anxiety about their homosexuality, and less fear of aging and death. These findings are consistent with those of Weinberg and Williams (1975: 286), who reported that men who are low in social involvement with other homosexuals have more psychological problems: lower self-acceptance, more depression, more loneliness, more anxiety about their homosexuality, and more frequent desire for psychiatric treatment.

Participation in homosexual institutions was measured by asking respondents to report the frequency with which they attended activities at gay political and social service organizations, bars or bathhouses, and social clubs. Surprisingly, this variable was not related to psychological adjustment. Participation in the more "public" aspects of the homosexual community is a limited measure of involvement with the gay community. It is possible, for instance, for an individual to attend homosexual bars and bathhouses regularly but still to have minimal "social" contact with other homosexuals. Our results suggest that the individual's friendships and patterns of socializing within the community are much more relevant to his positive psychological adjustment than is his participation in homosexual institutions.

Retirement

Research has generally shown that retirement has little effect on social and emotional adjustment. Characteristics such as life satisfaction and self-concept are not adversely affected by it (Atchley, 1977: 155ff.). Our findings were consistent with the literature. Respondents were asked to indicate whether they were fully or partially retired, and, if retired, whether they enjoyed retirement. As expected, neither retirement status nor attitude toward retirement was related to any measure of psychological adjustment.

Sex Life

For the most recent six-month period, respondents were asked to report how often they had had sexual relations with another man, the number of partners, and satisfaction with their sex lives. Table 11.1 shows that number of sex partners and sexual activity were generally not related to psychological adjustment. This is an important finding, in light of the popular notion (reinforced by some of the professional literature) that sexual promiscuity indicates psychopathology. Table 11.1 suggests that promiscuity and high levels of sexual activity are not indicators of psychological maladjustment; in fact, the opposite may be true, since respondents who maintained a high level of sexual activity were less likely to be anxious about their homosexuality. It may be that the direction of the relationship is not from sexual activity to adjustment, but the other way around–those individuals who are less anxious about their homosexuality (better adjusted) are more likely to engage in homosexual activity.

As predicted, satisfaction with one's sex life was significantly related to measures of psychological adjustment (with the exception of psychosomatic symptoms). Individuals who are high in self-acceptance are more likely to perceive themselves and their sex partner(s) in a more positive light; this may lead to high satisfaction with sexual activity. Although satisfaction with sex life has not previously been related to life satisfaction for older adults (perhaps due to an unarticulated belief on the part of researchers that sex is not important to seniors), our findings suggest that it may be an important component of overall life satisfaction and adjustment.

Commitment to Homosexuality

We measured commitment to homosexuality by asking the respondent to agree or disagree with the statements "I wish I were not homosexual" and "I would not want to give up my homosexuality even if I could." As noted earlier, an individual who is committed to homosexuality is more likely to be involved with the gay community and thus to be exposed to positive self-valuations. (In this study we did indeed find a significant positive relationship between commitment to homosexuality and integration in the homosexual community, $r = .305$, $p \leq .01$).

Such an individual would be well adjusted, and Table 11.1 confirms our predictions. Commitment to homosexuality was significantly related to all measures of psychological adjustment. Committed homosexuals were higher in self-acceptance, lower in depression, had fewer psychosomatic symptoms, greater life satisfaction, less anxiety about homosexuality, and less fear of aging and death. These findings are consistent with those of Weinberg and Williams, who reported a strong negative relationship between commitment to homosexuality and psychological problems for both younger and older homosexual males (1975: 215). Those who were more committed to homosexuality showed better self-acceptance, a more stable self-concept, fewer psychosomatic symptoms, less depression, less interpersonal awkwardness, less loneliness, and less anxiety about their homosexuality. In light of these findings it is ironic that so many interventions to improve the adjustment of homosexuals are directed toward decreasing their commitment to homosexuality.

Health

Respondents were asked to rate their present health as excellent, good, fair, or poor. As predicted, perceived health status was positively related to psychological adjustment, with respondents who reported good health indicating fewer psychosomatic symptoms, greater life satisfaction, less anxiety about homosexuality, and less fear of aging and death. Perceived health status was, however, independent of self-acceptance and depression.

Exclusive Relationship

We expected the presence of a lover or other individual to whom the respondent limited his primary involvement to correlate positively with psychological adjustment, since a lover is a steady source of positive valuation for the respondent. Respondents who reported a current exclusive relationship had higher life satisfaction, but they did not differ from other respondents in self-acceptance or other measures of adjustment. Although older homosexual men who had a current exclusive relationship were more satisfied with life, this finding was apparently independent of the effect of the relationship on their view of themselves (self-acceptance).

Age

The popular literature on homosexuality predicts a rapid decline in psychological adjustment with age. Our prediction was that age would not be related to adjustment, since the self-other processes which determine adjustment are independent of age. Our prediction was not confirmed. In fact, older respondents reported marginally significant *higher* levels of self-acceptance (Table 11.1). Older respondents also reported significantly less depression and fewer psychosomatic symptoms. These findings suggest that, in some aspects, psychological adjustment may actually increase with age for homosexual men.

Weinberg and Williams reported similar results. They found no age-related differences in self-acceptance, anxiety, depression, or loneliness. However, compared to younger homosexuals, older men were less effeminate, had more stable self-concepts, worried less about exposure of their homosexuality, and were less likely to desire psychiatric treatment (1975: 310-11).

There are several possible explanations for these findings. It may be that poor emotional adjustment in young adulthood and the middle years is due to failure to meet high personal expectations about one's life situation. As the individual enters his later years, his expectations are lowered. Thus what seems like a highly undesirable situation to a young adult may appear quite acceptable to his older counterpart. This perspective may also explain why a younger person might tend to believe (erroneously) that an older person "must be unhappy" (Weinberg and Williams, 1975).

Another possible explanation for an increase in psychological adjustment with age is contained in the "mastery of crisis" hypothesis. According to this idea, homosexuals, because of the absence of a family of procreation, face a crisis of independence early in adulthood. This developmental crisis, successfully resolved, strengthens their ability to cope with the crisis of aging later in life (Francher and Henkin, 1973; Kelly, 1974; Kelly and Johnson, 1978).

It is also possible (although less likely) that as potential respondents grow older, the healthiest and most successful come forward to complete a questionnaire. This factor alone could account for the age-related findings. That the present sample is above average in terms of income and education is consistent with this possibility. However, the fact that both our study and Weinberg and Williams' found a positive relationship of age to psychological adjustment makes it more difficult to dismiss our findings as dependent on sampling procedures.

Counseling Experience

An indirect way of assessing psychological adjustment is to determine whether the respondent has ever received or desired professional counseling. Each respondent was asked if he had ever received professional counseling specifically regarding his homosexuality. He was also asked if he had ever received counseling for other reasons.

Table 11.2 summarizes the relationships of respondent characteristics to counseling experience. These relationships were small, and almost all were insignificant. Like Weinberg and Williams, we found that a desire for counseling related to homosexuality diminished with age. As the individual grows older it makes less sense to try to change old ways. The respondent may feel that "you can't teach an old dog new tricks," that change becomes more difficult as we grow older. This finding may also represent a generational difference in perceptions about counseling, with the oldest respondents representing an age cohort for which counseling is considered unacceptable.

Consistent with our finding that individuals who are highly committed to their homosexuality had better adjustment was our finding that these individuals were also less likely to have desired or received counseling for their homosexuality or for other reasons. Respondents who were integrated into the gay community were less likely to have received counseling for their homosexuality–which is not surprising, in light of our earlier finding that well-integrated individuals had better adjustment. Those who actively participated in homosexual institutions (bars, clubs, organizations, etc.) were

TABLE 11.2. Correlations of Respondent Characteristics with Counseling Related to Homosexuality

Respondent characteristics	Counseling experience [a]			
	Ever received counseling?	Currently receiving?	Desires counseling?	Ever received counseling for reasons unrelated to homosexuality?
Concealment	.056	−.013	.126	.055
Known to others as homosexual	−.015	−.045	.089	−.090
Proportion of socializing with age peers	.109	.212*	.019	.011
Proportion of younger friends	−.064	.097	−.107	−.099
Anticipated negative reaction of the young	.008	.056	.055	−.010
Integration into homosexual community	−.199*	−.113	−.128	−.138
Participation in homosexual institutions	.168	.069	.026	.207*
Retirement status	.110	.098	.017	.107
Attitude toward retirement	.148	.000	.277	.277
Sexual activity	.052	.000	.087	.035
Number of sex partners	−.059	.191*	−.028	−.091
Satisfaction with sex life	−.064	.020	−.159	−.106
Commitment to homosexuality	−.206*	.001	−.299**	−.238*
Perceived health status	−.020	.043	−.116	−.021
Current exclusive relationship	−.187*	−.099	−.019	−.148
Age	−.171	.020	−.251**	−.148

[a] * $p < .05$
** $p < .01$

more likely to have received counseling for reasons other than homosexuality. Respondents with a current exclusive relationship were less likely to have received counseling. Finally, respondents with a greater number of sex partners over the past six months were more likely to be currently in counseling.

THE WELL-ADJUSTED OLDER HOMOSEXUAL

In order to identify respondent characteristics that were most significant in predicting positive psychological adjustment, we generated a series of stepwise multiple linear regression equations, with indexes of psychological adaptation as predicted variables and respondent characteristics as predictor variables. These equations are summarized in Table 11.3.

Contrary to the research hypotheses, age of respondent was the most important variable, accounting for performance on half of the measures of psychological adjustment. Age was associated with greater self-acceptance, fewer psychosomatic symptoms, and greater life satisfaction. The older male homosexual who is most likely to be psychologically well adjusted will be highly integrated into the homosexual community, unwilling to change his homosexuality, less concerned with concealment, perceiving his health as good or excellent, having a current exclusive relationship with another man, and reporting a high level of satisfaction with his sex life.

Work Life

One of the major life tasks facing a homosexual involves managing his identity at work. While he is known as gay among sexual and social contacts, he may be "in the closet" at work. We have already looked at data on how many people suspected or knew about the respondent's homosexuality. Among other homosexuals, heterosexual associates, relatives, and work associates, those at work were *least* likely to suspect or to know of the respondent's homosexuality. Many observers have noted that certain occupations such as artist, interior designer, and hairdresser are most likely to attract homosexuals. A more plausible view is that more homosexuals

TABLE 11.3. Effects of Respondent Characteristics on Psychological Adjustment

Psychological adjustment Predicted variables	Respondent characteristics Predictor variables	β	Significance level of β	R^2	Significance level of R^2
Model I Self-acceptance	Age	.0916	.0016	.1617	.0001
	Integration into homosexual community	.3747	.0037		
	Satisfaction with sex life	.5092	.0128		
Model II Depression	Commitment to homosexuality	−1.415	.0011	.0845	.0011
Model III Psychosomatic symptoms	Age	−.1176	.0000	.2671	.0000
	Integration into homosexual community	−.2431	.0150		
	Perceived health status	−1.2341	.0000		
Model IV Life satisfaction	Age	.1965	.0007	.2425	.0000
	Integration into homosexual community	.8667	.0007		
	Perceived health status	1.4927	.0381		
	Current exclusive relationship	.5557	.0383		
	Satisfaction with sex life	.8531	.0410		
Model V Anxiety about homosexuality	Commitment to homosexuality	−.7851	.0000	.2938	.0000
	Perceived health status	−.3192	.0173		
Model VI Fear of aging and death	Concealment	.3777	.0011	.1203	.0003
	Perceived health status	−.8271	.0114		

Note: The following respondent characteristics were entered as independent variables into a stepwise multiple linear regression analysis: age; anticipated negative reaction of the young; commitment to homosexuality; concealment; proportion of younger friends; integration into homosexual community; perceived health status; current exclusive relationship; sexual activity; satisfaction with sex life. A replacement-with-means method was used to estimate missing data values. Forward selection was used with a criterion of $p < .05$ for inclusion in the regression equation.

only appear to be so employed, because the public is particularly tolerant of open or known homosexuals in these occupations. (In fact, heterosexuals in these occupations are often assumed to be homosexual.)

Leznoff and Westley (1967) suggested that high-status occupations (professional and managerial) are less tolerant of open homosexuals than are low-status occupations (clerical and service positions, and the arts). Leznoff and Westley described the homosexual community as consisting of two separate communities with only minimal interactions between the two. One community consists of overt homosexuals, while the other is a secretive community of covert homosexuals who conceal their orientation from most people, particularly from non-homosexuals.

Presumably these separate communities arise from the need of the upward-mobile homosexual of high occupational status to avoid the loss of social status which would result if his deviance became known. In Erving Goffman's words (1963), while the overt homosexual is *discredited*, the covert homosexual is perpetually *discreditable*. The need to manage this "spoiled identity" explains the covertness of the high-status homosexual.

Leznoff and Westley presented data on forty covert and overt male homosexuals to confirm this theory. In their study of 1,057 male homosexuals Weinberg and Williams (1975) reported a similar finding: respondents of higher occupational status were more covert, more worried about exposure, and more bothered about being officially labeled homosexual. Weinberg and Williams suggested that homosexuals in higher-status occupations were more likely to need to socialize with heterosexual work associates; also, since higher-status individuals had a wider range of interests, they were more likely to socialize with heterosexuals. As a result, covertness became necessary.

We attempted to replicate these findings. We asked respondents to indicate their job title and to briefly describe what they did at work. (We asked retired respondents to describe their most recent full-time employment.) As described above, we classified each respondent as having low, medium, or high occupational status, using the same scale employed by Weinberg and Williams. Low-status positions included laborers, machine operators, and unskilled labor.

Medium-status positions included administrative personnel, small business owners, semi-professionals such as primary school teachers, clerical and sales workers, and technicians. High-status positions included business executives, proprietors of large and medium-size businesses, managers, and professionals.

We generated cross-tabulations between occupational status and a number of measures related to covertness: concealment, known to others as homosexual, integration into the homosexual community, participation in homosexual institutions, anxiety regarding homosexuality, and willingness to associate with a known homosexual. None of these relationships approached significance. When these cross-tabulations were computed separately for retired and employed respondents, the results were the same.

Weinberg and Williams also found that self-employed homosexuals were least concerned with concealment. Bell and Weinberg (1978) replicated this finding in a study of 977 male and female homosexuals in the San Francisco Bay area.

We rated type of employer on the basis of respondents' descriptions of their jobs. Following Weinberg and Williams (1975), we classified each respondent as self-employed, employed by a private firm or government agency, or employed by an educational institution. Agreement between two independent raters on this scale was 82 percent. Cross-tabulations were generated between type of employer and the measures of covertness noted above. Type of employer was not related to most of these measures, even when controlling for retirement status. There were, however, two important relationships which we have summarized in Tables 11.4 and 11.5. Self-employed respondents were much more likely to be highly integrated into the homosexual community; controlling for retirement status revealed that this relationship held true only for those respondents who were not currently retired (Table 11.4). There was also a non-significant tendency for self-employed respondents to express a greater willingness to associate with a known homosexual (Table 11.6). This relationship was not affected by controlling for retirement status.

Type of employer was not related to participation in homosexual institutions for the entire sample. However, for retired respondents, those who had been employed by an educational institution were much more likely to have a high level of participation in homosexual institutions (Table 11.5). (This result is based on a rather small sample of twenty-seven respondents.)

The present findings contradict the previous research, which found that male homosexuals in higher-status occupations were more likely to conceal their homosexuality (Leznoff and Westley, 1967; Weinberg and Williams, 1975). It is quite likely that this holds true only for younger homosexuals. The older man is more

TABLE 11.4. Effect of Type of Employer on Integration into the Homosexual Community (%)

	Type of employer						
	Self-employed	Private firm or government agency	Educational institution	N	X^2	ϕ	p
Integration into homosexual community							
All respondents							
Low	0	3	31	104	14.27	.37	.0065
Medium	36	54	31				
High	64	43	38				
Employed respondents only							
Low	0	2	40	77	15.24	.44	.0042
Medium	41	53	30				
High	59	44	30				
Retired respondents only							
Low	0	6	0	27	1.77	.26	.7776
Medium	17	56	33				
High	83	39	67				

Note: Variables adapted from Weinberg and Williams (1975).

likely to be secure in his job, and thus less likely to conceal. In addition, he may be less subject to implications of sexual deviance, since sexual motives in general are usually attributed to the young.

Our findings indicate that the self-employed older homosexual is more likely to be highly integrated into the homosexual community, and perhaps more willing to associate with a known homosexual. As suggested by Bell and Weinberg (1978), this association may be

TABLE 11.5. Effect of Type of Employer on Participation in Homosexual Institutions (%)

	Type of employer			N	X^2	ϕ	p
	Self-employed	Private firm or government agency	Educational institution				
Participation in homosexual institutions							
All respondents							
Low	61	76	38	104	4.99	.22	.2881
Medium	32	21	46				
High	7	3	15				
Employed respondents only							
Low	55	71	50	77	1.90	.16	.7546
Medium	36	24	30				
High	9	4	20				
Retired respondents only							
Low	0	0	0	27	7.21	.52	.0273
Medium	83	89	0				
High	17	11	100				

Note: Type of employer measured with item developed by Weinberg and Williams (1975).

TABLE 11.6. Effect of Type of Employment on Willingness to Associate with a Known Homosexual (%)

Willingness to associate		Type of employment					
	Self-employed	Employed by private firm or government agency	Employed by educational institution	N	X^2	ϕ	p
Low 1	3	10	8	104	13.94	.37	.0833
2	14	11	0				
3	0	15	8				
4	31	50	46				
High 5	52	15	38				

Note: Variables adapted from Weinberg and Williams (1975).

due to the fact that many self-employed homosexuals operate businesses catering to a homosexual clientele.

SUMMARY

Many stereotypes of the older homosexual male are discredited by our findings. Most older homosexuals questioned lived with a lover, roommates, or family members. The majority had experienced an exclusive sexual and emotional relationship with another man that had lasted at least one year, and a sizable minority had such a relationship at the time of the study.

The great majority of our respondents were psychologically healthy, as measured by such variables as self-acceptance, depression, and psychosomatic symptoms. There were few differences in psychological adjustment between our respondents and a comparable group of younger homosexuals; those differences that did emerge favored the older group. For example, fewer of the older men experienced anxiety regarding their homosexuality or worried about concealment. In general, the older men were more widely known as homosexual, did not worry about death (although most did worry about growing older), and had less exposure to professional counselors than did their younger counterparts. Most of their friends were other homosexuals, and they had a marked preference for socializing with age peers. Many older men believed that younger homosexuals had negative feelings about them. Although participation in homosexual institutions like bars, clubs, and political organizations was low, the level of sexual activity was generally high. Most of the men had sex at least once a week. Only about one-fourth reported that they were unsatisfied with their current sex life.

Predictions made from societal reaction theory were only partially confirmed. Compared to low concealers, high concealers reported more anxiety regarding their homosexuality and greater fears of aging and death, but they did not have poorer self-acceptance. Anticipating a negative reaction from younger homosexuals was not associated with poor self-acceptance, but it was associated with poor life satisfaction. Two of the strongest predictors of good adjustment were commitment to homosexuality (unwillingness to change sexual orientation) and integration into the homosexual community. Older respondents who associated with younger homosexuals showed the best adjustment. In some aspects of psychological adjustment, such as depression, being older was associated with better adjustment.

Although earlier findings have indicated that homosexual men in higher-status occupations are more covert, this relationship did not hold true for our sample. However, the older homosexual who was self-employed was more highly integrated into the gay community and more willing to associate with known homosexuals.

CHAPTER 12

The Older Homosexual Man in Perspective

Once my cousin asked, "Why didn't you ever get married?" and I answered, "Because it isn't legal to marry another man."

It is human nature for people to find someone in life who is beneath them.

Traditionally, homosexual behavior has been severely stigmatized by our culture. A very effective way to discourage behavior considered to be undesirable is to perpetuate beliefs that said behavior will result in catastrophic outcomes for the individual. In this context, common misconceptions about the effects of aging on homosexuals are comprehensible. The homosexual is told that his sexual orientation is not a viable life option–that he will "live to regret it." He is told that his friends and lovers place an inordinate emphasis on youth and good looks (more so than the heterosexual majority), meaning that he will become increasingly isolated from them as he ages. He will be "old" at thirty or forty. He will have an unhappy sex life and will have to resort to preying on young children, frequenting tearooms, and paying hustlers for sexual gratification. He is told that he will become increasingly effeminate–an "old queen"–and that his company will be unacceptable to others, gay or straight. As a result he will experience great loneliness, depression, and low self-esteem.

It is time for these myths to be laid to rest. Few of the men who participated in our study fit this description. Homosexual men over forty seem to be as well adjusted as their younger counterparts, and

on a measure of life satisfaction these men match or exceed comparable groups in the general population. In fact, contrary to the warn-
ings of our disapproving society, age has brought with it certain
advantages for these men, such as less need for concealment of
sexual orientation and greater self-acceptance. While most homosexual men over forty prefer to socialize with age peers in the gay
community, many of them have younger friends whose impact on
their psychological adjustment has been beneficial. Although participation in the visible aspects of the homosexual community de-
creases with age, few of the men fit the stereotype of the desperately
lonely and isolated old man. Most live with others, have regular
sexual relations, and have had an exclusive love relationship at
some time.

In the past decade homosexual lifestyles have received increasing public attention. Despite major setbacks, such as the repeal of
some local ordinances protecting against discrimination on the basis
of sexual orientation, there is a trend toward greater public acceptance of homosexuals. As part of this trend it is appropriate that the
reality of the aging process for gay men be examined. We suggest
that the quality of life as an individual ages is determined less by his
sexual orientation and more by factors which affect older persons in
general–health, finances, and social support.

No one comprehensive theory explains adjustment to homosexual identity or to aging. For both younger and older men, unwillingness to change sexual orientation and involvement in homosexual friendship and support systems are strong indicators of good
adjustment. Although causal relationships among these factors have
not been established, there is increasing reason to believe that helping professionals ought to direct their activities toward accepting
homosexual individuals as they are (Davison, 1974) and integrating
them into supportive social systems. This is just as true for the older
as for the younger homosexual man.

In the many hours we spent talking to respondents, we were able
to identify some common threads in their histories. We were particularly struck by the way these men described the process by which
they had arrived at their current view of themselves. All of them felt
they had traveled a long and tortuous road toward self-acceptance.
Most had consciously noticed early in life that they were attracted to

the same sex, and that they were therefore different from others; but this consciousness did not lead to immediate self-acceptance. Each individual struggled with his identity over a period of many years, torn by indecisiveness, ambivalence, and anxiety. The experience finally paid off in each man's deep commitment to his lifestyle and a feeling that he was at last comfortable with the role he had chosen.

This is not to imply that all of our respondents believed they had *chosen* to be homosexual; opinions were divided on this issue. However, every respondent we interviewed reported realizing at an early age that he was "different." For many respondents this realization occurred at a time when there were virtually *no* social or emotional supports to assist in coming to terms with a homosexual identity. Unlike the gay teenagers of today, many of these men were not able to simply show up at a gay bar to "look the scene over" and meet others. There were no gay social service organizations, rap groups, or crisis phone-counseling services, as there are today in every major city and in many smaller ones. The homosexual could not turn to sympathetic clergy or counselors, since these professionals considered homosexuality to be a moral abomination or a serious illness.

Our respondents told fascinating stories about the ways in which they had sought and contacted other homosexual men. Those who "came out" after World War II and had access to large metropolitan areas were able to frequent the few bars which catered to homosexuals. But these places were hidden away and were often difficult for the novice to find; once he got there, the atmosphere was less than relaxed. Dancing, touching, or any display of affection was not permitted, and drinks were watered down and expensive. Patrons were likely to give first names only and were often unwilling to meet outside the gay bar. Police raids were common. Friendship cliques met regularly, but it was often difficult to break into these. And if the individual held a professional or other responsible job, he might not want to join a clique whose members were too "obvious," lest his employment be endangered. He might also be hiding his involvement from family members.

One respondent described an event that gives a flavor of the secrecy of these times. A particular suburban house became a meeting place for a group of homosexual men. Invitations were solely by word-of-mouth; the host carefully screened each potential guest before informing him of the location, lest he be a police informer.

Guests were instructed to arrive only one at a time, in order to avoid attracting the neighborhood's attention. Guests who traveled to the area in small groups would split up before approaching the house.

Virtually all of our respondents were forced to come to terms with their sexual orientation under conditions like these. Many did not at first believe that there were other men like them; often this misconception and the resulting isolation lasted for many years. Considering the very adverse social conditions under which our respondents learned to deal with their sexual identities, it is remarkable that they manifest such high levels of self-acceptance and psychological adjustment. We can contrast their situation to that of younger men today, who (at least in the urban setting) can draw upon a resource network of gay social service organizations, professional counselors and clergy sympathetic to the gay lifestyle, and popular discussion of homosexuality in literature and in the media.

Although it is tempting to predict that younger homosexuals will be better adjusted than their older counterparts, on the basis of these considerations, our findings show few age-related differences in psychological adjustment. This may be due to an overall improvement in psychological health for homosexuals, as a result of improved societal conditions in the past decades. However, interviews with our respondents suggested strongly that most of these men had come to terms with their sexual identity and had reached a high level of self-acceptance long before the gay liberation movement of the 1970s. Matthew described this process, which occurred for him as a teenager in the 1920s: "I came to believe that I was born like everybody else and that my life too had come from God. If He had not wanted me to love other men, He would not have made me this way." Matthew and the men like him attest to the remarkable inner strength that many have had to muster in order to overcome sometimes unbearable social conditions. The homosexual men of Matthew's generation, lacking social supports for self-validation, had to draw on this inner strength in order to survive.

DIVERSITY

In writing about any group of people, it is all too easy to make generalizations. These generalizations should not obscure the sometimes very salient differences among individuals. Some differences among our respondents were so clear that they merit discussion.

One unfortunate result of popular misconceptions and ignorance about homosexuality is that, for many people, "homosexual" denotes one very specific type of person. Common descriptions associated with the label "homosexual" are male, effeminate, flighty, and unstable.

In many instances, the only difference between the homosexual and the heterosexual is his choice of sexual object. Alfred Kinsey, in his monumental study of male sexuality, recognized this:

> Males do not represent two discrete populations, heterosexual and homosexual. The world is not to be divided into sheep and goats . . . . It would encourage clearer thinking on these matters if persons were not characterized as heterosexual or homosexual, but as individuals who have had certain amounts of [sexual] experience. Instead of using these terms as substantives which stand for persons, or even as adjectives to describe persons, they may better be used to describe the nature of the overt sexual relations. (Kinsey, Pomeroy, and Martin, 1948: 617, 639)

Bell and Weinberg (1978) were so impressed with individual differences among their respondents that they titled their book *Homosexualities: A Study of Diversity among Men and Women.*

When we examine this issue closely, it is apparent that there are as many differences among homosexuals as among heterosexuals. Our in-depth interviews revealed many such differences. One man related socially and sexually only with age peers, while another had established a love relationship with a man thirty years his junior. One man cultivated a super-masculine image which involved leather clothing and participation in a motorcycle club; another had adopted a highly refined lifestyle and cultivated interests in art, classical music, and interior design. One man saw himself as a carefree single, perhaps a counterpart of the heterosexual "swinger," while another felt trapped in a long-term homosexual relationship, and still another was extremely devoted to his lover. One man, highly extroverted and assertive, was involved in a number of gay community activities; another, shy and withdrawn, spent his days quietly at home. Most respondents never married, but some had been married for many years and had several children. One man, whose wife and children did not know he was homosexual, was extremely concerned about concealment, while another was clearly "up front" and militant about his lifestyle. One man's very restrictive code of sexual conduct permitted relations only if the other person was a close friend. Another man regularly sought partners in cruising areas and sometimes paid for sexual favors. Some men were from the working class (laborer and mechanic), and others were professionals (lawyer, doctor, and judge).

PREJUDICE

Preoccupation with potential discrimination by outsiders often obscures actual discrimination within a minority group's own ranks. This is probably a universal characteristic of oppressed minority groups, and it is no doubt the case for the gay community. Derision of and prejudice against older gays have been described by several authors (e.g., Kelly, 1980: 3-6). One gay man in his forties described what he called the problem of "youthism" in the gay community: "Youthism is the unconscious belief that older people are inferior. We older gay men are looked upon as inferior in appearance, attractiveness, intelligence and sexual prowess. . . . Young people constantly use us. They use us to get a crash pad, money, food, jobs, contacts, and in return they condescend to let us do them" (Schaffer, 1972: 278). One author described the older gay as the "faggot's faggot," noting that the older person is highly stigmatized and often ridiculed within the gay community itself (Kochera, 1973: 6).

Many older gay men believe that younger gays react negatively to them. Most older gays feel that young people sometimes take advantage of them, do not welcome their company in bars, clubs, and bathhouses, do not care to associate or form friendships with them, and think they are dull company. Many of the older gay men in a particular support group were aware of how the younger person might "take advantage" of the older one, and several told of having provided jobs, clothing, housing, or other help to younger gays who subsequently disappeared from view with no thanks for the help. Although most members of the support group favored asking young gays to join it, some expressed the feeling that they had little to learn from "youngsters." The great majority of older gays socialize primarily with age peers.

It would be interesting to examine the attitudes of young gays in order to determine whether the older men's perceptions about the attitude of the young toward them are accurate. In a community where age cohorts are segregated, as they often are in the male homosexual community, there is always the danger that misperceptions and misunderstandings will be magnified. The male homosexual community is replete with situations that reveal disdain for the older homosexual: negative comments can often be heard coming from young gays, expressions such as "the wrinkle-bar" are common, and advertisements for bars and bathhouses provide incentives for the young gay, such as free admission for those under twenty-one.

The "youthism" Schaffer describes will continue as long as the gay community continues its age segregation. Older gay people ought to be encouraged to participate in political and social institutions and should be made welcome wherever gay people are welcome. In most gay social and political organizations, the older person not only remains in the minority, but he is also left outside the leadership and decision-making structure, in a reversal of the traditional role of the elder as advisor and statesman. These organizations must not only attract older members, but older persons must participate in their decision-making processes as well.

Other prejudices are evident in the male homosexual community, and older gays seem to be guilty of perpetuating some of them. Older gay men experienced a time when concealment of homosexuality was quite literally a prerequisite for survival, and some continue to view concealment as an absolute necessity (as do some younger gays). Under these conditions, a male homosexual whose outward appearance and public behavior is not appropriately heterosexual is derided and ostracized. Leznoff and Westley (1967), for instance, found that male homosexuals in high-status jobs were particularly likely to disdain overt homosexuals. One of our respondents objected to overt homosexuals by complaining, "Some gays are gayer than purple pancake batter." Some overtly effeminate homosexuals have described this ostracism. The most notable example is Quentin Crisp, a self-proclaimed effeminate homosexual who described his experiences to heterosexual and homosexual night club audiences.

As improving social conditions for male homosexuals diminish the need for concealment, the issue of effeminate or other overt behavior may assume less importance, although deeply ingrained attitudes about this type of behavior may change more slowly than social conditions. Unfortunately, standards which define a narrow range of acceptable behavior for homosexual men perpetuate the creation of the faggot's faggot. The issue of appropriate sex-role behavior must be resolved for our entire culture, not just for the homosexual minority.

Sexism and racism are also problems within the gay community, and they affect older gay men. We found that individual attitudes toward ethnic and racial minorities and women ranged from very sympathetic to very unsympathetic. It is significant that no older black or Latin America homosexual men were recruited for the study, despite efforts to secure their participation. A support group for older gay men was equally unsuccessful in this regard, despite the presence of large minority populations in the area. Indeed, minorities were conspicuously underrepresented in *all* the community groups approached for the study. Their low participation rates are probably due to a combination of factors, including the hostility of some racist individuals in gay community groups, the exclusionary practices of certain bars and clubs, and the premium that ethnic cultures place on masculinity, making it more difficult for male homosexuals to come out.

Participation by women in our study, and in social and political community organizations and bars, was also extremely low. This can only partly be explained by the lower incidence of homosexuality among women (Kinsey, Pomeroy, Martin, and Gebhard, 1953). Many homosexual men are unsympathetic to the demands of the feminist movement. In gay community organizations leadership roles are dominated by men, and lack of understanding or sympathy by these men for the feminist ideals of gay women may lead to intraorganizational disputes. For instance, some men may refuse to conform to feminist practices; they may balk at using non-sexist titles (e.g., "chairperson"). The use of drag queens (men dressed in women's clothing) at benefits has also alienated women who object to the exploitation of the traditional female role. A crucial issue is whether the interests of the gay and lesbian communities can continue to be represented by organizations dominated by male leaders. Although the feminist and gay liberation movements have a common goal in freeing society from rigid sex-role norms, this connection is missed by many gay men. The older gay man, accustomed to traditional roles for women, may find it even harder to see this connection.

ADJUSTMENT OF THE OLDER HOMOSEXUAL

For the most part we found striking similarities between the problems of our respondents and the problems of older individuals in general. The older person must adapt to the loss of physical attractiveness and to the limitations of poor health often associated with advanced age. Inability to accept these changes may lead to depression and denial for some older people, both heterosexual and homosexual. The absence of social and emotional support from family or friends seems to be equally a problem for both groups. While the heterosexual is more likely to rely on children and other relatives for support, the homosexual is more likely to rely on his friendship network.

There are, however, some differences between older heterosexuals and homosexuals. In discussing the problems of old age with our respondents, we were struck by the absence of allusions to finances. Although six out of every ten people over sixty-five are poor (Atchley, 1977: 125), few of our respondents mentioned financial problems. While our respondents had, on the average, higher incomes than most people their age, there were some poor respondents–11 percent of our questionnaire respondents reported annual incomes below $6,000.

There may be a factor operating here which is unique to the older homosexual. He is more likely to perceive at an early age that he must be independent. He knows he cannot expect support from children, and he is less likely to turn to other relatives. For these reasons he may be more prepared for the financial needs associated with retirement.

Another difference between older homosexuals and heterosexuals is embodied in the "mastery of crisis" hypothesis (Francher and Henkin, 1973; Kelly and Johnson, 1978). Many heterosexuals experience their first "crisis of independence" in old age. In earlier years they are integrated into their family of origin; when they leave this family, they move quickly into a family of procreation. Not until old age, when children have left home, work associates and friends have dwindled due to retirement and death, and the spouse has died, is the older person left alone. Old age is not the best time to develop the wherewithal necessary to negotiate these changes.

The older homosexual typically faces the crisis of independence much earlier, and he cannot usually look to a family of procreation for support. His need for concealment may distance him further from other family members. Because the crisis of independence must be resolved in young adulthood, his transition to old age and retirement is often less severe.

Although death of friends and family is a burden shared by older heterosexuals and homosexuals, the older homosexual is less likely to invest himself entirely in a single spouse. The issue of widow-hood or widowerhood is therefore less salient in the gay community. There are of course many instances where two homosexual men have invested themselves in a relationship lasting many years; the death of a partner is then a serious life disruption for the man who remains. But the homosexual, aware of his isolation at an early age, is perhaps more likely than the heterosexual to have developed strong friendship bonds, and these friendships are then used as a resource in crisis situations. Furthermore, because of the greater similarity in life expectancies for two men, the phenomenon of one spouse (the female) far outliving the other is less typical. The fact that average life expectancy for females is seven years longer than for males has led one observer to recommend homosexual compan-ionships as one solution to the problem of widow-widowerhood (Cavan, 1973).

Another difference in the aging process of heterosexuals and homosexuals is related to physical changes in older men. Diminu-tion in both sexual and non-sexual functions leads to increased passivity. For the heterosexual male, these changes are sometimes perceived as threats to masculinity; sexual changes in particular, such as increased arousal latency and decreased erectile ability (Masters and Johnson, 1966), can be a severe blow to the ego. It has been suggested that the older male homosexual is less concerned than his heterosexual counterpart with maintaining a masculine self-image. He is therefore less likely to experience "male menopause" (Simon and Gagnon, 1969), and less likely to experience a crisis related to physical prowess.

PSYCHOSOCIAL PROBLEMS

Despite the relative success with which most older homosexual men and women face the aging process, there are times when environmental demands exceed coping capacity. For the older homosexual unique environmental demands lead to psychosocial problems, the most common of which fall into four categories: (1) institutional policies, (2) legal problems, (3) emotional needs, and (4) medical needs.

Often the policies of institutions such as hospitals and nursing homes inadvertently create problems for the elderly homosexual. For instance, most hospital intensive care units allow only immediate relatives to visit. The patient's lover of twenty years may be excluded. If the elderly homosexual is unconscious or otherwise unable to make a decision about his treatment, only the signature of a blood relative is sought. This puts the elderly homosexual in the unenviable situation of having life-and-death decision making entrusted to an estranged or distant relative, rather than to a partner of long standing. Nursing homes rarely make provisions for the sexual expression of any of their residents, least of all for homosexual residents. Will the home allow conjugal visits with the resident's same-sex partner? Will the resident be placed in a home that is accessible to the partner? Will assignments be made so that older homosexuals in the same facility can share rooms? If staff and other residents become aware of the older person's homosexuality, will the quality of service decline? Will the person be ostracized?

The legal system, which was designed for the heterosexual majority, is another source of potential problems for the older homosexual. Since there are few precedents to follow and since most lawyers are not familiar with the needs of gay couples, few gay couples prepare wills. When one partner dies, the deceased's family can claim all of the inheritance. The ownership of a home or business may be left in one partner's name if the couple is concerned about hiding the relationship. If this partner dies, all of the property will pass to his family, despite the surviving partner's contributions. In some cases, even if a legal will has been prepared, relatives hostile to the relationship may contest the will on the basis of "undue influence" of the survivor.

The legal rights of homosexuals are limited in other ways as well. The homosexual cannot inherit the property of a deceased spouse's relatives, as can a legally married surviving spouse. In some states heterosexual couples can combine property in a legal device called tenancy by the entirety, which protects the property from creditors in the event of the spouse's death. Homosexuals do not have this option. Nor can they sue a third party for wrongful death, as can a heterosexual spouse.

The helping professional can assist homosexual couples to plan ahead to prevent some of these problems. Legally binding "relationship" contracts are becoming more common among homosexuals, as are wills and joint ownership of property. In addition, more lawyers are learning about the special needs of gay couples, and clients can be referred to them when appropriate.

Homosexuals are also subjected to other discriminatory practices. Some life insurance companies refuse to insure them; usually there is no legal recourse in this case. Elderly persons, particularly elderly homosexuals, are often the target of muggers or gangs of young hoodlums. In many areas police are openly sympathetic to those who attack homosexuals, and officers make few efforts to apprehend those involved or to prevent future attacks. Here again, few legal remedies are available for the victim.

Elderly homosexuals also have unique emotional needs. Although an agency provides bereavement counseling, it may not be prepared to counsel the surviving partner of a homosexual couple. Sensing this, the partner turns to friends rather than to professionals for support. But when friends are lacking, or when the partner's death leads to severe emotional problems such as prolonged depression, professional services ought to be available.

Helping professionals who counsel older homosexuals need special knowledge. They need to be familiar with local resources for meeting other older homosexuals. They should be familiar with the range of lifestyles among older homosexuals, with the effects of stigma within and outside the homosexual community, with the nature of concealment of a homosexual identity, and with the almost universal commitment to homosexuality displayed by older homosexuals.

Counseling strategies with homosexuals often focus on identifying causation (e.g., inappropriate relationship with parents), which encourages the client to avoid assuming responsibility for his or her own self-acceptance. A worker who attempts this approach with an elderly homosexual is doing the client a disservice. Older homosexuals, like older people in general, experience changes in their ability to function sexually, changes which sometimes lead to dysfunction. Because most older homosexuals continue sexual activity into their sixties and seventies, counseling services for sexual dysfunction in this group ought to be developed.

Counseling services for elderly homosexuals are impeded by professionals' lack of knowledge about relationship patterns in this group. Our research with older homosexual men revealed three basic life-long relationship patterns: committed, independent, and ambisexual. Committed homosexuals maintain long-term same-sex relationships, each lasting for a number of years. Sometimes the relationships occur in serial fashion; as one lover is lost due to incompatibility, geographical relocation, or death, a replacement is quickly found. These long-term relationships may or may not be monogamous. The partners begin with a sexual relationship but may evolve to a non-sexual status after the first few years, although the commitment to the relationship remains intact.

Independent homosexuals are those who limit their relationships to close friendships and brief affairs. One researcher has referred to these homosexuals as "loners," but few actually fit that stereotype. Most have at least two or three close friends, and many live with other homosexuals. Some are involved in gay community groups such as the Metropolitan Community Church and gay rights organizations.

Ambisexuals have had relationships with men and with women, both for substantial portions of their lives. Typically an ambisexual is married for at least several years and often has children. At some point he withdraws from the heterosexual relationship and begins homosexual relationships. The ambisexual may remain married while pursuing brief, furtive same-sex contacts, or he may separate from his wife and assume a complete homosexual lifestyle.

As this typology illustrates, older homosexuals are a diverse group. Understanding this diversity is basic to effective counseling. Older homosexual men have unique medical needs related to an increased incidence of sexually transmitted disease (Berger, 1977a). When an older homosexual man seeks medical help, the health care provider may commit two errors. The provider may assume (1) that the man is heterosexual because he looks the same as other men, and (2) that he is sexually inactive because older people purportedly have less interest in sex. To the contrary, the level of sexual activity among older homosexual men is quite high, and several partners may be involved. Both factors increase the likelihood of infection with Human Immunodeficiency Virus (HIV), Hepatitis-B, and other sexually transmitted diseases. Additional conditions of concern to homosexual men include pharyngeal and anal gonorrhea and anal fissures due to rectal penetration. Health care providers must ensure that the special procedures necessary to diagnose and treat these conditions are made available to patients. Often they are not, and the older homosexual is unaware of these procedures or too embarrassed to request them.

SERVICES AND POLICY FOR THE OLDER HOMOSEXUAL

With an increasing elderly population and a growing governmental role in providing services to it, talking about services for older homosexuals becomes more and more relevant. Although many homosexuals are undoubtedly among the older people who use these services, it is exceedingly rare for a service or program to take account of their needs.

One approach to the problem has been taken by the Gay Community Services Center in Minneapolis, which has established an "Affectional Preference and Aging" program. The agency sponsors two support groups: one for older gay men, and another for older lesbians. Groups meet twice a month to provide peer sharing, socialization, and social activities. However, the primary focus of the program is on community education, to train helping professionals and to sensitize them to the needs of older homosexual men and women. The program includes a phase to assess the attitudes of helping professionals toward older homosexuals and to ascertain the service needs of this group. The agency is also involved in disseminating information on older homosexuals to social service agencies through multi-media presentations, workshops, and conferences; it is developing training materials and a model training program.

This sort of educational program can have a great impact on the delivery of services to older homosexuals. For instance, a nursing home may begin taking into account sexual orientation when assigning patients to share rooms. A friendly visiting, telephone reassurance, or meals-on-wheels program may recruit volunteers from the gay community to provide services to older gays. A properly trained mental health counselor will be better able to counsel an older gay client.

Organizations for older homosexuals have also operated in other cities. The Gay Forty Plus Club in San Francisco became the first organization of older gay men when it had its first meeting in 1974. The organization, which has secured nonprofit status, has several purposes. A primary one is to help older gay men combat loneliness. This is achieved by creating a social alternative to the bars, bathhouses, and other gay community institutions in which many older gays are uncomfortable. Gay Forty Plus also attempts to facilitate understanding between younger and older gays. The group participates in community projects to help older gays (such as visits to nursing homes), assists researchers in studying the older gay population, and maintains liaisons with other groups in the gay community. Several attempts have been made to attract the interest of older lesbians. These attempts have not been very successful, although the group would like to establish a link between the men's and women's groups in the gay community.

The structure of Gay Forty Plus is highly informal, since the members feel that highly structured organizations get bogged down in organizational feuds and are not most conducive to an informal and relaxed atmosphere. Meetings are held in members' homes, rather than in an office or hall. Members share organizational responsibilities, and any member may suggest an activity for the group. If the others want to join in, they do so.

Membership is limited to individuals forty or older, since the club feels that members will be most relaxed in the company of age peers. Younger men are, however, permitted to attend as guests of a regular member for a limited number of meetings. There are two meetings each month. The first features a speaker from the gay community, and the second is devoted to socializing and discussion in small groups. Although the group does not offer professional therapy, members are able to share problems and concerns in these discussions. The chairperson of the Gay Forty Plus Club describes the usefulness of the group in this way: "Most of the persons who regularly attend our meetings comment that simply mixing with so many of their peers who are still attractive, enjoy life, and are leading busy, fulfilling existences alters their attitude toward growing older."

In New York City, Senior Action in a Gay Environment (SAGE) is a nonprofit, tax-exempt organization designed to provide social services to older homosexual men and women. The SAGE Statement of Purpose explains:

Our society is beginning to recognize the great cultural wealth offered by its older adults, and is just beginning to recognize and address their needs so that they may continue to lead full lives. However, a group within this older population has contributed equally to our culture and also to a long culture of their own, but whose needs have neither been recognized nor met. It is for this reason that a coalition of professionals in the fields of gerontology and social services and concerned members of the gay community have created Senior Action in a Gay Environment (SAGE). SAGE's program is aimed at those older gay people who are not part of a supportive friendship network, or whose friendship network has been decimated by death, disability or geographic scattering. SAGE will identify and assess the needs of these men and women as they relate to their physical, emotional, environmental and social well-being.

Without espousing the cause of separatism for gay people, SAGE believes that prejudices against those with affectional preference for their own sex remain so strong that most traditional programs for older adults do not provide a comfortable or comforting ambience for the older gay woman or man. The history of social harassment is such that many cannot bring themselves to trust fully even the increasingly numerous broadminded members of the heterosexual world. Too many older gay people are invisible to the helping professionals and therefore live in isolation rather than chance further rebuff and social disapproval. It is to solace and ease the aging of these individuals and bring them into their own social and cultural community that SAGE has been brought into existence.

Among the services provided by SAGE are telephone reassurance, friendly visiting, escort services, personal shopping, support groups, and bereavement counseling. With support from volunteers, private contributions, and a grant, SAGE has opened an office from which these services are coordinated. It will soon implement volunteer training, research, and evaluation programs.

In the city where this study was conducted, the author organized a support and discussion group for older homosexuals called Gray Is Good. The group met for two hours every other week from 1977 to 1979 but is no longer active. Activities of the group included speakers on a variety of topics, growth group exercises, and discussion of various issues such as misconceptions about older gays, conflict between younger and older gays, nutrition, sex and older gays, and adjusting to the physical changes of aging. The group participated in a workshop in which members described their experiences in coming out between the 1920s and 1940s. The goals of the group were strikingly similar to those of the Gay Forty Plus Club: (1) to help younger gays understand growing older, (2) to learn how to cope with loneliness and to use the group to overcome loneliness, (3) to learn to deal with the problems of being older and gay, and (4) to help dispel the myths and fabrications about the older gay within the gay community. Initially, the author planned all activities. As the group progressed, members took on more responsibility for organizational tasks until the group was run entirely by the members. Members prepared articles and advertisements for a local gay community publication, arranged for speakers and meeting places, and called members to remind them of meetings and to arrange transportation.

In addition to these services, which could become available in many other locales, a number of changes in federal, state, and local policy would benefit the older homosexual. The most apparent ones would benefit the homosexual community as a whole. For instance, it is important for state legislatures to decriminalize consenting adult sexual behavior in private. Several states have made this change, but some have decriminalized this behavior for heterosexuals only, thus singling out the homosexual for punishment. Although these laws are rarely enforced, they are a threat to the security of gay people, are used selectively against gays, and have a chilling effect on efforts to improve social conditions for gays.

Another change that would benefit the community as a whole would involve enactment of regulations to protect homosexuals from discrimination in housing, employment, and public accommodations. Although such laws were repealed in highly publicized campaigns in Dade County, Florida, St. Paul, Minnesota, Wichita, Kansas, and Eugene, Oregon, over 100 localities have antidiscrimination ordinances or executives orders.

Of course, legislated changes have little meaning if they are not put into practice. In this regard the harassment of homosexual individuals and organizations by law enforcement agencies must stop.

Additional policy changes would have a more direct impact on the older homosexual. For instance, in planning for the service needs of the elderly, the specific needs of homosexuals should be considered. The Area Agencies on Aging, established by the federal government in 1973, coordinate services for the elderly and plan for improved service delivery. These agencies should be required to direct their needs assessment and planning functions to the homosexual community, much as they are required to plan for other elderly minorities.

A final policy recommendation involves redefining the "family unit" for government agencies and public and private service providers. Many goods and services in our society are made available to the traditional nuclear family. However, our society increasingly consists of individuals and groups who do not fit the nuclear family model, and these groups are, in effect, punished for their status. The single person, for instance, pays higher automobile insurance premiums, and is ineligible for some social service programs. The "single" individual may in fact be someone who is living in a nontraditional family setting, or he or she may be a homosexual living with a lifelong partner.

Redefinition of the family unit would help all of these individuals. Such a redefinition would benefit not only homosexuals but many others as well, such as unmarried older persons who live together, most of whom are heterosexual. A redefinition of this policy might allow any two or more individuals who share a household to declare themselves a family unit. The composition of the unit could change from year to year, or it could dissolve entirely, allowing for the ever-changing relationships we are experiencing in our society. In addition, those who choose to live in single-person households should not be penalized regarding access to goods or services.

CONCLUSION

In discussing the issues of homosexuality and aging, one of our respondents commented very astutely that "preconceptions of any sort tend to color one's responses." Nowhere is this maxim more true than in our preconceptions about the categories of "old people" and "homosexuals." Perhaps *Gay and Gray* will help dispel some of the more inaccurate preconceptions among both young and old, heterosexual and homosexual.

If we look deeply into the lives of our respondents, we see a startling truth about the nature of the preconceived categories into which we are so fond of placing ourselves and others. To the extent that each of us is a sexual being with needs for affection, there are no heterosexuals or homosexuals–there are only human beings with sexual and affectional needs to be fulfilled in a variety of ways. To the extent that each of us is a survivor of life, we are all aging. While we must not ignore real differences among people's ages and sexual needs, we must also be ready to challenge our preconceptions about the significance of these differences.

PART III: ADDITIONAL PERSPECTIVES ON GAY AGING

CHAPTER 13

Age-Status Labeling in Homosexual Men

Fred A. Minnigerode

Age-status labels, such as "young," "middle-aged," and "old," are readily defined by the general population in terms of chronological age. Neugarten, Moore, and Lowe (1965) found that the majority of their middle-aged sample judged a young man to be between eighteen and twenty-two years of age, a middle-aged man to be between forty and fifty years, and an old man to be between sixty-five and seventy-five years. The extent to which homosexual men use these same chronological ages to delineate young, middle, and old age remains unknown.

Folk wisdom suggests accelerated aging in homosexual men. This view is promulgated in journalistic accounts of homosexuality (Stearn, 1961), in homosexual publications (Humphreys, 1972; Kyper, 1974), and in plays about homosexual men (Crowley, 1968). More objectively, Francher and Henkin (1973) similarly suggest that homosexual men, compared with heterosexual men, experience

Fred Minnigerode, PhD, is in the Department of Psychology, University of San Francisco, San Francisco, California 94117.

This chapter was originally published in *Journal of Homosexuality*, Vol. 1(3), 1976.

an earlier onset of middle and old age since they adapt to aging and other "life crises," such as role loss, earlier in life.

The purpose of the present study was to obtain information regarding the loci of middle and old age in the life cycle of homosexual men. It was expected that homosexual men anticipate an earlier onset of middle and old age than do heterosexual men.

METHOD

Subjects

Ninety-five homosexual men between twenty-five and sixty-eight years of age participated in the study. All subjects indicated that they were either exclusively or predominantly homosexual on a seven-point Kinsey-like scale. The sample included five men in their twenties, forty-nine men in their thirties, twenty-seven men in their forties, twelve men in their fifties, and two men in their sixties. While most of the subjects were not in therapy, 11 percent were currently undergoing some form of psychiatric treatment regarding their homosexuality.

Of the ninety-five subjects, 40 percent were obtained through homosexual organizations (Dignity, Gay Teachers' Caucus, Gay Forty Plus) and a local motorcycle club, another 40 percent through friendship networks, and 10 percent from bars. Most subjects were middle- or upper-middle-class and white. Nonwhite subjects constituted 11 percent of the sample.

Procedure

All subjects completed a questionnaire that included items to assess relevant demographic characteristics, perceived health status, and general life satisfaction (Spreitzer & Snyder, 1974). The following items were added to obtain information regarding age-status labeling: "Do you consider yourself (a) young, (b) middle-aged, or (c) old?" "When does middle age begin?" "When does old age begin?" Finally, all subjects were asked to complete Gough and Heilbrun's (1965) Adjective Checklist.

Subjects completed the questionnaires at their convenience and returned them either directly to the experimenter or by mail. Although self-addressed, stamped envelopes were not provided, the return rate averaged 65 percent to 70 percent. All respondents remained anonymous.

RESULTS AND DISCUSSION

When asked to indicate whether they were "young," "middle-aged," or "old," all subjects in their twenties described themselves as young. On the other hand, 20 percent of those in their thirties, 72 percent of those in their forties, and all those over fifty years of age described themselves as middle-aged. The mean chronological age given for the onset of middle age was 41.29 years ($SD = 9.11$) and for the onset of old age was 64.78 years ($SD = 7.89$).

These data do not substantially differ from those of Neugarten, Moore, and Lowe (1965) who found that their middle-aged sample from the general population judged a middle-aged man to be between forty and fifty and an old man to be between sixty-five and seventy-five. The present findings contradict suggestions of accelerated aging in homosexual men.

Seventy-two percent of the men in their forties considered themselves middle-aged; the remainder considered themselves young. Comparisons between these two groups revealed that those considering themselves young were significantly younger than those considering themselves middle-aged ($t = 2.92$, $df = 25$, $p < .01$). Their respective mean ages were 41.85 years ($SD = 2.47$) and 45.33 years ($SD = 2.91$). No significant differences between those considering themselves young and middle-aged were obtained on the Adjective Checklist scales (all t's < 1, or in perceived health status and general life satisfaction, both χ^2's < 1).

Unexpectedly, chronological age correlated significantly with age given for the onset of old age (+.24, $df = 93$, $p < .05$), but not with the age given for the onset of middle age (+.15). In addition, the age given for the onset of old age correlated significantly with the Personal Adjustment scale on the Adjective Checklist (+.24, $df = 93$, $p < .05$) and perceived health status (+.23, $df = 93$, $p < .05$). These correlations did not attain significance with the age given for the onset of middle age (all r's <.11). Those scoring higher on Personal Adjustment and those judging themselves to be in better physical health estimated that old age occurred later in the life cycle than did those scoring lower on Personal Adjustment or those judging themselves to be in poorer physical health. This perceived distance from old age as a correlate of psychological and physical well-being is consistent with findings that old people who identify themselves as old, while objectively correct in doing so, are more maladjusted or more physically sick than those who label themselves either middle-aged or young (Bennet & Eckman, 1973).

The present data do not support popular suggestions that homosexual men enter middle and old age earlier than heterosexual men and that homosexual men experience accelerated aging. These data do suggest that homosexual men who anticipate an early onset of old age might possess poorer physical and/or psychological health than those who do not have such expectations. In terms of age-status labeling, homosexual men appear to be more similar to heterosexual men than different from them.

CHAPTER 14

Natives and Settlers:
An Ethnographic Note on Early Interaction
of Older Homosexual Men
with Younger Gay Liberationists

John Grube

A flood of studies of "gay community" over the past decade has not only made this a "buzz topic" (Murray, 1984, p. 60) in social science, but has given the impression that a stable and elaborate gay community is a post-Stonewall (post-1969) phenomenon. Not so. Homosexuals prior to Stonewall were not merely atomistic individuals in search of others of their kind. They had a historical culture, whether "underworld" or not, with points of entry, established territories, initiation procedures, annual festivities, and "circles"

John Grube, MA, AOCA, teaches English and Creative Writing at the Ontario College of Art.

Correspondence may be addressed to the author at: Ontario College of Art, Department of Liberal Arts Studies, 100 McCaul St., Toronto, Ontario, Canada M5T 1W1.

The author would like to thank Dr. Stephen O. Murray and Professors Richard J. Hoffman, John Alan Lee, and Victor Marshall for their helpful criticisms of earlier versions of this chapter.

This chapter was originally published in *Journal of Homosexuality*, Vol. 20(3/4), 1990.

with leaders ("queens") (Hooker, 1961; Leznoff & Westley, 1963; Simon & Gagnon, 1967). To make a distinction important to this chapter, I refer to the pre-Stonewall gay world as the *traditional gay community*. The more institutionally complete post-Stonewall community with openly declared leaders (Lee, 1977, 1978; Murray, 1979) will be termed the *organized gay community*.

An important yet often neglected feature of the *traditional gay community* was its ideology about the patterns of adaptation in which members of the subculture might resolve the tensions between their stigmatized status and the world at large. These patterns varied from becoming a "flaming queen" or "flaunting" homosexual (Crisp, 1983) to leading a double life in which one's public status was entirely heterosexual (married, with children), while one's private sexual outlet was known only to a very few.

One of the first sociological studies of the *traditional gay community* (Leznoff & Westley, 1963) simplified these patterns into *overt* and *covert* homosexual roles. Barry Dank (1971, 1972) published the first psychosociological studies of the processes by which a new recruit to the gay world made his choice between alternative patterns of "coming out" and marrying (or not). These decision-making processes may be usefully compared with those facing an immigrant to a "new world." Decisions must be made about how much of a former culture to retain, how much of the new setting to assimilate. But host environments rarely offer a single route to accommodation, and forerunners among the immigrant group often provide models for different kinds of accommodation (Gordon, 1961). A young person "coming out" as a homosexual likewise has to decide among models of adaptation to the heterosexual culture, and this process has been made more complex by the multiplication of such models since Stonewall.

There were few models of the "public and respectable" gay individual before 1969, for this role was largely restricted to the brave, famous, and independently well-off (e.g., André Gide). Even less common was the model of "Spokesperson" of an openly homosexual organization (e.g., Magnus Hirschfeld). For most homosexuals the choice was clear. If they wanted success and high status in the dominant culture defined as heterosexual reality (Adam, 1978), they had to hide their homosexual activity in a secret culture

(Warren, 1977). In other words, they learned to accommodate to the prevailing heterosexual world. Let us think of them as similar to the indigenous people or "natives" before white settlers arrive. By contrast the gay liberationists were like settlers who arrive, ignore the indigenous population, and set out to transform the landscape, in this case using as a model an existing pattern of heterosexual leftwing political activism. Many of the early gay activists adopted not only the leftist faith in the possibility of social change, but also much of their value system and lifestyle.

Adopters of each route have often left the others to go their own way, while occasionally applying epithets to the other choice ("closet queens" vs. "boat rockers" and "militants"). The alternative choice of patterns of accommodation has sometimes erupted into open conflict over the "politically correct strategy" to take in surviving as a homosexual.

The evidence is certainly not conclusive yet, but there does appear to be a greater likelihood of older homosexuals, whose earlier socialization was in the *traditional gay culture*, to be less ready to assimilate to the *organized gay community* and its ideology than young homosexuals born after 1960. Early in the conflict of natives versus settlers, some older gay men ventured from the native into the settler camp to become gay liberationists, but soon found the *organized gay community* offered no welcome for older homosexuals (e.g., Schaffer, 1973; cf. also Lee, 1987).

Certain observers suggest there is now a condition of "mutual avoidance" between older and younger homosexuals. For example, Berger (1982, p. 161) notes that "public gay institutions . . . are frequented mostly by younger gays" while "older gays rely on social networks (sometimes one or two friends), dinner parties, and other 'private' mechanisms." I shall argue that a more insightful understanding of the difficulties of aging in the immensely significant period of homosexual history following Stonewall can be furthered by an analysis of gay experience in terms of the different models of accommodation by "natives" and "settlers."

METHODOLOGY

During the period 1983-1987, thirty-five gay men were interviewed as part of a larger project, Project Foolscap, dedicated to recovering the oral history of earlier gay life in Toronto. The main concern of this project is to recover memories concerning the early development of the modern gay community, including the adaptation of members of the *traditional gay community* to the new gay liberation.

Respondents ranged in age from forty to ninety-two and almost all had spent their adult lives in Toronto. An unstructured private interview of each man was conducted, lasting about four hours, covering a list of key topics which included initiation into the "gay community" as defined at that time; interaction with the police or with psychiatric therapy; interpersonal relationships; perceptions of gay social structure (ranging from "the only one in the world" experience to membership in extended circles); first contact with gay liberationist individuals and ideas; membership, if any, in post-Stonewall organizations; and personal experience of contact and conflict between the new gay "radicals" and the *traditional gay community*. All quotations in this paper, unless otherwise specified, are taken from transcripts of these interviews.

From these interviews emerged central themes that are the topic of this chapter: (a) A distinction had to be made between the *traditional gay community* and the modern, *organized gay community;* (b) The *organized gay community* is largely modeled on heterosexual institutions with a gay "United Appeal," gay business council, gay counseling service, and so forth; (c) The basic structural unit of the *traditional gay community* appeared to be the mentor-protégé pair (Grube, 1986); (d) Older gay men socialized into the *traditional gay community* understand and perceive the nature of gay relationships and community quite differently from the new gay liberationists. The two conceptual models frequently come into conflict.

Rather than attempt a survey approach at this still early stage in the research of Project Foolscap, I have chosen three men to represent three distinctive patterns of adaptation among the 35 men interviewed. First, I briefly review the socialization of older gay men as "natives" into the *traditional gay community.* Then I briefly review the influence of nongay, leftist radicalism in the 1960s leading to a gay ideology of accommodation as "settlers" and its early conflict with the established accommodation pattern. Then I present the three men as examples of adaptation to the conflict between the adaptation patterns.

SOCIALIZATION
INTO THE TRADITIONAL GAY COMMUNITY

All dominated groups experience intense pressure to assimilate and the history of *traditional gay communities* is a history of accommodative survival (Adam, 1978; Bérubé, 1981; Boswell, 1980; Cory, 1951; and many others). Maurice Leznoff's pioneering study of Montreal's traditional gay community of the early 1950s (Leznoff & Westley, 1963) perceptively noted the strong pressures to assimilate to heterosexual society; that is, to "pass." Open homosexuals existed but these men either had occupations with "traditionally accepted homosexual linkages in the popular image" such as artists, interior decorators, or hairdressers, or they held low-status occupations such as bellhops. Leznoff and Westley (1963) quote an upwardly mobile informant, Robert, who had just become the manager of an appliance store and who felt he had to cut himself off from his openly gay friends if he was to assimilate into the heterosexual and heterosexist corporate structure:

My promotions have made me more conscious of the gang I hang around with. You see, for the first time in my life I have a job that I would really like to keep and where I can have a pretty secure future. I realize that if word were to get around that I am gay I would probably lose my job. I don't see why that should be, because I know that I'm the same person gay or not. But that's the way it works. I don't want to hang around with Robert any more or any of the people who are like Robert. I don't mind seeing them once in a while at somebody's house, but I won't be seen with them on the street any more.

Robert was, in Leznoff's words, "an overt queen" and this was in the 1950s. If he really did assimilate to the role models the appliance company executives provided, he may well have risen to the top of the corporate structure, gaining in the process not only monetary rewards but the esteem of his straight colleagues.

The same pressure to assimilate was still reported to me by older gay people in Toronto in 1987. For example, Del, a man of fifty-five, socialized into the *traditional gay community,*

Quite a few of my very close gay friends are still very closeted: they hold excellent jobs that are very highly paid and they have parties, house parties . . . and some of them, like the ones who are the wealthiest, they hire models or call-girls, whatever you want, just to go along as escorts to company parties, as a camouflage.

It is startling to realize that for many Toronto homosexuals, especially older men such as Del's business friends, very little has changed since Leznoff and Westley's investigation thirty-five years ago. There are the discreet little house-parties, the ruses with employers, the continued attempts to 'pass' or accommodate to the existing (heterosexual) social landscape.

LIBERATION: SETTLERS TRANSFORMING THE LANDSCAPE

The American origins of a "liberated" gay community are now well-documented (e.g., Marotta, 1981; D'Emilio, 1983), as are its European ancestors (e.g., Lauritsen & Thorstad, 1974; Steakley, 1975; Adam, 1987). Work on the origins of Canadian gay liberation has also been published (Kinsman, 1987). Although there is good reason to believe in the "survival of domination" (Adam, 1978) of a heterosexist reality, to date little attention has been paid to the social pressures felt by liberation activists to accommodate to the heterosexual definition of reality. While proposing to transform the social landscape, many of the new "radicals" actually adopted existing (in this case, leftist political) heterosexual models of social change.

Many young gay activists were deeply imbued with the values of the New Left. This is no longer a controversial point with most scholars, but if it is less than obvious, then compare, for example, the New Left essays in Long (1972), with the gay liberationist essays in McCaffrey (1972), and Humphreys (1972). Many of the early radical gay liberationists angrily rejected the covert life of the *traditional gay community* and tried to 'reform' it along heterosexual lines. There is irony here that the "liberators" of homosexuals also had their images shaped by a heterosexual politics.

It is often overlooked today that the beginning of organized gay liberation was signaled by a revolt of the natives of the *traditional gay community*–the so-called Stonewall riot. But with the progress of gay liberation, the "settlers" (or activists) steadily distanced themselves from the "natives." Marotta's careful micro-historical study of the warring gay liberation factions in New York City in the early 1970s shows a pattern that was replicated in Toronto and, no doubt, in many other locations.

Most vocal and visible is the radical faction. Marotta (1981, p. 147) describes the founders' of the New York Gay Liberation Front point of view: "The radicals who ran GLF, believing the Movement their community, worked to establish GLF as a homosexual division in the radical vanguard." The Movement was straight, active, macho. Therefore, any gay liberation movement that was basically one of its divisions would also have to be straight, active, macho–as far as gay men really can assimilate to this model.

Although Marotta does not say so, when there were chants at demonstrations, they were often modeled on football yells ("two, four, six, eight, gay is twice as good as straight"), football being one of the most macho sports in North America. It followed, of course, that these gay radicals would see the *traditional gay community*–so different from the *organized gay community* they wished to construct–in terms of disapproved stereotypes. As Marotta (1981) points out:

> When they discussed what it was like to be gay, radical male GLFers rapidly agreed that they found gay life unpleasant and unsatisfying. This led them to conclude that male homosexuals who wanted to be fulfilled sexually had to abandon traditional styles of promiscuity and to avoid subcultural institutions like bars, bathhouses, and pornographic bookstores. What they neglected to consider was that some homosexuals found participation in the gay male subculture genuinely fulfilling. Instead of arguing "each to his own," the radical males tended to

generalize their personal preferences and to condemn traditional gay male patterns as "unliberated." (p. 105)

This led to one GLF manifesto assertion that "GLF must demand the complete negation of the use of gay bars, tea rooms, trucks, baths, streets, and other traditional cruising institutions" (Marotta, p. 121). In other words, they proposed abolition of many of the long-established social institutions of the *traditional gay community*, which was admittedly much less "institutionally complete" (Lee, 1978; Murray, 1979) but had nevertheless survived since anyone could remember. Rather like the first American pioneers who saw themselves as establishing a New World blithely overlooked the existence of a long-established native community, the new gay liberationists on occasion treated the "natives" as backward aborigines or as passive lepers hiding in ghettos (Humphreys, 1972, p. 14; Hunter, 1972).

By contrast, the group Marotta calls cultural reformists decided to celebrate the gay community they found and endow it with cultural institutions. The Gay Activists' Alliance did this as a conscious political act (Marotta, 1981):

GAA's Firehouse, as it continued to be known, rapidly became the base for gay cultural enterprises of unprecedented scope and variety. New committees explored gay themes in literature, theater, film, art, and music. . . . By institutionalizing the cultural reformist approach to gay liberation, GAA took a giant step in the direction of legitimizing homosexual interests and promoting the idea that enjoying traditional gay pastimes was not only moral and salutary, but political. As more and more homosexuals, often without appreciating the political outlook most responsible for legitimizing and encouraging their activities, followed the lead of the first cultural reformers, there was a surfacing of the gay subculture and a proliferation of identifiably gay bars, discos, restaurants, bathhouses, bookstores, sex shops, artistic enterprises, publishing ventures, hotels, community centers, and neighbourhoods. (p. 193)

Political analysts of the dynamics of leftist social change, especially Marcuse (1974), have often warned of the power of the dominant culture, especially of its economic and commercial institutions, to "co-opt" social change through "repressive desublimation." In some respects, the new organized gay communities are a clear example of the ironic extent to which radical efforts to liberate homosexuals have led to the very "mimicry of straight society" that the radical liberationists condemned (e.g., Wittman, 1972, p. 161).

THREE EXAMPLES OF ACCOMMODATION

Many gay men in Toronto, especially those socialized before Stonewall, have made very little accommodation to the *organized gay community*. They continue in their private circles. It is almost startling today, considering the widespread media and public awareness of gay life, to meet young men from small towns somewhat distant from Toronto who arrive in the city and have little or no knowledge of the *organized gay community* or of the *traditional gay community*, often spending many months before making their first contact. Neither the older gay man who has made no effort at accommodation nor the naive younger man of today are discussed here. Instead, the three men below are chosen to shed light on the experiences of those who made some accommodation to the dynamics created by the two patterns of accommodation.

Ken

Ken has been a dedicated Toronto radical leader since the early 1970s. Like many individuals born and educated in Toronto, he went to the U.S. for graduate study, to Cornell, in 1968. It was there he realized for sure that he was gay, and began going to Mory's in his off hours:

> It was a weird, weird bar because it was not only for people at the two universities and townies but it was also a gay bar, a black bar, and a drug-addict bar, I mean it was, like, everything that Republican Ithaca reviled, gathered in that bar, and so it was rather an interesting institution. At one point the owner tried to throw the gay people out, didn't want them there, and the bar was seized by gay people a few nights later.

Ken took part in that operation, and was deeply influenced by the Cornell atmosphere:

> You have to understand that the campus within weeks after I arrived was in chaos, because the black students, armed, had taken over the student center . . . generally there was a loosening of all those props that sort of, you know, guide you in what you think of as acceptable behavior . . . there were certain (gay) events that were directly inspired by what had been going on in connection with the racial question.

At Cornell he came into marginal contact with some queen-and-entourage formations of the *traditional gay community* (Leznoff & Westley, 1963), formed an unfavorable impression of them, and so continued to be influenced socially and politically by the basically straight behavior and values of those men leading the campaigns against the U.S. involvement in Vietnam and in favour of black liberation. Gay radicals such as Ken looked up to such men–the gravitational pull of assimilation operates almost imperceptibly.

Back in Toronto some years later, Ken and his radical friends took up the fitness craze and ran into a group of gay men already entrenched at the local YMCA. How did he and his radical gay friends relate to these men socialized in the pre-Stonewall era? Ken is remarkably candid: "We were like the settlers arriving among the Indians, you know, they just didn't exist for us, we were bringing social organization with us." This perspective is worth pondering, because it underlies much of the *oranized gay community's* thinking. In this view the *traditional gay community* before Stonewall had no structure and does not merit serious study or respect–except for a few illustrious predecessors who were gay radicals before their time. Just as the white men arrived among "primitive," therefore expendable, Indians, so the young gay radicals of the early 1970s occupied gay spaces reported by early observers (e.g., Cory, 1951) without consulting the indigenous inhabitants. The old YMCA was classic gay space, but Ken reported:

> We only realized, gradually realized, that there already was an existing gay network, within the Y, there was this layer of older men in particular who you'd see were always looking at

you with squinty eyes, and would never speak to you or anything, obviously because for one they were terrified and two they were afraid we were going to blow it for them all, and later on too I discovered that in fact there was this guy called Al, who was one of the instructors there who was in fact one of these queen-bees, and the center of a social circle and peoples' careers rose and fell on whether they got invited to his dinner parties or not, and he didn't like us very much, and of course his whole world had been swept aside, in a sense, or this other center suddenly appeared full-blown in his midst you know, and he had no purchase on it and of course we were totally unaware of any of this . . . that little group of men who looked at you through slitty eyes, very few of them ever came over into the group that I belonged to. Some did. Yeah, there got to be a breaking down of the boundaries there but there was always this residue, this hard-core residue of what I take to be self-hating gay men who resented us for, like, disturbing their little grotto for one thing, and probably for not being available for another. And also for carrying on our little sexual thing right there, you know, right in the showers, and so on and so forth, whereas they were very furtive about it, we were scandalously, and from their point of view, dangerously, more open.

In the end the Toronto YMCA, like many others, started aggressively marketing family memberships to upwardly mobile straights in its brand new building and is no longer primary gay space. Ken has a record of fifteen years' work in Toronto as a full-time gay radical helping to construct the *organized gay community* he and his friends would like to see. Their vision is not one that includes the "natives," those gay men socialized before 1969. Here is a potential problem for gays who are aging and whose "whole world had been swept aside," as Ken put it. There is little space for the "natives" in the radical vision.

Michael

Elements in Michael's life story shed light on the "born-again" gay radical without leadership aspirations. Michael was born, grew up, and was educated in English-speaking Montreal. He experienced the usual pressures to conform. The assimilationist pressures were so strong at McGill University that, although he couldn't make the football team, or even be an official cheerleader, he felt the need to associate himself with the football cult:

> I spent most of my . . . second year at McGill as a cheerleader, for the football team, of all bizarre things . . . I wasn't an official one, you had to be a sort of fraternity boy to be in that . . . so I was, like, freelance cheerleader, which nobody asked for, and nobody particularly wanted, and so I went there, and I'd get myself drunk . . . and I'd go and make a fool of myself.

His unwillingness to accept a gay identity was so great that he voluntarily underwent aversion therapy: "It was like an act of faith in a way, a sort of desperate faith, I mean faith doesn't involve thinking through things, faith involves saying 'I give myself to this.' "

Shortly after breaking off his therapy in 1972 he went on a trip to Europe and North Africa. In Athens he had the "conversion" experience that was to lead him into radical gay liberation:

> One of the things that happened was in Athens, there happened to be the first of the student demonstrations against the colonels, and terrible police smashing of this and beating up of students and I saw all that, and if was the first time in my life, this is after lots of Vietnam demonstrations and so on here but I never, it was as if those things were outside my world. It was the first time, and suddenly, amazing, on that one day, it was as if a veil was removed from me, and suddenly I saw the world completely in the reverse from everything I had done before that, totally in political terms, without any theory, I had no Marxist theory, but everything I looked at from then on was to do with power and wealth and control, and powerlessness and revolution and struggle.

On his return to Toronto, where he had moved, he phoned the Community Homophile Association of Toronto hotline, and began to understand about bathhouses, dances, sexual encounters. Shortly afterward he discovered that Gay Alliance Toward Equality, a radical gay organization, was more to his liking:

I was becoming involved in a quite militant way with gay liberation, so I was, I was very quickly becoming intolerant of people who were sort of downtown bar, very puritanical in a way . . . anyway my political coming-out far outpaced my sexual coming-out. Far. I was desperately fumbling around sexually, but meanwhile taking this extremely militant stance, and being right, like, at the edge of things . . . everything was for gay liberation, I mean it was total, for me it was like a full-time job.

Michael took up gay journalism, the first activity at which he was an unqualified success. His monthly column was:

. . . essentially whatever I was thinking about when I wrote it, whatever I was doing and saying, and which is why I think I was so popular, it was like a very direct expression of gay liberation, no theory, just practice, and anger one month, funny another month, bitchy another month, whatever was going came out in the column, and at the same time for GATE we were producing materials and we were organizing educationals, as we called them which were meetings where there'd be speakers, and movies and so on.

This was unpaid, voluntary work, but for Michael and many others it helped organize their life and give it meaning.

Michael's contact with the "natives" of the *traditional gay community* was almost non-existent and he felt "extremely angry with people who wouldn't come out." He does recall vividly one contact with a "native":

I'd been to a party and I remember this person, this well-dressed, well-coiffed, well-turned-out person, with a good job, lots of money and privilege and so on, the party was like that, it was a high-rise apartment block, people with lots of money and comfort, I got into an argument with this person about gay liberation, he being one of many people then who probably still I suppose would say "oh you people rocking the boat, you, you're the ones who cause our problems, if you'd just keep quiet we'd be all right," and I remember screaming at

him, shouting at him that it was people like him, chains, something about chains, people like him they had their chains in
their head, and I wrote this column then, immediately after-
wards . . . saying how I wanted to drag these people by their
Vidal Sassooned hair out of the closet, and kicking and
screaming force them to, and I was damned if I was going to
put myself on the front line for other people. It always did
make me angry, that, I mean distributing literature in bars and
having people refuse it.

Although Michael felt fulfilled in many ways by his discovery of
gay liberation, he began to feel that the movement was narrowing
the ground on which it stood to "the right of gay men to their
bath-houses, when it should have been part of a vast, world-wide
struggle of all progressive forces." As he now says:

I realized only a couple of years ago that in fact my gay
liberation had not been a sexual liberation, in fact it had been a
justice struggle, because I never achieved sexual liberation for
myself through it, and that's one of the reasons in fact that I
eventually abandoned it, I was never a sexual liberationist, I
was always a human rights fighter, that was very different.

He sadly realized in the end that he didn't have "what real revo-
lutionaries have, which is a very long vision, you work and you
work and you work," so he abandoned gay journalism and moved
into a variety of other progressive causes.

Ken and Michael Contrasted

Ken absorbed directly the values and attitudes of the straight
movement men who led the antiwar campaign at Cornell. He also
has integrity and a fine mind which has given him self-assurance
and staying power, something he has needed to remain a radical gay
leader for fifteen years. At forty he is even beginning to mellow in
his relations with members of the *traditional gay community.* Michael, by contrast, came into the *organized gay community* already
constructed by Ken and his friends. For the first time he felt welcome in a group, for the first time his writing skills were properly

utilized, gay liberation had started with a "conversion" experience ("it was as if a veil was removed from me"), and his life now had meaning and direction. But he picked up negative attitudes toward the *traditional gay community*, the "natives," from his new mentors who themselves had absorbed these attitudes from straight movement men. The accommodation of Ken, an original "settler," was to the straight left. The accommodation of Michael was to the world these "settlers" had constructed. He lacked Ken's Marxist belief-system, and he lacked roots in the tribal rituals of the *traditional gay community*. So he had nothing to fall back on. As a result the effect of his secular "conversion" began to wear off and he ceased to be a gay activist at all.

George

The man Michael met and disliked (in the party anecdote above) is probably still giving downtown Toronto parties and telling all gay activists he meets–radical or reformist–not to rock the boat. If anyone is going to bring him over into the *organized gay community* it is probably the reformist George.

George was born into a working-class Toronto family sixty-three years ago, started work in a factory at sixteen, helped organize a radical union there, was fired for his union organizing at another job, came into contact with the arts through Communists (the Labor Arts Guild), and through them with the Toronto gay community of the mid-1940s. Although George had been cruising parks, cans, and moviehouses since early adolescence, and had been servicing his high-school jock peers sexually, it took Communist Party members interested in bringing along working-class youths to get him into the Toronto gay community and to arrange an acting scholarship at a prestigious institution.

As George says of this 1943-46 era: "I came to the conclusion that everybody in the arts was homosexual and leftist because that was the world I was presented with." He was never able to commit himself to any party, then or later, but this early experience with Marxist dialecticians made it possible to understand the mind-set of the gay radicals, the "settlers," such as Ken and his friends whom he encountered in the 1970s. George remembers fun, stimulating parties in the 1940s "in lofts at Bathurst and Queen and draughty dusty rehearsal studios," with actors, writers, puppeteers, and visual artists; in fact, he experienced the *traditional gay community* in all its rich variety.

George was also close to the one Toronto figure who tried to promote a Canadian homophile movement as early as 1948 (Champagne, 1986). This man, Jim Egan, was a well-known and respected member of the *traditional gay community,* gave parties where homosexual rights ideas were canvassed, kept in touch with the homophile movement in other countries, and published on such subjects under his own name in the popular press. The closest he got to starting a homophile movement in Toronto was the founding of a small weekly discussion group at a gay club, whose activities were written up favorably in the mainstream press (Katz, 1964). It was in this context that George's reformist political ideas were formed.

In the fall of 1969 the first local above-ground gay organization was formed at the University of Toronto with George present. The political context had changed dramatically. Demonstrations and sit-ins were the order of the day, Marxist theory had become fashionable again for the first time since the 1940s. However, as George says, "soon we were having these splits . . . along the militant lines, political action, take to the streets, attack, versus the back-stage approach," the gay radicals versus the reformists who were mostly former homophiles. George therefore spearheaded the formation of a community group:

> In the Fall of '70-'71 it became apparent that we needed a community group, that many people in the community wouldn't come to the university, though it was an intellectual group, they were uncomfortable, and my thrust had been towards helping people to come to terms with their homosexuality, and the beginning of organization along the lines of social services work. Where can I get a doctor? Where can I get a lawyer?

The conflict between George and the radicals soon surfaced again, and it was partly a matter of age and socialization. George was what Ken thought of as a "native," having deep roots in the *traditional gay community,* an early inoculation against Marxism, and social service concerns for his community. The radicals, or "settlers," came with straight left socialization. George describes the community organization he helped found as:

> . . . a discussion group, we were a help group, a self-help group. And leaning towards social services. I was very concerned about people being arrested and I set up the first organization going to courts, and monitoring courts, and since my bent was that way, and I was–the leader, quote–I felt there was room for the political arm, but it wasn't long before those that were into radical politics were fed up with this namby-pamby approach as they saw it of helping people, that we had to attack the institutions of our oppression, and we had to get out of the closets and into the streets, and we had to protest and storm the barricades, and build barricades of our own, with which we could defend ourselves.

The radicals soon left and started their own organizations. As George recognized, specialist gay organizations arose to deal with the social service needs of the gay community. He himself made a good run for alderman in 1980, became an investor in the gay bath-bar scene, helped start the local chapter of the Lambda Business Council, and in spite of strong and sustained radical attempts to damage his credibility, he still remains the unofficial mayor of gay Toronto as he enjoys his seventh decade.

CONCLUSION

It has become almost conventional wisdom among gay liberationists (at least the many holding a social constructionist view) to question the existence of a gay community before 1969. It has also become somewhat commonplace to question, if not blame, the extent to which traditional homosexuals hid themselves, accommodated to the prevailing heterosexist ideology through marriage and other forms of the double life, and otherwise declined to challenge heterosexist domination.

But if traditional homosexuals are to be questioned for their accommodation to the heterosexual world they survived in, then it is equally just to question the accommodation of gay liberationists.

In many ways, modern gay communities in large North American centers have become mirror images of their heterosexual counterparts, with their entertainment institutions, financial institutions, business councils, United Appeal, and even their own telephone directories.

In the traditional or "native" gay community, with basic structural units such as the mentor/protégé couple (Grube, 1986), the queen-and-entourage formation (Leznoff & Westley, 1963), and the party and dinner circles, communities were formed in which older men had privileges and duties. Older men introduced young men, for example, to their social circle, sometimes in exchange for sex, often for the glamorous social company of youth. As a man grew older in these "native" communities, he was able to command a modest respect as long as he had some money and reasonable health.

This is not true of the post-1969 *organized gay community,* which lacks an effective equivalent of the mentor/protégé tradition, so useful in training new leaders. It lacks attractive social institutions dedicated to the needs of homosexuals as they age; the difficulties of organizing sustainable institutions for older gays are well-known (Berger, 1982; Dawson, 1982; Lee, 1987). Older men socialized in the *traditional gay community* have reason to feel "aversion" (Berger, 1982: p. 167) to the new "liberated" community; they may well have reason to reject a liberationist movement which has, in two decades, ironically led to a gay version of heterosexual reality, and one in which they are not especially welcome.

No one in his right mind would want to go back to the oppression and underground communities of the pre-Stonewall era. We owe a great debt to the dynamic energy of the radicals and the institution-building of the reformists. But the time has come to take a second look at the *traditional gay community* into which men who are now middle-aged or elderly were first socialized. Their experience can offer much in the way of survival techniques, the training of new leaders, the transmission of culture, as well as provide an honorable and welcome place in the community for homosexuals as they grow old. After all, even attractive young radicals do age.

CHAPTER 15

Sexual Attitudes
and Behavior
in Midlife
and Aging Homosexual Males

Mark Pope
Richard Schulz

INTRODUCTION

Even though research has been done on gay people, little has been done on the aging gay male. This chapter discusses some of the findings of a study of eighty-seven homosexual males between the ages of forty and seventy-seven in the Chicago metropolitan area. Using a self-report questionnaire, data were gathered on the sexual attitudes and behavior of this group.

The stereotype of the aging gay male is being changed (Kelly,

Mark Pope, EdD, is President of Career Decisions (A Career Counseling and Consulting Firm) and Adjunct Professor at the University of San Francisco, Golden Gate University, and at John F. Kennedy University as well as Clinical Supervisor in Stanford University's Counseling and Health Psychology Program.

Richard Schulz, PhD, is Professor and Director of the Gerontology Program at the University of Pittsburgh's Western Psychiatric Institute.

This chapter was originally published in *Journal of Homosexuality*, Vol. 20(3/4), 1990.

1977). Kelly's study stated the societal myths of the aging gay man include the following: That he no longer goes to bars, having lost his physical attractiveness and his sexual appeal to the young men he craves. He is oversexed, but his sex life is very unsatisfactory. He has been unable to form a lasting relationship with a sexual partner, and he is seldom sexually active anymore. When he does have sex, it is usually in a "tearoom" (public toilet). He has disengaged from the gay world and his acquaintances in it. He is retreating further and further into the "closet"–fearful of disclosure of his "perversion." Most of his associations now are increasingly with heterosexuals. He is labeled "an old queen," as he has become quite effeminate.

Kelly, in this pioneering study, stated that the aging gay men in this study bear little resemblance to this stereotyped composite image. The sex life of the older gay man was, characteristically, quite satisfactory, and he desired sexual contact with adult men, especially those near his own age. The subjects were not, however, currently involved in a gay liaison, defined in Kelly's study as an emotional and sexual relationship of one year's duration or longer. The number of persons in liaisons increased with age until the forty-six to fifty-five-year-old category. Above fifty-five partnerships decreased to almost none. Two reasons for this decline often mentioned by older gays were the death of the loved one and the rejection of the notion of having a single lifelong lover.

Kleinberg (1977) stated that the aging gay male was better off than his heterosexual counterpart. Attributing this to having lived through the "long closeted life," the gay males in this study were survivors of the widowhood, loneliness, and loss of social place that are many times terminal grief for the heterosexually oriented person.

All of the gay males in the Kimmel (1977) study were sexually active and their sexual relationships continued to be an important part of their lives. Several respondents reported that sex was less important now than when they were younger, but several indicated that sex was more satisfying for them now. Kimmel's subjects also pointed out some of the advantages in aging for the gay male: more awareness of one's responsibility for self; non-reliance on family or children; more "continuity of life" (not having to cope with children leaving home); no limiting "male"/"female" roles in performing necessary tasks of life such as cooking, shopping, managing finances; having lived alone before, living alone now is not an ego-shattering experience; and having a friendship network on which to rely for social and sexual companionship and support.

Berger (1982) administered a questionnaire to 112 gay males from forty-one to seventy-seven years old and then selected ten subjects for an extensive interview. This comprehensive study also reported data on sexual activity and satisfaction of the subjects. Berger stated that the reported level of sexual activity was quite high for this sample, and that almost 75 percent of the questionnaire sample were satisfied with their sex lives.

None of the above-cited studies, however, included data by consistent age cohort. Berger (1982) did not categorize the subjects into age categories when presenting the data on sexual activity or sexual satisfaction. Kelly (1977) used varying age categories in reporting the data, using a fifty to sixty-five age bracket for sexual satisfaction and a forty-six to fifty-five age bracket for number of gay partnerships (coupling). Kelly also did not provide any tabular data for these categories. Neither Kimmel (1977) nor Kleinberg (1977) had large enough samples (less than fifteen each) to make cohort analysis meaningful.

METHOD

Historically, there has been no gay reference group in the research literature that took into account the racial, socioeconomic, or age parameters of the American gay subculture. Because of the unique character of this subculture–that is, ability to conceal sexual orientation, fear of reprisals in various life situations, et cetera–effective population sampling techniques have not been utilized. Almost all studies to date of noninstitutionalized gay men have used gay organizations (Evans, 1969; Hooker, 1956), gay bars (Myrick, 1974), friendship networks (Loney, 1972), gay newspaper advertising (Laner, 1978; Lee, 1976), or a combination of these methods (Berger, 1982; Kelly, 1977; Minnigerode, 1976; Saghir & Robins, 1973; Weinberg & Williams, 1974). Further, some of the above referenced studies had very small samples. For instance, the Kleinberg (1977) and Kimmel (1977) studies only considered five and fourteen subjects, respectively.

The data in this study were collected through questionnaires mailed to 235 members of Maturity, a social group for gay men forty years of age or older (see Appendix 15.A). Maturity was the only organized group of this type in the metropolitan Chicago area at the time. Also, Maturity provided an opportunity to contact a large aging gay male population.

The decision to use the questionnaire format for data collection was made on the basis of the Pfeiffer et al. researchers. Pfeiffer, Verwoerdt, and Wang (1968) conducted a similar study using interviews. Four years later, Pfeiffer, Verwoerdt, and Davis (1972) did a follow-up study, but used questionnaires instead of the interview. In the latter study, increased response rates were noted.

The questionnaire used here was accompanied by a letter from the co-chair of the National Caucus of Gay and Lesbian Counselors (now Association for Gay, Lesbian, and Bisexual Issues in Counseling), a group of mental health counselors in the American Personnel and Guidance Association (now American Association for Counseling and Development). In the recent past the policy of mental health professional organizations such as the American Psychological Association, the American Association for Counseling and Development, and, especially, the American Psychiatric Association was that a homosexually oriented individual was inherently "mentally ill." Although these organizations have repudiated these policies, it was felt that there might continue to be a virulent distrust of this type of psychological research, that somehow this research might be "used against" gay people. By accompanying the questionnaire with this letter, inviting the subjects to participate in this study, it was felt that many of these fears could be assuaged and increased response would be the outcome.

RESULTS

Some interesting descriptive data were garnered through the questionnaires. Of the 235 questionnaires which were mailed, 101 were returned. Fourteen of the returned questionnaires were from gay males under forty years of age and were not used in this analysis. The ages of the respondents ranged from forty to seventy-seven years. Thirty-seven (43 percent) of the respondents were between the ages of forty and forty-nine, twenty-nine (33 percent) were in the fifty to fifty-nine age cohort, and twenty-one (24 percent) were in the sixty-plus age category. While the mean income level for the total group fell in the $15,000 to $20,000 per year category, 44 percent of the sixty-plus age group earned less than $10,000 per year. Sixty-three percent of the respondents rented their residence and 33 percent owned their house or apartment. It was also an overwhelmingly urban group with 73 percent residing in cities with over 100,000 population, 15 percent in suburban areas, 15 percent in small cities, and only one percent in rural areas. No information was gathered on the racial makeup of the group. Because of the difference in the income level of the sixty-plus age group, there may be some psychological dissonance inherent in their economic situation as they see many of the younger gay men living much better than they do.

Reported Current Frequency of Sex

In the forty to forty-nine age group, 54 percent of the respondents reported that they had sex more than once per week, 34 percent of the fifty to fifty-nine age group respondents reported similarly, while only 5 percent of the sixty-plus age category reported sex more than once per week. This latter group, however, did report 38 percent having sex once-per-week. Each of these percentages is the statistical mode for their cohort. (See Table 15.1.)

Percentage of Respondents Remaining Sexually Active

Ninety-one percent of the total respondents reported that they were still sexually active. Ninety-seven percent of the forty to forty-nine age category were active currently, 86 percent of both the fifty to fifty-nine and 60-plus categories reported that they had not stopped sexual activity. Twenty percent of the sisxty-plus age group, however, did not report a specific frequency. They instead considered themselves "active," but declined to categorize themselves in the once-per-month to more-than-once-per-week groups. (See Table 15.1.)

Reported Current Level of Sexual Feelings (Interest)

There did seem to be a decline in sexual interest with age; however, over 45 percent of the respondents in each of the age groups

TABLE 15.1. Current Frequency of Sexual Relations in Percentages for Gay Men (N = 87)

Age Group (years)	Number	None	Once Per Month	Once Per Two Weeks	Once Per Week	More Than Once Per Week	Other But Active
40 - 49	37	3	3	8	27	54	5
50 - 59	29	14	10	7	14	34	7
60+	21	14	9	14	38	5	20

reported currently having strong sexual feelings. In all age categories, over 90 percent of all respondents reported a moderate or strong sexual interest. There was a tendency for the forty to forty-nine age group to report a strong interest (62 percent) while the sixty-plus age group reported a weaker interest percentage (48 percent); nevertheless, even in this latter group, this represented the statistical mode. Still, in the over sixty group, almost half of those responding indicated a moderate degree of sexual interest. (See Table 15.2.)

Percentage of Respondents Reporting Continued Sexual Feelings (Interest)

All of the respondents reported having a current interest in sex; 5 percent of the forty to forty-nine group reported a weak interest, while only 10 percent of the sixty-plus category responded similarly. (See Table 15.2.)

Change in Level of Reported Enjoyment of Sex

Sixty-nine percent of the respondents reported no change in their enjoyment of sex from their younger years to the present, 13 percent reported an increase, and 16 percent a decrease. The age of the respondents had no effect on this measure.

TABLE 15.2. Current Level of Sexual Interest in Percentages for Gay Men (N = 87)

Age Group (years)	Number	None	Weak	Moderate	Strong
40 - 49	37	0	5	33	62
50 - 59*	29	0	0	38	52
60+	21	0	9	43	48

* Percentages do not equal 100 here as two respondents marked two choices and one respondent did not answer.

DISCUSSION

This is one of the few studies of older gay men to utilize this large a sample. Most of the previous studies have used less than fifteen subjects, with the notable exceptions of Berger (1982), Minnigerode (1976), and Weinberg and Williams (1974). Because of the sampling methodology, however, the findings of this study cannot be applied as representative of all aging gay males. This sample of eighty-seven men can, however, provide additional information on the older gay male in modern American society.

It is obvious, however, that these older gay men have maintained both their interest in sex as well as their ability to function sexually. Similar findings have been reported by both Kelly (1977) and Berger (1982). This may be a function of the predominant male sexual attitudes in current American society as well as the particular institutions in the gay male subculture, for example, bars and baths, which both foster these attitudes and provide a testing ground for their concomitant behavior.

Vacha (1985) specifically dedicated his book to the "survivors of an era beset by greater persecution than present." From several of the written comments returned with the completed questionnaires, it became clear the older gay men in this study who did provide comments have also developed coping mechanisms that have allowed them to function in their particular environments. These older gay men, who have functioned for almost all of their years in a more homosexually oppressive society than today's younger gay generations, have adapted to the specific mores of the society in which they found themselves. Several of the written comments returned with the completed questionnaire indicated that these coping mechanisms were not acquired easily.

The method of acquisition of these coping mechanisms is not within the scope of this study; however, further research using these age categories might yield data on these areas. One possible approach might be to do a study using younger gay men, younger heterosexually oriented men, and same age-categoried midlife and aging heterosexually oriented men as additional comparison groups. Using these groups would allow an examination of the type and nature of the coping mechanisms to see if there are differences on the basis of age and sexual orientation. For purposes of this study, it is sufficient to note that the older gay males in this sample seem to have both the desire and the ability to function in sexual situations.

Also, neither sexual "activity" nor sexual "relations" were operationally defined for the respondents before responding to the survey. It was left to the individual to interpret the questions. For purposes of this analysis, these two phrases have been defined as equivalent. It is, however, noted that a relatively large percent (20 percent) of the sixty-plus age group in the gay male sample refused to categorize themselves as to frequency of sexual "relations," but indicated that they continued to remain "active." The questionnaire specifically asked about sexual "relations." Asking about sexual "activity" may have elicited a different response as "relations" may seem to exclude masturbation or any self-erotic behavior. Future studies should include self-erotic behavior as a separate category in order to analyze the contribution of this category to sexual "activity."

Further, the data for this study were gathered during 1978, before Acquired Immune Deficiency Syndrome (AIDS) became a national health issue. It is beyond the scope of this study to assess the direct effect of AIDS on this population.

This study should be seen as the beginning of a more generalized study of older gay male sexuality. Other areas must be explored in a comprehensive study. Especially in the aging male and female who for many reasons are relatively isolated, a classification of self-erotic behavior or masturbation may take on added prominence. Unless specific information is asked about this form of sexual activity, there may be a bias on the part of most respondents to omit this classification. Also, using consistent age cohorts in future research will enable cohort comparisons to be made much more easily.

The current study of eighty-seven midlife and aging gay males' sexual behavior and attitudes is a unique study which paves the way for additional studies of this often misunderstood area of human sexuality.

APPENDIX 15.A
Questionnaire

1. If you were to rate your enjoyment of sex in your younger years, would you rate this as:
   ( ) None   ( ) Mild   ( ) Very much

2. Please classify your sexual feelings in your younger years:
   ( ) None   ( ) Weak   ( ) Moderate   ( ) Strong

3. How much do you enjoy sexual feelings at the present time?
   ( ) None   ( ) Mild   ( ) Very much

4. How would you rate your sexual feelings at the present time?
   ( ) None   ( ) Weak   ( ) Moderate   ( ) Strong

5. What is your present frequency of sexual relations?
   ( ) None   ( ) Once per week
   ( ) Once per month   ( ) More than once per week
   ( ) Once every two weeks   ( ) Other, but active

6. If your sexual relations have stopped, when did this occur?
   ( ) Not stopped   ( ) 6-10 years ago
   ( ) One year ago or less   ( ) 11-20 years ago
   ( ) 2-5 years ago   ( ) 20 years ago or more

CHAPTER 16

Older Lesbian and Gay People:
A Theory of Successful Aging

Richard A. Friend

As a group, older lesbian and gay people are best described as diverse (Kimmel, 1978). The most common unifying elements for this group are the facts that today's older gay and lesbian people have all developed some type of homosexual identity and all grew up in a particular socio-historical period. The popular image of older lesbian and gay people is extremely negative. Older gay men are frequently depicted as lonely, depressed, oversexed, and living a life without the traditional support of family and friends (Kelly, 1977). Older lesbian women are often described as unattractive, unemotional, and lonely (Berger, 1982a). This common negative

Richard A. Friend, PhD, is on the faculty of the Human Sexuality Education Program at the University of Pennsylvania's Graduate School of Education as well as an Adjunct Assistant Professor at the College of Allied Health Sciences at Thomas Jefferson University.

Correspondence may be addressed to the author at: University of Pennsylvania, Graduate School of Education, Human Sexuality Education Program, 3700 Walnut Street, Philadelphia, PA 19104.

The author would like to acknowledge special thanks to Professor Kenneth D. George for his help and support.

This chapter was originally published in *Journal of Homosexuality*, Vol. 20(3/4), 1990.

image conflicts, however, with the descriptions of older gay and lesbian adults from the research literature.

Kelly (1977) argues that the popular negative stereotypes of older gay men are myths that do not accurately reflect the lives of the men he studied. Like Kelly, Berger (1980, 1982a, 1982b), Friend (1980), Kimmel (1978), Francher and Henkin (1973), and Weinberg (1970) all report on samples of older gay men who are described as psychologically well adjusted, self-accepting, and adapting well to the aging process. Almvig (1982), Martin and Lyon (1979) and Raphael and Robinson (1980) also describe the majority of older lesbian women they studied as happy and well adjusted, contrary to popular stereotypes.

It is argued here that these disparate views of older gay and lesbian people reflect two responses to the social construction of homosexuality as a negative identity. Some people internalize the negative discourse of what homosexuality means, while others reconstruct its meaning in positive and affirmative ways. The purpose of this chapter is to present a theory of successful aging. According to this theory, by achieving a positive lesbian or gay identity, certain skills, feelings, and attitudes are also acquired that function as resources facilitating adjustment to aging.

Using social construction theory, this chapter discusses a model of the diverse ways in which older lesbian women and gay men form their individual sexual identity. By highlighting the relationship between the social construction of lesbian and gay identities and the individual psychology of older gay and lesbian people who have worked to make their lives meaningful within the context of a particular socio-historical period of time, a theory of what it means to successfully grow old emerges.

This chapter begins with an explanation of social construction theory and presents a model of the relationship between the development of popular ideology and the individual psychology of identity formation. Next, the diverse ways in which older lesbian and gay people have made their lives meaningful and formed their identities are discussed using this model. Finally, a theory of successful aging is offered based on this analysis. Included in this discussion is the potential impact this theory has on the lives of younger lesbian and gay people. Recommendations for future research are also offered.

SOCIAL CONSTRUCTION THEORY
AND HOMOSEXUALITY

Social construction theory suggests that sexual functions and feelings have no intrinsic or essential meaning of their own, but are given meaning by the ideological systems developed for their explanation (Foucault, 1978; Weeks, 1977, 1981; Weinberg, 1983; Vance, 1984). This constructionist view contrasts with the more common essentialist view which conceptualizes sex as

> an overpowering force in the individual that shapes not only the personal but the social life as well. It is seen as a driving, instinctual force, whose characteristics are built into the biology of the human animal, which shapes human institutions and whose will must force its way out, whether in the form of direct sexual expression or, if blocked, in the form of perversion or neurosis. (Weeks, 1981, p. 2)

Foucault (1978) argues that certain knowledge is created through discourse (beliefs, theories, and ideas) that constructs our notions of reality and functions as a powerful mechanism of control over individual sexuality. According to this perspective, the great interest of medical authorities during the late nineteenth and early twentieth centuries in describing and documenting sexual behavior functioned to change popular constructions of homosexuality from the notion of sin to sickness (Foucault, 1978; Weeks, 1977, 1981). Weeks (1981) says that while meanings of homosexuality have varied throughout history, it was not until near the turn of the century that a distinction was made between homosexual behavior and homosexual roles and identities.

Homosexual identities fell under the category of what Foucault (1978) called the "perverse adult." Foucault (1978) argues that the construction of an identity known as the "perverse adult" generated control over individual sexuality not through repression, but through the creation of detailed taxonomies and definitions which set up specific notions of what homosexuality meant, and, hence, a limitation on the possibilities of creating individual meaning.

Weeks (1981) says that the notion of a homosexual person or identity (rather than simply homosexual behavior) served two inter-related functions. First, it provided clear definitions of acceptable and unacceptable behavior. In other words, it legitimized heterosex-ism. Heterosexism is defined as the assumption that everyone is heterosexual, and if they are not, that they should be heterosexual. As a socially constructed belief system, heterosexism facilitates the development of homophobia. Homophobia is a dimension of indi-vidual psychology and is defined as the irrational fear and hatred of homosexuality in one's self and in others (Weinberg, 1972). Sec-ond, the creation of something known as a homosexual identity facilitated the emergence of a homosexual subculture that allowed some people access to each other and created a system of resistance for challenging heterosexism.

Regarding this latter function, Foucault (1978) describes the re-verse discourse of resistance during the turn of the century:

> Homosexuality began to speak in its behalf, to demand that its legitimacy or "naturality" be acknowledged, often in the same vocabulary, using the same categories by which it was medi-cally disqualified. (p. 101)

In terms of individual psychology, heterosexism and the socially constructed notion of sickness associated with homosexual identities were resisted by some lesbian and gay people and clearly internal-ized by many others. Weeks (1981) comments on the relationships between heterosexist discourse and either affirmative resistance or internalized homophobia. He says,

> The striking feature of the "history of homosexuality" over the past hundred years or so is that the oppressive definition and defensive identities and structures have marched together. Control of sexual variations has inevitably reinforced and re-shaped rather than repressed homosexual behaviour. In terms of individual anxiety, induced guilt and suffering, the cost of moral regulation has often been high. But the result has been a complex and socially significant history of resistance and self-

definition which historians have hitherto all too easily ignored. (p. 117)

A PROPOSED MODEL FOR IDENTITY FORMATION

Resistance and internalized homophobia are two different responses for managing the heterosexist discourse that constructed the homosexual identity during the turn of the century into the mold of sickness. It is argued that for today's older lesbian and gay adults who grew up close to this particular socio-historical period, resistance or internalized homophobia are the end-points of a continuum of potential cognitive/behavioral responses to heterosexism. Associated with this cognitive/behavioral continuum is a range of potential emotional responses that each action can generate.

In the process of developing an identity as a lesbian or gay person, individuals must make meaning out of the messages they have received about homosexuality. This process of identity formation reflects the relationship between individual psychology and social construction. Given social norms, each person is challenged to interpret these in a way that results in a style of individual meaning for that person. There are a variety of ways in which this can be accomplished. The model presented here suggests that these styles can be described along a set of two continuums.

One continuum represents cognitive/behavioral responses. At one end-point of this continuum is the internalization of the pervasive heterosexist ideologies. This results in the belief that homosexuality is sick and/or otherwise negative. At the other end of the continuum is a cognitive/behavioral response to heterosexism which involves challenging or questioning the validity of these negative messages. As a result, there is a reconstruction of what it means to be lesbian or gay into something positive and affirmative. This affirmative reconstruction is the foundation of the reverse discourse of resistance described by Foucault (1978).

Associated with this cognitive/behavioral continuum is a set of corresponding affective responses. For example, if one end of the cognitive/behavioral continuum is the negative evaluation of homosexuality, the corresponding emotional response to these beliefs is internalized homophobia. Feelings of self-hatred, low self-esteem, and minimal or conditional self-acceptance may result. Associated with the other end of the cognitive/behavioral continuum (a gay or lesbian identity reconstructed as positive) are the feelings of increased self-acceptance, high self-esteem, personal empowerment, and self-affirmation.

The model of cognitive/behavioral and affective continua as processes involved in the development of homosexual identities corresponds with other developmental models regarding lesbian, gay, and bisexual identity formation (Cass, 1979; Coleman, 1981/82; Dank, 1971; Lee, 1977; Minton & McDonald, 1983/84). These models suggest that one early stage of acquiring a homosexual identity involves the internalization of the prevailing norms regarding homosexuality. The last stage, according to Minton and McDonald, involves the realization that social norms can be critically evaluated, and can result in the potential acceptance of and commitment to a positive gay identity. The notion of two continua that is offered here, while consistent with the other developmental models, highlights the significance of and relationship between cognitive/behavioral and affective processes.

THE IDENTITIES OF OLDER GAY
AND LESBIAN PEOPLE

Dawson (1982) estimates that there are currently at least 3.5 million lesbian and gay people over the age of sixty. As a group, one factor older gay and lesbian people have in common is living the major part of their lives through historical periods described as actively hostile and oppressive toward homosexuality (Almvig, 1982; Dawson, 1982; Kimmel, 1977, 1978). As indicated earlier, given this socio-historical context, a significant part of the lives of of older gay and lesbian people involves managing heterosexism. It is suggested here that there is a range of cognitive/behavioral and emotional responses in this process which characterize at least three distinct groups of older lesbian and gay adults.

Those older gay and lesbian people whose identities conform to the stereotype of being lonely, depressed, and alienated, represent people whose cognitive/behavioral responses to heterosexism are in the direction of extreme internalized homophobia. As a group, they represent one set of end-points on the two continua. This group is referred to here as "Stereotypic Older Lesbian and Gay People" and are the ones identified in the popular myths.

Those older gay and lesbian adults who are described in the research literature as psychologically well adjusted, vibrant, and adapting well to the aging process represent those whose response to heterosexism is one of reconstructing a positive and affirmative sense of self. They are at the other end of the two continua. This group is referred to as "Affirmative Older Lesbian and Gay People."

The mid-range of these continua reflect men and women who accommodate heterosexism by marginally accepting some aspects of homosexuality but still believing that heterosexuality is inherently better. This group is called "Passing Older Lesbian and Gay People." While some older adults in this middle group may, under certain circumstances, label themselves as lesbian or gay, they have a strong investment in either passing as non-gay or non-lesbian, or at least not appearing to be stereotypically lesbian or gay.

These three groups, which represent different places along the two continua reflect three possible styles of identity formation among older lesbian and gay people. Given that this model is based on continua, there are certainly many more styles that are possible. This model is offered to facilitate the conceptualization of a complex process and move toward developing a theory of successful aging. As such, this model is limited by its own linear structure. As Weinberg (1984) suggests, it is not clear whether social identities follow a linear pattern of development. Models constructed in this fashion are problematic because human beings are flexible, creative, and individualistic in their developmental patterns. Linear models tend to ignore human wavering and developmental patterns which occur at rates which are not uniform. As such, this model does not necessarily assume that there are no other developmental sequences that can be adapted and which result in the same or different outcomes as those suggested here.

Stereotypic Older Lesbian and Gay People

Those individuals described as "Stereotypic Older Lesbian and Gay People" conform to the popular negative images as a result of internalizing powerful heterosexist ideology. Dawson (1982) describes their common socio-historical context and those people who internalized the messages. He says,

> When today's older gays were young, they faced an unrelieved hostility towards homosexuality that was far more virulent than it is today. They were labeled "sick" by doctors, immoral by clergy, unfit by the military, and "a menace" by police and legislators. If identified as homosexual, they risked the loss of job, home, friends, and family. The need for secrecy caused an isolation which imperiled their most intimate relationships. And the greatest damage was done to those gay people who *believed* what society said about them, and thus lived in corrosive shame and self-loathing. (p. 5)

Kimmel (1977) describes the older gay men who were loners in his study, as living lives "of relatively little sexual intimacy. Typically these men had repressed their sexuality and were often fearful that their homosexuality would be discovered" (p. 388). Similarly, Almvig (1982) reports that while lesbianism has gained increased acceptance in recent years, many older lesbian women have led invisible lives of secrecy and personal danger.

The "Stereotypic" group may never associate with openly lesbian and gay people and, therefore, may have never had an opportunity to challenge their own heterosexist belief system. Having internalized extremely negative ideas about themselves, the men and women in this group may also lead lives punctuated by very little intimacy with non-lesbian and non-gay people as well. Isolation of this sort may reflect the assumption that "no one would want to be close with me."

The guilt, anxiety, self-hatred, and low self-esteem which characterize this group of older people may interfere with the process of forming meaningful relationships with others. Emotional distance in interpersonal relationships reflects the extent to which a poor relationship with oneself impacts on relationships with others. Other potential responses to the internalization of extreme homophobia include loneliness, despair, depression, and suicide. Those older lesbian and gay people whose lives are described as reflecting the internalized homophobia end-points of the identity continua, are also the people identified by popular stereotypes.

Passing Older Lesbian and Gay People

The group of people characterized by the mid-range of the continua are the "Passing Older Lesbian and Gay People." They believe the heterosexist sentiments with which they were raised while also acknowledging and marginally accepting their homosexuality. Many manage the conflict that results by marrying heterosexually and/or distancing themselves from anything defined as stereotypically lesbian or gay. Married older gay men in this group may be like Miller's (1979) "Trade Fathers" who engage in sexual encounters with other men but define these behaviors as only "genital urges." Historically, many gay men and lesbian women have married heterosexually assuming this was their only option for some degree of happiness (Martin & Lyon, 1973; Miller, 1979). Many of these older persons who are married may wait for their spouse to die before managing their sexuality in a different way (Kimmel, 1977; Martin & Lyon, 1979).

Not all gay and lesbian people who marry heterosexually are necessarily trying to pass and many are in fact happily married bisexual people. Wolf (1985) reports on twenty-six married couples in which the husband was bisexual. He describes these marriages as stable and that the partners were satisfied with the quality of their relationships in those marriages where the husband was open and not trying to "pass."

Matteson (1985) reports that more recent marriages involving a bisexual partner are made for positive reasons as opposed to an escape from or a cover for homosexuality. Matteson compared acknowledged and secretive bisexual marriages and argues that a positive homosexual identity can be developed in the former type of marriages. Matteson says that husbands in acknowledged bisexual marriages "not only accepted their homosexual experience but also affirmed and felt positive about being homosexual" (p. 167). These men have higher levels of self-acceptance in addition to their affirmative homosexual identity, according to Matteson.

It is argued here that "Passing Older Lesbian and Gay People" who are married are more likely to be in secret marriages. Their internalization of the negative messages about homosexuality would prevent them from sharing their sexual orientation with their marital partner, as well as other lesbian and gay people. Given the strength of heterosexist discourse, being secretive and trying to pass is probably more representative of older lesbian and gay people who marry than it is of younger lesbian and gay people. In fact, Matteson (1985) reports that husbands in secret bisexual marriages were older than husbands in acknowledged bisexual marriages.

Married or unmarried, older lesbian and gay adults who try to pass as heterosexual may have some contact with other lesbian and gay people or even form long-term same gender relationships. Much energy is spent, however, in appearing heterosexual. Compartmentalizing the various aspects of their lives is not uncommon among this group. Given marginal or conditional self-acceptance, there is a perceived need to live in two mutually exclusive worlds. This may result in a fragmented sense of self and a lack of authenticity in interpersonal relationships. According to Minton and McDonald (1983/84), "In choosing to hide an essential part of the self, individuals are left with a gnawing feeling that they are really valued for what others expect them to be rather than for who they really are" (p.102).

The energy of "passing" is reflected in very complicated styles of living that include separate bedrooms, phones, or even housing for the purpose of concealing same-sexed relationships. Martin and Lyon (1979) report on a lesbian couple who wrote:

> We are in our fifties, have been together for 18 years, but have never declared our love for each other in front of a third party. When we shut our doors at night we shut the world out. We have no gay friends that we know of. We are looking for companions, friendship and support, but in the lesbian organizations we've contacted we find only badge-wearing, drum-beating, foot-stomping social reformers. They consider our conservative life 'oppressed,' and we think of their way of life as 'flagrant.' There must be more like us, but how do we meet them? (pp. 140-141)

Emotional issues that are common among this group include heightened levels of anxiety and self-consciousness generated by the possibility of being "found out," conditional self-acceptance, and the absence of emotional supports during crises and times of need. According to Martin and Lyon (1979),

> Other women who had been in lesbian relationships of long standing poured out their grief over the death of a lover. These couples had no gay friends, and the surviving partner felt bereft and alone. True, some of them had straight friends or relatives who knew, but it had never been discussed. (p. 140)

Affirmative Older Lesbian and Gay People

Some older gay and lesbian people live lives of internalized homophobia; still others marginally accept their sexual orientation while accommodating heterosexist sentiments. However, as a social service provider for older lesbian and gay people, Dawson (1982) says while some "have suffered brutal repression for their sexuality and have been growing old in isolation . . . these people are very much in the minority" (p. 5). Dawson indicates that the largest percentage of older gay and lesbian adults with whom he works are vibrant, active, and independent.

"Affirmative Older lesbian and Gay People" manage heterosexism by reconstructing what it means to be gay or lesbian into something positive, and are reflected in the research literature. According to the literature, the vast majority of older lesbian and gay people studied have managed to attain a high level of self-acceptance and psychological adjustment, even within the hostile and unaccepting historical periods in which they were raised (Almvig, 1982; Berger, 1982a, 1982b; Francher & Henkin, 1973; Friend, 1980; Kelly, 1977; Kimmel, 1977, 1978; Raphael & Robinson, 1980; Weinberg, 1970).

Some of the "Affirmative Older Lesbian and Gay People" presented in the literature may be described as activists engaged in resistance. Foucault (1978) would argue that this resistance is an effort to gain self-empowerment by reconstructing the meaning of a homosexual identity–an attempt to control one's sexuality. These men and women may be engaged in a purposeful attempt to challenge and alter the prevailing and oppressive socio-sexual ideologies and hence their identity reflects this process.

While some may be engaged in resistance as an active attempt for social change, this is likely not true for all of the older lesbian and gay adults in this group. For others, self-acceptance and social integration may not be a conscious sociopolitical form of resistance. Rather, it may simply illustrate people living lives that comfortably reflect individualistically who they are without struggling to change dominant socio-sexual ideologies. In order to manage the conflicts that being lesbian or gay in a heterosexist environment generates, people in this group may reconstruct the meaning homosexuality has for them individually without being committed to a purposeful attempt for social change.

The disparate views of older lesbian and gay people reflect the end-points of the continua model described here. The popular image of older gay and lesbian adults as lonely, depressed, and isolated reflects the group described here as "Stereotypic Older Lesbian and Gay People." The image of older lesbian and gay adults provided by the research literature describes the group referred to here as "Affirmative Older Lesbian and Gay People." Paradoxically, both are consequences of responses to the social oppression of heterosexism.

At this time it is impossible to assess the extent to which any of these groups are represented in the general population. While a majority of those older lesbian and gay adults described in the literature do not conform to popular negative stereotypes, given sampling bias and limited access to older lesbian and gay people, conclusions about the general population of older lesbian and gay people must be accepted with caution.

Harry (1986) discusses the source-related sampling problems of research on gay men. Specifically, access to research samples is limited primarily to lesbian and gay people who have some degree of involvement in the gay and lesbian communities. Since the oldest and youngest age groups are least likely to be involved in these community resources, Harry (1986) argues that "our studies of homosexuality are largely studies of active gays, those for whom their sexual orientation constitutes a lifestyle" (p. 22). Given limitations of current research, those who internalize heterosexist discourse and whose sexuality may be repressed and/or altered as a result, are not easily accessible for research.

It is argued that the ways in which "Affirmative Older Lesbian and Gay People" reconstruct the meaning of homosexuality also results in growing old successfully. By examining more closely the ways in which they shape their lives and the effects these new ideologies have on events associated with growing old, a theory of successful aging is offered.

A THEORY OF SUCCESSFUL AGING

Even within the hostile and unaccepting historical periods in which they were raised, the vast majority of older lesbian and gay people are described in the research literature as psychologically well adjusted, partially defined as having high levels of self-acceptance and comfort with being lesbian or gay (Almvig, 1982; Berger, 1982a, 1982b; Francher & Henkin, 1973; Friend, 1980; Kelly, 1977; Kimmel, 1977, 1978; Raphael & Robinson, 1980; Weinberg, 1970). It is argued here that these older lesbian and gay adults (labeled here as "Affirmative Lesbian and Gay People") have achieved these high levels of adjustment, in part, as a response to the pervasive negative messages about homosexuality with which they were raised.

In fact, some authors suggest that as a result of managing what it means to be lesbian and gay in a heterosexist world, many lesbian and gay adults develop skills for managing their lives that facilitate their adjustment to the aging process (Francher & Henkin, 1973; Friend, 1980; Kimmel, 1977). A theory of successful aging is presented here to describe these processes.

If the purpose of theory is to explain or predict, the theory of successful aging offered here is valuable in its potential to explain whether or not a particular older lesbian or gay person has aged successfully. Given the individual's particular cognitive/behavioral and affective identity style, one should be able to predict the success of their aging with this theory. Aging can be viewed as falling along a continuum ranging from successful to unsuccessful. This theory argues that those lesbian and gay people who will age successfully are those whose identities are formed in the affirmative direction. Those lesbian and gay people who are in the passing or stereotypic groups of the identity continua will age less successfully according to this theory. This theory examines the process of successful aging which is a result of the reconstruction of homosexuality as something positive within the following contexts: individual psychology; social and interpersonal dimensions; and legal and political advocacy.

Individual Psychology

While sexual orientation appears to be established very early in the life span, it is during adolescence when lesbian and gay people become aware of their sexual feelings and perhaps not until later in life that they begin to manage what these feelings mean (Cass, 1979, 1983/84; Coleman, 1981/82; Martin, 1982). Kimmel (1978) describes this process as a potential crisis, and the extent to which it occurs early in the life span, it is

> one that can involve extensive family disruption, intensive feelings and sometimes alienation from the family–maybe one of the most significant a gay person will face. Once resolved, it may provide a perspective on major life crises and a sense of crisis competence that buffers the person against later crises. (p. 117)

This "crisis competence" is a dimension of individual psychology which is functional in terms of adjusting to aging. An example of crisis competence is reflected in the fact that part of managing issues associated with sexual orientation involves dealing with the potential loss of family and friends. Therefore, some older lesbian and gay people may have already developed psychological skills for dealing with the losses which occur when family and friends move away or die.

Another aspect of individual psychology which facilitates successful aging is challenging, in addition to homosexuality, other socially constructed identities. These identities include gender and old age.

Confronting rigid gender role definitions can be functional to the aging process (Dawson, 1982; Francher & Henkin, 1973; Friend, 1980, 1984). Given the prevalence of traditional gender role definitions, many older people today may have a limited number of skills for managing daily living. Rigid gender role definitions may mean that a recently widowed heterosexual woman may have to learn to read the electric meter, repair household appliances, or even balance the checkbook. A widowed heterosexual man may have to learn how to do laundry or cook.

If part of reconstructing the meaning of homosexuality as something positive involves confronting the somewhat arbitrary ways in which sexual feelings get defined as "appropriate" or "inappropriate," then this same analysis easily applies to the arbitrary construction of traditional gender role definitions. As a result, throughout their lives older lesbian and gay adults have had the potential for greater freedom to learn skills that may be considered non-traditional.

Greater flexibility in gender role definitions may allow older gay and lesbian people to have developed ways of taking care of themselves that feel comfortable and appropriate. These skills may be less developed among heterosexual women and men who may be used to having or expecting a husband or wife to care for them.

Challenging the arbitrary social construction of gender roles may be more threatening to the sexual identities of older heterosexual people than older lesbian and gay adults. Having addressed the issues of gender roles and sexual orientation earlier in life, many older lesbian and gay people may feel more comfortable when it comes to engaging in non-traditional gender role definitions.

In our culture what it means to be an older person is also the result of a particular set of socially constructed beliefs and attitudes. Attitudes about aging and older people generally are negative, and views of older women are frequently more negative than those of older men (Bennett & Eckman, 1973; Francher, 1962; Green, 1981; Palmore, 1971; Sontag, 1975).

Ageism, which refers to this set of negative attitudes, describes the overt discrimination which occurs based simply on age (Schaie & Geiwitz, 1982). Ageism also generates "gerontophobia," the irrational fear of aging and the elderly (J. Turner, personal communication, May 1985). Ageist assumptions include the beliefs that the elderly are all unproductive, senile, incompetent, overly dependent, asexual, and unattractive. Given that these stereotypes and myths are the foundation for many people's attitudes regarding older people and the aging process, ageism and gerontophobia can be challenged and reconstructed in positive and affirmative ways in much the same way as homosexuality and gender.

Access to diverse models of what it means to be an older person is essential to this process of challenging stereotypes. These models include older people who are active, productive, sexual, and self-determining individuals. A diversity of styles of adjusting to aging provides evidence that stereotypical images are arbitrarily constructed and have the potential for change.

Older gay and lesbian people who have had experience in reconstructing the arbitrary definitions of what homosexuality and gender mean, are also more likely to be able to transfer these affirmative processes to their identities as older people.

Crisis competence, flexibility in gender role, and reconstructing the personal meanings of homosexuality and aging so they are positive have powerful effects on the individual psychology of older lesbian and gay people. At a cognitive level there is the adoption of a set of beliefs that affirm personal worth. At a behavioral level, adaptive skills that promote both daily living and a sense of competence and empowerment are developed. As previously suggested, these cognitive and behavioral dimensions impact positively on emotional factors such as self-acceptance and self-esteem. According to this theory of successful aging, these factors of individual psychology function to promote adjustment to the aging process in the ways described.

Those lesbian and gay people who are either passing or have internalized negative and stereotypic messages are less likely to have developed the type of crisis competence and gender role flexibility that "Affirmative Older Lesbian and Gay People" have developed. If crisis competence as an aspect of individual psychology is based on resolving potential losses and conflicts, it is not clear whether the "passing" and "stereotypic" groups have indeed come to this stage of resolution. Additionally, by definition, "passing" and "stereotypic" older lesbian and gay people have not reconstructed the negative social constructions of homosexuality. Therefore, they may be less likely to have challenged the arbitrary constructions of gender and old age as well.

Social and Interpersonal Dimensions

Reconstructing the meaning of homosexuality as positive involves social and interpersonal dimensions as well as individual psychological process. Family, friends, and community can all be sources of affirming homosexuality as positive in a way that facilitates successful aging.

Dawson (1982) reports that many adults grow old believing that their children or extended family will provide for them in their old age. With greater longevity and current changes in family patterns, this type of family support for the elderly is not ensured. Dawson (1982) reports that "gay people have been less likely to assume that their families would provide for them in old age" (p. 6) and are more likely to have carefully planned for their own future security. Through considering real or imagined loss of family support earlier in life, older gay and lesbian people may be better prepared for the realities of old age.

Another potential resource in adjusting to old age is the re-definition of family which occurs for many lesbian and gay people. Francher and Henkin (1973) report in their study that for older gay men who lost family support, this support was replaced with a strong network of friendships. Bell and Weinberg (1978) describe these friendship circles as a "surrogate family." Almvig (1982) says, " 'family' for the older lesbian can be made up of a current lover, past lovers and friends, besides her own blood-line family" (p. 148).

Likewise, rather than simply replacing lost family support with the support of friends, Friend (1980) reports that in his sample there was overall gain of *reinforcing* family supports with those of friends. According to Friend, many gay men expected to lose the support of family when they came out, but this did not happen. He concludes that, "This in turn facilitates adjustment for older gay men and gives them a broad network on which to rely in times of instrumental or socio-emotional need" (Friend, 1980, p. 244).

The resources provided by all of these family arrangements can also be strengthened by the presence of an empowering community. In many places, the lesbian and gay communities offer many opportunities for cultural, social, political, and religious activity and support that are open to older people. In larger urban areas, there may even be intergenerational organizations like the New York based Senior Action in a Gay Environment (SAGE), which provides a variety of social and support services specifically for older lesbian and gay adults.

Intergenerational associations in groups such as SAGE are important in that "Affirmative Older Lesbian and Gay People" can serve as role models for younger gay and lesbian people. It has been argued that the negative and stereotypic images of older lesbian and gay adults have functioned as a form of social control to keep younger lesbian and gay people from "choosing" an openly lesbian or gay lifestyle or developing greater self-acceptance (Friend, 1980, 1984; Kimmel, 1978). Kimmel (1978) writes:

> Since development of a positive identity involves a sense of the future course of that identity, the lack of information about gay adult development has allowed the stigma of homosexuality to intertwine with the stereotypes about aging in our society. Thus, highly negative views of gay aging have been produced, leading to even greater difficulty in the development of a positive gay identity among young homosexuals. Fears about aging as a gay person have been used to dissuade young people from accepting their homosexuality, further hindering self-acceptance. (p. 114)

These intergenerational associations can be powerful sources of socioemotional support and strength for both the younger and the older people involved. For the older people, they may also provide a sense of generativeness or guiding of the next generation (Erikson, 1963). For the younger people they can also provide a sense of hope for the future, a model for achieving one's goals, and a clear sense of the possibilities associated with developing a positive lesbian or gay identity.

The "stereotypic" group, given their alienation from others, are least likely to develop any type of surrogate family system. Likewise, their low self-esteem may also preclude careful and thoughtful financial and emotional planning for their own future. Those who are "passing" and invested in being perceived as heterosexual will have fewer non-heterosexual family arrangements and non-heterosexual community involvements. Heterosexually married, the older lesbian or gay adult faces the same financial and emotional uncertainties as the older heterosexual person where support is not ensured.

Legal and Political Advocacy

In the process of achieving an affirmative lesbian or gay identity, many older people have developed advocacy skills for managing heterosexism and ageism in a direct fashion. Others familiarize themselves with advocacy organizations which provide them additional resources for ensuring their rights. For example, the difficulties of managing terminal or chronic illness may be magnified by the policies of intensive care units which exclude everyone except next of kin (Kimmel, 1978; Martin & Lyon, 1979). The attitudes of nursing staff and physicians may create an unaccepting atmosphere (Anderson, 1981; Lief, 1973) and the expression of affection between lovers and/or same-sex friends may be discouraged (Weinberg, 1982). An openly lesbian or gay relationship may be used by family members as evidence of senility in contesting a will. Being acknowledged as next of kin or as legal spouse can be complicated when writing wills, making funeral arrangements, or participating in other aspects of the mourning process. All of these issues require some knowledge of the legal and health care systems and can be managed by either addressing them in advance of a crisis or having another person act as a legal or social advocate. Older lesbian and gay people who have a comprehensive support system which includes family, friends, and community are more likely to have the resources for managing these issues.

In addition to health care, areas where the elderly face discrimination include housing, employment, and traditional social service systems. As a result of crisis competency, supportive friends, family, and community, as well as positions of advocacy, "Affirmative Older Lesbian and Gay People" may have certain resources for ensuring their rights that many other older people have not developed.

Older lesbian and gay people described as "stereotypic" or "passing" are not only unlikely to seek out or participate in legal and political advocacy, but they are unlikely even to perceive the need for this type of action. Advocacy is based on the belief of supporting and ensuring human rights. Self-hatred, low self-esteem, and the general "I'm not worth it" attitude of the "stereotypic" group is in conflict with the assumptions of advocacy. Persons in the "passing" group would actually distance themselves from any form of advocacy that might be lesbian or gay identified.

The model presented here suggests that developing an affirmative identity as a gay or lesbian person involves restructuring the meaning of homosexuality as something positive. As a result of this process, certain attitudes, skills, and emotional resources are gained that function to promote successful aging according to this theory. These resources include: individual psychological processes, social and interpersonal dimensions, and legal and political advocacy.

This theory of successful aging has clear value for mental health practitioners and policymakers, as well as researchers. This theory's ability to predict successful aging provides specific areas for assessment in health care and program planning. By more clearly explaining and describing the diverse ways in which lesbian and gay people age, and the relationship between successful aging and identity formation, greater focus is provided for future research.

RECOMMENDATIONS AND CONCLUSIONS

Based on the proposed model and theory, several recommendations for future research emerge. The model of identity formation along two corresponding continua presented here contends that those who positively reconstruct the meaning of homosexuality develop resources which promote successful aging. The theory of successful aging described here delineates the specific areas in which these resources are developed.

Additional research is needed in order to verify and refine the theory presented here. Research that examines the degree to which the factors within each area outlined by the theory contribute individually and collectively to adjustment to the aging process is necessary. Experimental research of this type would not only help to validate the theory, but provide necessary information regarding a significant segment of the older adult population.

The model of identity formation contends that "stereotypic" and "passing" older lesbian and gay adults are least represented in the research literature and additional information regarding these groups is necessary. As such, research that examines special problems, needs, and potential resources of these groups, as well as information regarding how to safely identify them within their current contexts is very important. Research that examines attitudes regarding aging among younger lesbian and gay people who have contact with older gay and lesbian people who may or may not serve as role models is necessary.

Cohort analyses that examine the management of heterosexism by older gay and lesbian adults versus younger gay and lesbian people are also needed. The age groups could be further broken down into the three groups described here which represent different places on the identity continuums. The type of research that examines differences between groups of older and younger lesbian and gay people as a result of aging or as a result of living in different socio-historical periods would not only provide valuable information about the lives of these women and men, but also about the transhistorical and context-specific qualities of heterosexism. Given the Supreme Court ruling (*Bowers v. Hardwick,* 1986), which upheld the State of Georgia's sodomy law, and the ever-growing fears about AIDS, understanding the extent to which these events are unique or transhistorical would be useful for developing strategies to challenge their potentially oppressive outcomes.

A history of managing heterosexism is a significant factor which has influenced the ways in which the identities of older lesbian and gay people have been constructed. Some of these people have internalized these negative ideologies; others have accommodated to them, while still others have shaped their lives around a reconstructed set of positive and affirmative beliefs. The power of older gay and lesbian adults to challenge the negative messages about homosexuality and to create new meanings of affirmation and happiness provides an important lesson. Not only are these older lesbian and gay adults potentially significant role models for younger lesbian and gay people, but they may also offer valuable insights for all people regarding what it means to grow old in ways which promote independence, self-determination, and a sense of engaging in life.

APPENDIX A: ADVERTISEMENTS

HOW MUCH LONGER WILL YOU PERMIT SOCIETY TO CLOSE ITS EYES TO GAYS AND LESBIANS WHO ARE FORTY AND OLDER?

Dr. Raymond M. Berger needs to hear from you if you are gay/lesbian and forty or older.

You can help in two ways: (1) By filling out a questionnaire that will take approximately 25 minutes to complete. Anonymously. Confidentially. No records of names kept, or even asked. (2) We also need a few to participate in in-depth interviews at your convenience. We will meet at a place of your choice.

If you are willing to answer the questionnaire, be interviewed, or both, please call Dr. Berger or Rosita Perez at [phone number]. If they are not in, please leave a first name and number and your call WILL be returned.

Share with us. Without you, this study cannot be done.

[Advertisement that appeared in publications of local homosexual groups.]

HOW MUCH LONGER WILL YOU PERMIT SOCIETY TO CLOSE ITS EYES TO GAYS AND LESBIANS WHO ARE GRAY?

A pilot project is now being conducted by Raymond M. Berger, PhD, to study the gay/lesbian, *forty and older.* Basically, this study addresses the following questions:

1. The lack of descriptive information about this group–What are you like?
2. How have you adjusted to growing older?

Today there are over twenty million older Americans. As many as two million of these older people are homosexual. Yet, when was the last time you heard the needs of the older gay/lesbian discussed? The lack of attention directed toward the older homosexuals in our communities is reflected in the limited agency services and other community resources, as well as in research.

In order to compile the necessary data, your help is needed. If you are forty or older and are gay or lesbian, you can help by filling out a questionnaire, which will take about 25-30 minutes. You remain anonymous. No records of names are kept, or even asked. Your confidentiality is assured. A few older men and women will also be asked to participate in in-depth interviews at their convenience. The interview will last about 1 1/2 hours. You may choose to fill out the questionnaire only. Either way, by helping us today, you will be preparing the way for more comprehensive studies that will bring older gays and lesbians into the mainstream of social services planning and delivery. Aren't you tired of society pretending you don't exist?

Dr. Berger and his research associate, Rosita Perez, will be present at a [local gay organization] meeting in the near future to ask you to fill out a questionnaire or volunteer to be interviewed.

For more information, please call Dr. Berger or Rosita Perez at [phone number]. Is "gay" and "gray" good? Only you can possibly know. Share with us. Our work depends on your interest today so that others will be interested tomorrow.

Thank you!

[Article that appeared in publications of local homosexual groups.]

APPENDIX B: INTERVIEW SCHEDULE

ADAPTATION TO AGING:
THE HOMOSEXUAL FEMALE AND MALE

Instructions to Interview Respondents

(*Interviewer:* Read the following to each respondent.)

This interview will last about an hour to an hour and a half. The interview is part of a study being conducted by Dr. Raymond Berger at [University]. The purpose of the study is to find out what gay men and women over the age of forty are like, and how they have adjusted to growing older.

I will be asking you questions about your current and past life, your family, your experiences in "coming out," and your feelings about growing older, as you observed on the interview schedule you have just read. We are aware that you may have already answered many of these questions on the written questionnaire. We are asking you to answer some of the questions again in order to allow you to elaborate a little more on questions that are difficult to answer with a "Yes" or "No." Your help in answering these questions is very important to us because little is currently known about gay people over the age of forty.

Although I will write your name down, please be assured that this interview and the questionnaire you have completed (will complete) are strictly confidential.

May I have your permission to tape record our discussion? (Interviewer: Explain need for tape recorder and set it up while he/she looks through the interview schedule.)

All tapes and materials will be placed in a locked cabinet, and all names will be removed from these materials at the end of the study. The final results will be presented in such a way that no individual can be identified.

You should also know that your participation in this study is completely voluntary.

Before we begin, do you have any questions?

(*Interviewer:* EXPLAIN INFORMED CONSENT FORM
TO RESPONDENT)

1. SOCIAL LIFE:
Will you tell me about your current social life?
- How many of your friends are gay/straight?
- How much of your leisure time do you spend socializing with other gays/straights?
- What proportion of your leisure-time socializing is with people (gay or non-gay) who are within ten years of your age or older?
- Are you satisfied with your current social life?
If no, How could it be improved?

2. INVOLVEMENT WITH HOMOSEXUAL COMMUNITY:
- Are you involved with any gay organizations such as local gay rights groups, gay religious groups like the Metropolitan Community Church, etc.? How do you feel about these organizations?
- Do you ever go to gay bars, bathhouses, beaches, or places known as gay "cruising" areas?
Why or why not?
If yes, How often?
How do you feel about these places?

3. INVOLVEMENT WITH FAMILY:
I would like to know about members of your *immediate* family–spouse, parents, children, or siblings. How many brothers and sisters do you have (living or dead)? What is your birth order? Eldest? Youngest?
- Do you have a spouse, parents, children, or siblings who are living?
- At the present time, are you regularly in touch?
- Do they know you are gay? *If yes or no,* How does this affect the relationship?

4. RETIREMENT STATUS:
- At the present time are you retired or partially retired?
If yes or no, How do you feel about this?

5. EXCLUSIVE RELATIONSHIPS:
- Do you currently have a lover?
  If yes, What is this relationship like?
  Do you live together?
  What things do you do together/apart?
- Have you had a lover sometime in the past?
  (*Interviewer:* Repeat same two questions as above.)
- How did the relationship end?

6. COMING OUT:
  Now I would like to ask you some questions about coming out.
- What does "coming out" mean to you?
- Can you tell me about your first sexual experience with a member of your own sex? (I am referring to any sexual experience with another person or persons, even if there was no orgasm.)
  How old were you? How old was the other person? What was your relationship to your partner(s)–friend, relative, stranger, etc.?
- When did you first realize you were attracted to the same sex? When did you first admit to yourself that you were gay? How did you feel about this?
  Did you discuss it with others? *If yes,* With whom?
- When did you first get to know other gay people? What was it like being a homosexual when you first came out?

7. SEX LIFE:
  May I ask you about your current sex life? I am interested in any sexual activity with another person or persons over the past six months.
- Over the past six months, how often have you had sexual relations? What was your relationship to your partner(s)–lover, friend, stranger, etc.?
  (If respondent has *not* had sexual relations in the past six months, rephrase the two questions below as appropriate.)
- How is your sex life different now from when you were younger?
- Overall, how satisfied are you with your sex life over the past six months?
  If not satisfied, How could it be different?

8. INTERGENERATIONAL ATTITUDES:
  I would like your opinion about one aspect of the gay community. When I say "gay community" I am referring to *both* men and women.

- In your estimation, how do gays under thirty feel about gays over forty years of age?
- How do gays over forty feel about gays under thirty years of age?
- How do you feel about gays under thirty?

9. DISCRIMINATION–SEXUAL PREFERENCE:
- Do you feel you have ever been discriminated against because of your homosexuality? For instance, have you lost or been denied a job, an apartment, a service, etc.?
  If yes, When? What were the circumstances?
  What did you do about it?

10. DISCRIMINATION–AGE:
- Do you feel you have ever been discriminated against because of your age? In the gay community or anywhere else?
  If yes, When? What were the circumstances?
  What did you do about it?

11. ADAPTATION:
A major purpose of this study is to find out what makes older gays/lesbians adjust well to growing older.
- In your opinion, what things make a gay/lesbian over the age of forty adjust well to growing older?
- What can a homosexual person do to help him (her) self adjust to growing older?

12. ACCOMPLISHMENT:
I would like you to think back over your life.
- What has been the most important accomplishment of your life?

13. LEAST SATISFACTION:
- What aspect of your life has been *least* satisfying to you?

14. GROWING OLDER:
- What is the worst thing about growing older?
  What are some other negative aspects of growing older?
- What is the best thing about growing older?
  What are some other positive aspects of growing older?

15. YOU HAVE BEEN VERY HELPFUL. IS THERE ANYTHING ELSE YOU'D LIKE TO TELL OR ASK ME? THANK YOU FOR ALLOWING ME TO INTERVIEW YOU.

APPENDIX C: QUESTIONNAIRE

QUESTIONNAIRE STUDY ON HOMOSEXUALITY AND AGING

This questionnaire will take 25 to 30 minutes to complete. Before you complete the questionnaire, you should know the answers to the following questions.

1. Who is conducting this study?
The study is sponsored by the [University]. The project director is Dr. Raymond M. Berger. If you have any questions about the study, or if you want a copy of the results, call Dr. Berger or research associate Rosita Perez at [phone number].

2. Will my answers be confidential?
Yes. Please do not write your name anywhere on these forms. Your completed questionnaire will be placed in a locked cabinet. The final results will be presented in summary form so that no individual can be identified.

3. Am I required to complete the questionnaire?
Absolutely not. You may be asked to complete the questionnaire by a social service organization or some other group. If this is the case, the services you receive from this group will in no way be affected by your decision to participate or not. You may refuse to continue completing the questionnaire at any time.

4. Who should answer this questionnaire?
You should answer this questionnaire if you are a gay man, or lesbian, over the age of forty. In this questionnaire, the word "homosexual" refers to both women and men.

5. How will this study be used?
This study will be used to shed some light on a group of people who have been ignored and sometimes abused, older gay men and lesbians; therefore, we urge you to help us by carefully completing this questionnaire.

Remember, do not write your name anywhere on this questionnaire.

Please place a check mark here to indicate that you have read this page.

Thank you very much!   Place check here
_____

INFORMED CONSENT FORM

NUMBER: __ __ __ __

In order to insure your rights, we would like to give you the opportunity to certify that you have participated in this study.

This is for your benefit. If you wish, you may devise a four-digit number that we will keep in our records. You may write this number at both the top and bottom of this page. After you've done this, detach the number at the bottom and retain for your records.

Do this only if you wish to be able to certify that you filled out a questionnaire.

We do not keep any records of names.

------------------------ (cut) ------------------------

NUMBER: __ __ __ __

If you have any questions about this study, call Rosita Perez or Raymond Berger at [phone number].

INDICATE THE EXTENT TO WHICH YOU AGREE THAT THE STATE-MENTS BELOW CHARACTERIZE YOU AND YOUR FEELINGS.

AFTER READING EACH STATEMENT:

CIRCLE:	*IF YOU:*
SA	STRONGLY AGREE
A	AGREE
?	ARE NOT SURE
D	DISAGREE
SD	STRONGLY DISAGREE

1. I am not as happy as others seem to be. SA A ? D SD

2. I wish I could have more respect for myself. SA A ? D SD

3. In the gay/lesbian community young people sometimes take advantage of older people. SA A ? D SD

4. In gay/lesbian bars, clubs, and bathhouses older patrons are just as welcome as younger ones. SA A ? D SD

5. I feel that I'm a person of worth, at least on an equal plane with others. 5A A ? D SD

6. I get a lot of fun out of life. SA A ? D SD

7. All in all, I am inclined to feel that I am a failure. SA A ? D SD

8. On the whole, I am satisfied with myself. SA A ? D SD

9. I take a positive attitude toward myself. SA A ? D SD

10. On the whole, I think I am quite a happy person. SA A ? D SD

11. Most young homosexuals would like to associate with older homosexuals. SA A ? D SD

12. I certainly feel useless at times. SA A ? D SD

13. In general, I feel in low spirits most of
    the time.   SA   A   ?   D   SD

14. I often feel downcast and dejected.   SA   A   ?   D   SD

15. I feel that I have a number of good
    qualities.   SA   A   ?   D   SD

16. Young people in the homosexual
    community are often eager to make
    friends with older homosexuals.   SA   A   ?   D   SD

17. I wish I were not homosexual.   SA   A   ?   D   SD

18. I would not want to give up my
    homosexuality even if I could.   SA   A   ?   D   SD

19. In the gay/lesbian community most
    young people do not want to make
    friends with an older person.   SA   A   ?   D   SD

20. At times I think I am no good at all.   SA   A   ?   D   SD

21. I am able to do things as well as most
    other people.   SA   A   ?   D   SD

22. Most young homosexuals think that older
    homosexuals are pretty dull.   SA   A   ?   D   SD

23. I do not like to associate socially with a
    person who has a reputation (among
    heterosexuals) of being homosexual.   SA   A   ?   D   SD

24. I do not care who knows about my
    homosexuality.   SA   A   ?   D   SD

25. I would not mind being seen in public
    with a person who has the reputation
    (among heterosexuals) of being
    homosexual.   SA   A   ?   D   SD

26. I feel I do not have much to be proud of. SA   A   ?   D   SD

FOR EACH OF THE FOLLOWING QUESTIONS, PLEASE CIRCLE ONE *AND ONLY ONE* LETTER.

27. Taking all things together, how would you say things are these days? Would you say you are:
    a. Very happy
    b. Pretty happy
    c. Not too happy
    d. Very unhappy

28. Which category best describes your social situation among gay people?
    a. Not really known among gay people
    b. Not really a part of the group
    c. Well accepted
    d. Popular socially
    e. Very popular socially

29. Of all your current friends, how many are (to your knowledge) gay/lesbian?
    a. All
    b. Most
    c. About half
    d. Only a few
    e. None

30. What proportion of your leisure-time socializing is with gay/lesbian people?
    a. All
    b. Most
    c. About half
    d. Only a small amount
    e. None

31. What proportion of your leisure-time socializing is with people (homosexual or heterosexual) who are within ten years of your age or older?
    a. All
    b. Most
    c. About half
    d. Only a small amount
    e. None

32. Now think about all the people whom you would call *friends*.

    Do not include family members.

Specify the exact number of people whom you consider to be
your *friends.*
(e.g., 0, 1, 2, 3, 4, . . .)   _____
                                       NUMBER

Of these friends, write the number that are   _____
gay/lesbian . . .   NUMBER

AND

Write the number that are more than twenty
years younger than you are. . .   _____
                                        NUMBER

33. Of the following gay/lesbian organizations, *check* how
    frequently you attend activities or utilize services of that
    organization.

	More than once a week	About once a week	About once every other week	About once a month	About once every few months	Never
Political/social service organizations*						
Homosexual bars and/or bathhouses						
Homosexual religious organizations: MCC, MCS, Dignity, Integrity, Lutherans Concerned, etc.						
Homosexual social clubs or dinner clubs**						
Other (Specify) ____						

  * A list of political and social organizations appeared here, but has been omitted in order
    to protect anonymity of respondents.
 ** There were several such clubs in the area where the study took place, including a
    private dinner club, and a club whose interest was in leather clothing and motorcycles.

34. Of the following people check *how many* suspect or know that you are gay/lesbian:

	Not appli-cable	All	Most	More than half	About half	Less than half	Only a few	None
Straight people whom you know								
Relatives (spouse-parents-siblings-children, etc.)								
Work associates								
People whom *you* know are gay/les-bian								

35. HOW OFTEN DO THE FOLLOWING THINGS HAPPEN TO YOU? (For each question, place a check under the appropriate answer.)

	Nearly all the time	Pretty often	Not very much	Never
a. Do you ever have any trouble getting to sleep or staying asleep?				
b. Have you ever been bothered by nervousness, feeling fidgety and tense?				
c. Are you ever troubled by headaches or pains in the head?				
d. Do you have loss of appetite?				
e. How often are you bothered by having an upset stomach?				
f. Do you find it difficult to get up in the morning?				

	Many times	Some- times	Hardly ever	Never
g. Have you ever been bothered by shortness of breath when you were not exercising or working hard?	___	___	___	___
h. Have you ever been bothered by your heart beating hard?	___	___	___	___
i. Do you ever drink more than you should?	___	___	___	___
j. Have you ever had spells of dizziness?	___	___	___	___
k. Are you ever bothered by nightmares?	___	___	___	___
l. Do you tend to lose weight when you have something important bothering you?	___	___	___	___
m. Do your hands ever tremble enough to bother you?	___	___	___	___
n. Are you troubled by your hands sweating so that you feel damp and clammy?	___	___	___	___
o. Have there ever been times when you couldn't take care of things because you just couldn't get going?	___	___	___	___

36. FOR THE FOLLOWING QUESTIONS, PLEASE CHECK WHETHER YOU MAINLY AGREE, MAINLY DISAGREE, OR ARE NOT SURE. PLEASE ANSWER ALL QUESTIONS.

	Agree	Disagree	Not sure
As I grow older, things seem better than I thought they would be.	___	___	___
I have gotten more of the breaks in life than most of the people I know.	___	___	___
This is the dreariest time of my life.	___	___	___

I am just as happy as when I was
younger.   ___   ___   ___

These are the best years of my life.   ___   ___   ___

Most of the things I do are boring or
monotonous.   ___   ___   ___

The things I do are as interesting to me
as they ever were.   ___   ___   ___

As I look back on my life, I am fairly
well satisfied.   ___   ___   ___

I have made plans for things I'll be
doing a month or a year from now.   ___   ___   ___

When I think back over my life, I didn't
get most of the important things I
wanted.   ___   ___   ___

Compared to other people, I get down
in the dumps too often.   ___   ___   ___

I've gotten pretty much what I expected
out of life.   ___   ___   ___

In spite of what some people say, the lot
of the average person is getting worse,
not better.   ___   ___   ___

FOR EACH OF THE FOLLOWING QUESTIONS, PLEASE
CIRCLE ONE AND ONLY ONE LETTER.

37. Does knowing that you are homosexual "weigh on your mind"
(make you feel guilty, depressed, anxious, or ashamed)?
   a. A great deal
   b. Somewhat
   c. Not very much
   d. Not at all

38. At the present time do you ever experience shame, guilt, or anxiety after
having sexual (homosexual) relations?
   a. Nearly always
   b. Pretty often
   c. Not very much
   d. Never

39. Does the thought of growing old occur to you?
    a. Never
    b. Very infrequently
    c. Sometimes
    d. Often
    e. Constantly

40. Do you worry about growing old?
    a. Never
    b. Very infrequently
    c. Sometimes
    d. Often
    e. Constantly

41. Does the thought of dying occur to you?
    a. Never
    b. Very infrequently
    c. Sometimes
    d. Often
    e. Constantly

42. Do you worry about dying?
    a. Never
    b. Very infrequently
    c. Sometimes
    d. Often
    e. Constantly

43. At the present time, how is your health?
    a. Excellent
    b. Good
    c. Fair
    d. Poor

44. REGARDING YOUR HOMOSEXUALITY: *CIRCLE ONE:*

    a. In the past have you ever received counseling from a mental health pro-
    professional such as a psychiatrist, psychologist, social worker, or
    counselor?

                                              Yes   No

    b. Are you presently receiving such counseling?

                                              Yes   No

If no, answer "c" and "d"

c. Would you like to obtain such counseling regarding your homosexuality?

Yes   No

d. Have you ever had (or are you presently receiving) counseling for reasons *other than* your homosexuality?

Yes   No

45. At the *present* time, are another gay/lesbian person and yourself limiting your sexual relationships primarily to each other?
   a. No
   b. Yes, we have been for less than a month
   c. Yes, we have been for one to six months
   d. Yes, we have been for six months to a year
   e. Yes, we have been for more than a year

46. At some time *in the past,* did another gay/lesbian person and yourself limit your sexual relationships primarily to each other? (This should refer to a different relationship than the one considered in the previous question.)
   a. No
   b. Yes, for less than a month
   c. Yes, for between one and six months
   d. Yes, for between six months and a year
   e. Yes, for more than a year

47. Over the *last six months*, how often, on the average, have you had sexual relations with a member of your *own* sex?
   a. Never
   b. Once a month or less
   c. More than once, but less than four times a month
   d. About once a week
   e. More than once a week, up to twice a week
   f. Three times or more a week

FOR QUESTION #47:

How many partners did this involve in addition to yourself?
   a. Only one
   b. Two
   c. Three
   d. More than three
   e. I have not had sexual relations with a member of my own sex in the last six months.

48. Over the *last six months*, how often, on the average, have you had sexual relations with a member of the *opposite* sex?
    a. Never
    b. Once a month or less
    c. More than once, but less than four times a month
    d. About once a week
    e. More than once a week, up to twice a week
    f. Three times or more a week

    FOR THE ABOVE QUESTION, HOW MANY PARTNERS BESIDES YOURSELF DID THIS INVOLVE?

    a. Only one
    b. Two
    c. Three
    d. More than three
    e. I have not had sexual relations with a member of the opposite sex in the last six months.

49. Overall, how satisfied are you with your sex life *over the last six months?*
    a. Very unsatisfied
    b. Unsatisfied
    c. Somewhat satisfied
    d. Satisfied
    e. Very satisfied

50. *At the present time* how would you rate your sexual orientation?
    a. Exclusively heterosexual
    b. Primarily heterosexual, only slightly homosexual
    c. Primarily heterosexual, but more than slightly homosexual
    d. Just about equally homosexual and heterosexual
    e. Primarily homosexual, but more than slightly heterosexual
    f. Primarily homosexual, only slightly heterosexual
    g. Exclusively homosexual

51. How old are you? (Indicate the number of years.) _____

52. What kind of work do you do for a living? What is your job called, what kind of business or industry do you work in, and *what do you do?*

For example: "I was a sales clerk, waited on customers in a department store" or "doctor of internal medicine in private practice."

(If you are fully retired, indicate what your job was right before you retired.)

ANSWER HERE: _____

_____

_____

53. At the present time are you:
   a. Fully retired
   b. Partially retired
   c. Not retired

   ANSWER THE NEXT QUESTION IF YOU ARE CURRENTLY RETIRED OR PARTIALLY RETIRED.

54. In general, how do you feel about your retirement?
   a. I enjoy being retired.
   b. I have no feelings about retirement one way or the other.
   c. I would prefer *not* being retired.

55. What is your sex?
   a. Male
   b. Female

56. PLEASE CHECK YOUR APPROPRIATE ETHNIC IDENTITY:

   a. _____ ASIAN (includes Japanese, Chinese, Korean, Filipino descent)

   b. _____ BLACK, NON-HISPANIC (includes Afro-American, Jamaican, Trinidadian, West Indian, and African descent)

   c. _____ HISPANIC (includes Mexican, Puerto Rican, Cuban, Latin American, or Spanish descent regardless of race)

   d. _____ INDIAN, AMERICAN

   e. _____ WHITE, NON-HISPANIC

   f. _____ OTHER (includes others not covered above and should include Pakistani and East Indian descent, Aleut, Eskimo, Malayan, Thai and Vietnamese)

57. With whom do you currently live?
    a. Alone
    b. With your lover only
    c. With your lover and roommate(s)
    d. With roommate(s) only
    e. With your family only (spouse, children, relatives)
    f. Other (please explain)_____

58. At the present time what is your *legal* marital status?
    a. Never married
    b. Married
    c. Divorced
    d. Separated
    e. Widowed

59. What is the highest level of education you have completed?
    a. Grade school
    b. High school
    c. Some college
    d. College graduate
    e. Master's degree
    f. PhD, MD, or other advanced degree

60. How would you describe your political views?
    a. Very liberal or radical
    b. Somewhat liberal
    c. Moderate
    d. Somewhat conservative
    e. Very conservative

61. At the present time, what is your yearly income?
    a. Less than $3,000
    b. $3,000-$5,999
    c. $6,000-$8,999
    d. $9,000-$11,999
    e. $12,000-$14,999
    f. $15,000-$18,000
    g. Over $18,000

62. What is your present religious preference?
    a. No religious preference, atheist, or agnostic
    b. Protestant
    c. Roman Catholic

d. Jewish
e. Other (please specify) _____

THANK YOU VERY MUCH FOR ANSWERING THIS
QUESTIONNAIRE.

REFERENCES

PART I AND PART II

Adelman, M. (1991). Stigma, gay lifestyles, and adjustment to aging: A study of later-life gay men and lesbians. In J. A. Lee (Ed.), *Gay midlife and maturity* (pp. 7-32). New York: Harrington Park Press.

Allen, C. (1961). The aging homosexual. In I. Rubin (Ed.), *The third sex*. New York: New Book.

Atchley, R. C. (1977). *The social forces in later life*. 2nd ed. Belmont, CA: Wadsworth.

Becker, H. S. (1963). *Outsiders: Studies in the sociology of deviance*. New York: Free Press.

Bell, A. P., & Weinberg, M. S. (1978). *Homosexualities: A study of diversity among men and women*. New York: Simon and Schuster.

Berger, R. M. (1977a). Report on a community based venereal disease clinic for homosexual men. *Journal of Sex Research, 13*(1), 54-62.

Berger, R. M., (1977b). An advocate model for intervention with homosexuals. *Social Work, 22*(4), 280-283.

Berger, R. M. (1982). *Gay and gray: The older homosexual man*. Urbana, IL: University of Illinois Press.

Berger, R. M., & Kelly, J. J. (1981). Do social work agencies discriminate against homosexual job applicants? *Social Work, 26*(3), 193-198.

Bergler, E. (1958). *Counterfeit-sex: Homosexuality, impotence, frigidity*. 2nd ed. New York: Grune and Stratton.

Bieber, I., Dain, H. J., Dince, P. R., Drellich, M. G., Grand, H. G., Gundlach, R. H., Kremer, M. W., Rifin, A. H., Wilbur, C. B., & Bieber, T. B. (1962). *Homosexuality: A psychoanalytic study*. New York: Basic Books.

Blair, R. (1975). Counseling and homosexuality: Keynote address of the 1975 national conference series of the *Homosexual Counseling Journal, 2*(3), 94-106.

Cavan, R. S. (1973). Speculations on innovations to conventional marriage in old age. *Gerontologist, 13*(4), 409-411.

Comptroller General. (1979). *Entering a nursing home: Costly implications for Medicaid and the elderly*. General Accounting Office Publication PAD-80-12. Washington, DC: U.S. Government Printing Office.

Cumming, E., & Henry, W. E. (1961). *Growing old: The process of disengagement*. New York: Basic Books.

Davison, G. C. (1974, November). *Homosexuality: The ethical challenge*. Presidential address presented at the meeting of the Association for Advacement of Behavior Therapy, Chicago.

Dawson, K. (1982, November). Serving the older gay community. *SIECUS Report, 11*(2), 5-6.

DeCrescenzo, T. A., & McGill, C. (1978). *Homophobia: A study of the attitudes of mental health professionals toward homosexuality.* Unpublished manuscript, University of Southern California School of Social Work.

Festinger, L. (1957). *A theory of cognitive dissonance.* New York: Harper and Row.

Figliulo, M. C., Shively, M. G., & McEnroe, F. (1978). The relationship of departures in social sex-role to the abridgment of civil liberties. *Journal of Homosexuality, 3*(3), 249-256.

Francher, J. S., & Henkin, J. (1973). The menopausal queen: Adjustment to aging and the male homosexual. *American Journal of Orthopsychiatry, 43*(4), 670-674.

Friend, R. A. (1980). GAYging: Adjustment and the older gay male. *Alternative Lifestyles, 3*(2), 231-248.

Friend, R. A. (1987). The individual and social psychology of aging: Clinical implications for lesbians and gay men. *Journal of Homosexuality, 14*(1/2), 307-331.

Friend, R. A. (1989). Older lesbian and gay people: Responding to homophobia. *Marriage and Family Review, 14*(3/4), 241-263.

Garfinkle, E. M., & Morin, S. F. (1978). Psychologists' attitudes toward homosexual psychotherapy clients. *Journal of Social Issues, 34*(3), 101-112.

Gochros, H. L. (1972). The sexually oppressed. *Social Work, 17*(2), 16-23.

Goffman, E. (1963). *Stigma: Notes on the management of spoiled identity.* Englewood Cliffs, NJ: Prentice-Hall.

Gough, H. G., & Heilbrun, A. B. (1965). *The adjective checklist.* Palo Alto, CA: Consulting Psychologists Press.

Gray, H., & Dressel, P. (1985). Alternative interpretations of aging among gay males. *Gerontologist, 25*(1), 83-87.

Halleck, S. (1971). A psychiatrist looks at the uses of abnormality. *The Progressive, 35*(6), 29-33.

Harrington, M. (1962). *The other America: Poverty in the United States.* New York: Macmillan.

Hooker, E. (1957). The adjustment of the male overt homosexual. *Journal of Personality Assessment, 21,* 18-31.

Hooker, E. (1965). Male homosexuals and their "worlds." In J. Marmor (Ed.), *Sexual inversion: The multiple roots of homosexuality.* New York: Basic Books.

Humphreys, R. A. L. (1970). *The tearoom trade: Impersonal sex in public places.* Chicago: Aldine.

Huyck, M. H. (1974). *Growing older.* New York: Prentice-Hall.

Kameny, F. E. (1971). Homosexuals as a minority group. In E. Sagarin (Ed.), *The other minorities.* Waltham, MA: Xerox.

Kantrowitz, A. (1976, June 16). Dirty old men: We don't want to be reminded that it's going to happen to us. *Advocate,* 21-29.

Katz, J. (1976). *Gay American history: Lesbians and gay men in the U.S.A., a documentary.* New York: Thomas Y. Crowell.

Kelly, J. J. (1974). Brothers and brothers: The gay man's adaptation to aging. PhD dissertation, Florence Heller Graduate School for Advanced Studies in Social Welfare, Bradeis University. University Microfilms No. 75-24, 234.

Kelly, J. J. (1977). The aging male homosexual: Myth and reality. *Gerontologist, 17*(4), 328-332.

Kelly, J. J. (1980). Homosexuality and aging. In J. Marmor (Ed.), *Homosexual behavior: A modern reappraisal.* New York: Basic Books.

Kelly, J. J., & Johnson, M. T. (1978). Deviate sex behavior in the aging: Social definitions and the lives of older gay people. In O. J. Kaplan (Ed.), *Psychopathology and aging.* New York: Academic Press.

Kimmel, D. C. (1978). Adult development and aging: A gay perspective. *Journal of Social Issues, 34*(3), 113-130.

Kinsey, A. C., Pomeroy, W. B., & Martin, C. E. (1948). *Sexual behavior in the human male.* Philadelphia: W. B. Saunders.

Kinsey, A. C., & Gebhard, P. H. (1953). *Sexual behavior in the human female.* Philadelphia: W. B. Saunders.

Kochera, B. (1973, September 1). The faggot's faggot: Gay senior citizens and gay S&M. *Pittsburgh Gay News,* p. 6.

Laner, M. R. (1978). Growing older male: Heterosexual and homosexual. *Gerontologist, 18*(5), 496-501.

Larson, R. (1978). Thirty years of research on the subjective well-being of older Americans. *Journal of Gerontology, 33*(1), 109-125.

Lee, J. A. (1987). What can homosexual aging studies contribute to theories of aging? *Journal of Homosexuality, 13*(4), 43-71.

Lee, J. A. (1989). Invisible men: Canada's aging homosexuals. Can they be assimilated into Canada's "liberated" gay communities? *Canadian Journal on Aging, 8*(1), 79-97.

Lee, J. A. (Ed.). (1991). *Gay midlife and maturity.* New York: Harrington Park Press.

Levitt, E. E., & Klassen, A. D., Jr. (1974). Public attitudes toward homosexuality: Part of the 1970 national survey by the Institute for Sex Research. *Journal of Homosexuality, 1*(1), 29-43.

Leznoff, M., & Westley, W. A. (1967). The homosexual community. In J. H. Gagnon, & W. Simon (Eds.), *Sexual deviance.* New York: Harper and Row.

Liljestrand, P., Petersen, R. P., & Zellers, R. (1978). The relationship of assumption and knowledge of the homosexual orientation to the abridgment of civil liberties. *Journal of Homosexuality, 3*(3), 243-248.

Lipman, A. (1986). Homosexual relationships. *Generations, 10*(4), 51-54.

Marmor, J. (Ed.) (1965). *Sexual inversion: The multiple roots of homosexuality.* New York: Basic Books.

Masters, W. H., & Johnson, V. E. (1966). *Human sexual response.* Boston: Little, Brown.

Masters, W. H., & Johnson, V. E. (1979). *Homosexuality in perspective.* Boston: Little, Brown.

Miller, M. (1971). *On being different: What it means to be a homosexual.* New York: Random House.

Minnigerode, F. A. (1976). Age-status labeling in homosexual men. *Journal of Homosexuality, 1*(3), 273-276.

Minnigerode, F. A., & Adelman, M. (1976, October). *Adaptations of aging homosexual men and women.* Paper presented at the convention of the Gerontological Society, New York.

Mischel, W. (1968). *Personality and assessment.* New York: Wiley.

National Council on Aging. (1975). *The myth and reality of aging in America.* 2nd printing. Washington, DC.

Neugarten, B. L., Havighurst, R. J., & Tobin, S. S. (1961). The measurement of life satisfaction. *Journal of Gerontology, 16,* 134-143.

Oregon Task Force on Sexual Preference. (1977). *Preliminary report.* Reprinted in *Sexual Law Reporter, 3*(4), July/October.

Pincus, A. (1970). Reminiscence in aging and its implications for social work practice. *Social Work, 15,* 47-53.

Pope, M., & Schulz, R. (1990). Sexual attitudes and behavior in midlife and aging homosexual males. *Journal of Homosexuality, 20*(3/4), 169-177.

Reiss, A. J. (1967). The social integration of queers and peers. In J. H. Gagnon and W. Simon (Eds.), *Sexual deviance.* New York: Harper and Row.

Robinson, M. K. (1979). The older lesbian. Master's thesis, California State University at Dominguez Hills.

Rogers, E. (1978). Older gays: Our neglected roots. *Alive, 1*(11), 20-25.

Saghir, M. T., & Robins, E. (1973). *Male and female homosexuality: A comprehensive investigation.* Baltimore: Williams and Wilkins.

Schaffer, R. S. (1972). Will you still need me when I'm 64? In K. Jay, & A. Young (Eds.), *Out of the closets: Voices of gay liberation.* New York: Douglas-Links.

Siegelman, M. (1972). Adjustment of male homosexuals and heterosexuals. *Archives of Sexual Behavior, 2,* 9-25.

Silverstein, C. (1977). *A family matter: A parents' guide to homosexuality.* New York: McGraw-Hill.

Simon, A. (1968). The geriatric mentally ill. *Gerontologist, 8,* 7-15.

Simon, W., & Gagnon, J. H. (1969). Homosexuality: The formulation of a sociological perspective. In R. W. Weltge (Ed.), *The same sex.* Philadelphia: Pilgrim.

Socarides, C. W. (1968). *The overt homosexual.* New York: Grune and Stratton.

Stearn, J. (1961). *The sixth man.* New York: McFadden Publishers.

Steinman, R. (1991). Social exchanges between older and younger gay male partners. In J. A. Lee (Ed.), *Gay midlife and maturity* (pp. 179-206). New York: Harrington Park Press.

Suppe, F. (1982a). Homosexuality and Masters and Johnson's research program. Manuscript.

Suppe, F. (1982b). The Bell and Weinberg study: Future priorities for research on homosexuality. Manuscript.

Szasz, T. S. (1970). *The manufacture of madness: A comparative study of the Inquisition and the mental health movement.* New York: Harper & Row.

Tripp, C. A. (1975). *The homosexual matrix.* New York: McGraw-Hill.
Truax, C. B., & Carkhuff, R. R. (1967). *Toward effective counseling and psychotherapy: Training and practice.* Chicago: Aldine.
Wallach, M. A., & Kogan, N. (1961). Aspects of judgment and decision making: Interrelationships and changes with age. *Behavioral Science, 6,* 23-36.
Warren, C. A. B. (1977). Fieldwork in the gay world: Issues in phenomenological research. *Journal of Social Issues, 33*(4), 93-107.
Weinberg, G. (1973). *Society and the healthy homosexual.* Garden City, NY: Doubleday/Anchor.
Weinberg, M. S. (1970). The male homosexual: Age-related variations in social and psychological characteristics. *Social Problems, 17*(4), 527-537.
Weinberg, M. S., & Williams, C. J. (1975). *Male homosexuals: Their problems and adaptations.* New York: Penguin.
Wolf, D. G. (1978, November). Close friendship patterns of older lesbians. Paper presented at the convention of the Gerontological Society, Dallas.
Wood, V., Wylie, M. L., & Sheafor, B. (1969). An analysis of a short self-report measure of life satisfaction: Correlation with rater judgments. *Journal of Gerontology, 24*(4), 465-469.

PART III

Chapter 13

Bennet, R., & Eckman, J. (1973). Attitudes toward aging: A critical examination of recent literature and implications for future research. In C. Eisdorfer, & M. P. Lawton (Eds.), *The psychology of adult development and aging.* Washington, DC: American Psychological Association.
Crowley, H. (1968). *The boys in the band.* New York: Farrar, Straus & Giroux.
Francher, J. S., & Henkin, J. (1973). The menopausal queen: Adjustment to aging and the male homosexual. *American Journal of Orthopsychiatry, 43,* 670-674.
Gough, H. G., & Heilbrun, A. B. (1965). *The adjective checklist.* Palo Alto, CA: Consulting Psychologists Press.
Humphreys, L. (1972). *Out of the closets: The sociology of homosexual liberation.* Englewood Cliffs, NJ: Prentice-Hall.
Kyper, J. (1974). Over the hill at 30? *Gay Sunshine, 20.*
Neugarten, B. L., Moore, J. M., & Lowe, J. C. (1965). Age norms, age constraints, and adult socialization. *American Journal of Sociology, 70,* 710-717.
Spreitzer, E., & Snyder, E. E. (1974). Correlates of life satisfaction among the aged. *Journal of Gerontology, 29,* 454-458.
Stearn, J. (1961). *The sixth man.* Garden City, NY: Doubleday.

Chapter 14

Adam, B. D. (1978). *The survival of domination.* New York: Elsevier.

Adam, B. D. (1987). *The rise of a gay and lesbian movement.* Boston: Twayne.

Berger, R. (1982). *Gay and gray.* Urbana, IL: University of Illinois Press.

Bérubé, A. (1981, October 15). Marching to a different drummer. *Advocate.*

Boswell, J. (1980). *Christianity, social tolerance and homosexality.* Chicago: University of Chicago Press.

Champagne, R. (1986). Canada's pioneer gay activist: Jim Egan. *Rites, 3*(7), 12-14.

Cory, D. W. (1951). *The homosexual in America.* New York: Greenberg.

Crisp, Q. (1983). *The naked civil servant.* New York: New American Library.

Dank, B. (1971). Coming out in the gay world. *Psychiatry, 34,* 180-197.

Dank, B. (1972). Why homosexuals marry women. *Medical Aspects of Human Sexuality, 6,* 12-23.

Dawson, K. (1982, November). Serving the gay community. *Sex Information and Education Council of the United States Report, 11*(2).

D'Emilio, J. (1983). *Sexual politics, sexual communities.* Chicago: University of Chicago Press.

Gordon, M. (1961). Assimilation in America: Theory and reality. *Daedalus, 90,* 363-365.

Goffman, E. (1963). *Stigma.* New York: Prentice Hall.

Grube, J. (1986). Queens and flaming virgins: Towards a sense of gay community. *Rites, 2*(9), 14-17.

Hooker, E. (1961). The homosexual community. *Proceedings of the 16th International Congress of Applied Psychology.*

Humphreys, L. (1972). *Out of the closets.* Englewood Cliffs: Prentice Hall.

Hunter, J. F. (1972). *The gay insiders.* New York: Stonehill.

Katz, S. (1964, February 22/March 7). The homosexual next door. *Maclean's.*

Kinsman, G. (1987). *The regulation of desire: Sexuality in Canada.* Montreal: Black Rose Books.

Lauritsen, J., & Thorstad, D. (1974). *The early homosexual rights movement (1864-1935).* New York: Times Change Press.

Lee, J. A. (1977). Going public. *Journal of Homosexuality, 3*(1), 49-78.

Lee, J. A. (1978). *Getting sex.* Toronto: General Publishing.

Lee, J. A. (1987). What can homosexual aging studies contribute to theories of aging? *Journal of Homosexuality, 13*(4), 43-71.

Leznoff, M., & Westley, W. A. (1963). The homosexual community. In H. Ruitenbeck (Ed.), *The problem of homosexuality in modern society.* New York: E. P. Dutton.

Long, P. (1972). *The new left.* Boston: Porter Sargent.

Marcuse, H. (1974). *Eros and civilization: A philosophical inquiry into Freud.* Boston: Beacon Press.

Marotta, T. (1981). *The politics of homosexuality.* Boston: Houghton Mifflin.

McCaffrey, J. (Ed.). (1972). *The homosexual dialectic.* New York: Prentice Hall.

Murray, S. O. (1979). Institutional elaboration of a quasi-ethnic community. *International Review of Modern Sociology, 9,* 165-178.

Murray, S. O. (1984). *Social theories, homosexual realities.* New York: Gay Academic Union of New York.

Schaffer, R. (1973). Will you still need me when I'm 64? *The gay liberation book.* San Francisco: Ramparts Press.

Simon, W., & Gagnon, J. (1967). Homosexuality, the formulation of a sociological perspective. *Journal of Health and Social Behaviour, 8,* 177-185.

Steakley, J. (1975). *The homosexual emancipation movement in Germany.* New York: Arno Press.

Warren, C. (1977). *Identity and community in the gay world.* New York: Wiley.

Wittman, C. (1972). A gay manifesto. In J. McCaffrey (Ed.), *The homosexual dialectic.* New York: Prentice Hall.

Chapter 15

Berger, R. M. (1982). *Gay and gray: The older homosexual man.* Boston: Alyson Publications.

Evans, R. B. (1969). Childhood parental relationship of homosexual men. *Journal of Consulting and Clinical Psychology, 33,* 129-135.

Hooker, E. (1956). A preliminary analysis of group behavior of homosexuals. *Journal of Psychology, 42,* 217-225.

Kelly, J. (1977). The aging male homosexual. *The Gerontologist, 17,* 328-332.

Kimmel, D. C. (1977, November). Patterns of aging among gay men. *Christopher Street,* pp. 28-31.

Kleinberg, S. (1977, November). Those dying generations: Harry and his friends. *Christopher Street,* pp. 7-26.

Laner, M. R. (1978). Growing older male: Heterosexual and homosexual. *The Gerontologist, 18,* 496-501.

Lee, J. A. (1976). Patterns of gay love and gay liberation. *Journal of Homosexuality, 1*(4), 401-418.

Loney, J. (1972). Background factors, sexual experiences, and attitudes toward treatment in two "normal" homosexual samples. *Journal of Consulting and Clinical Psychology, 38,* 57-65.

Minnigerode, F. A. (1976). Age-status labeling in homosexual men. *Journal of Homosexuality, 1,* 273-276.

Myrick, F. (1974). Attitudinal differences between heterosexually and homosexually oriented males and between covert and overt male homosexuals. *Journal of Abnormal Psychology, 83,* 81-86.

Pfeiffer, E., Verwoerdt, A., & Wang, H. S. (1968). Sexual behavior in aged men and women. *Archives of General Psychiatry, 19,* 753-758.

Pfeiffer, E., Verwoerdt, A., & Davis, O. C. (1972). Sexual behavior in middle life. *American Journal of Psychiatry, 128,* 1262-1267.

Saghir, M. T., & Robins, E. (1973). *Male and female homosexuality.* Baltimore: Williams & Wilkins.

Vacha, K. (1985). *Quiet fire: Memoirs of older gay men*. Trumansburg, NY: The Crossing Press.

Weinberg, M. S., & Williams, C. J. (1974). *Male homosexuals*. New York: Oxford University Press.

Chapter 16

Almvig, C. (1982). *The invisible minority: Aging and lesbianism*. New York: Utica College of Syracuse University.

Anderson, C. L. (1981). The effect of a workshop on attitudes of female nursing students toward male homosexuality. *Journal of Homosexuality, 7*, 57-70.

Bell, A. P., & Weinberg, M.S. (1978). *Homosexualities*. New York: Simon and Schuster.

Bennett, R., & Eckman, J. (1973). Attitudes toward aging: A critical review of recent literature and implications for future research. In C. Eisdorfer, & M. P. Lawton (Eds.), *The psychology of adult development and aging*. Washington, DC: American Psychological Association.

Berger, R. M. (1980). Psychological adaptation of the older homosexual male. *Journal of Homosexuality, 5*, 161-175.

Berger, R.M. (1982a). The unseen minority: Older gays and lesbians. *Social Work, 27*, 236-242.

Berger, R.M. (1982b). *Gay and gray*. Urbana: University of Illinois Press.

Bowers v. Hardwick, No. 85-140 S. Ct. (1986).

Cass, V. C. (1979). Homosexual identity formation: A theoretical model. *Journal of Homosexuality, 4*, 219-235.

Cass, V. C. (1983/1984). Homosexual identity: A concept in need of definition. *Journal of Homosexuality, 9*, (2/3), 105-126.

Coleman, E. (1981/1982). Developmental stages of the coming out process. *Journal of Homosexuality, 7*, (2/3), 31-43.

Dank, B. M. (1971). Coming out in the gay world. *Psychiatry, 34*, 180-197.

Dawson, K. (1982, November). Serving the older gay community. *SEICUS Report, 5-6*.

Erikson, E. (1963). *Childhood and society*. New York: W.W. Norton.

Foucault, M. (1978). *The history of sexuality, volume 1: An introduction*. New York: Vintage Books.

Francher, S. J. (1962). American values and the disenfranchisement of the aged. *Eastern Anthropologist, 22*, 29-36.

Francher, S. J., & Henkin, J. (1973). The menopausal queen. *American Journal of Orthopsychiatry, 43*, 670-674.

Friend, R. A. (1980). GAYging: Adjustment and the older gay male. *Alternative Lifestyles, 3*, 231-248.

Friend, R. A. (1984, June). *A theory of accelerated aging among lesbians and gay men*. Paper presented to the combined annual meeting of American Association of Sex Educators, Counselors, and Therapists and The Society for the Scientific Study of Sex, Boston, MA.

Green, S. K. (1981). Attitudes and perceptions about the elderly: Current and future perspectives. *Aging and Human Development, 13,* 95-115.

Harry, J. (1986). Sampling gay men. *The Journal of Sex Research,* 22(1), 21-34.

Kelly, J. (1977). The aging male homosexual: Myth and reality. *The Gerontologist, 17,* 328-332.

Kimmel, D. C. (1977). Psychotherapy and the older gay man. *Psychotherapy: Theory, Research and Practice, 14,* 386-393.

Kimmel, D. C. (1978). Adult development and aging: A gay perspective. *Journal of Social Issues, 34,* 113-130.

Lee, J. A. (1977). Going public: A study in the sociology of homosexual liberation. *Journal of Homosexuality, 3,* 49-78.

Lief, H. I. (1973). Obstacles to the ideal and complete sex education of the medical student and physician. In J. Money, & J. Zuben (Eds.), *Contemporary sexual behavior: Critical issues in the 1970's.* Baltimore: Johns Hopkins University Press, 441-453.

Martin, D. (1982). Learning to hide: The socialization of the gay adolescent. *Adolescent Psychiatry, 10,* 52-65.

Martin, D., & Lyon, P. (1973). Lesbian mothers. *Ms., 2,* 78-82.

Martin, D., & Lyon, P. (1979). The older lesbian. In B. Berzon, & R. Leighton (Eds.), *Positively gay.* Millbrae, CA: Celestial Arts.

Matteson, D. R. (1985). Bisexual men in marriage: Is a positive homosexual identity and stable marriage possible? *Journal of Homosexuality, 11* (1/2), 149-171.

Miller, B. (1979). Unpromised paternity: Life-styles of gay fathers. In M.P. Levine (Ed.), *Gay men: The sociology of male homosexuality.* New York: Harper and Row.

Minton, H. L., & McDonald, G. J. (1983/1984). Homosexual identity formation as a developmental process. *Journal of Homosexuality, 9,* 91-104.

Palmore, E. (1971). Attitudes toward aging as shown by humor. *The Gerontologist, 11,* 181-187.

Raphael, S. M., & Robinson, M. K. (1980). The older lesbian. *Alternative Lifestyles, 3,* 207-229.

Schaie, K. W., & Geiwitz, J. (1982). *Adult development and aging.* Boston: Little, Brown & Company.

Sontag, S. (1975). The double standard of aging. In *No longer young: The older woman in America.* Proceedings of the 26th Annual Conference on Aging, The University of Michigan, Wayne State University, 31-39.

Turner, J. (1985, May). Personal communication.

Vance, C. S. (1984). Pleasure and danger: Toward a politics of sexuality. In C.S. Vance (Ed.), *Pleasure and danger: Exploring female sexuality.* Boston: Routledge and Kegan Paul.

Weeks, J. (1977). *Coming out: Homosexual politics in Britain, from the nineteenth century to the present.* London: Quartet.

Weeks, J. (1981). *Sex, politics and society.* London: Longman Group.

Weinberg, G. (1972). *Society and the healthy homosexual.* New York: St. Martin's.

Weinberg, J. S. (1982). *Sexuality: Human needs and nursing practice.* Philadelphia: W. B. Saunders Company.

Weinberg, M. S. (1970). The male homosexual: Age-related variations in social and psychological characteristics. *Social Problems, 17,* 527-537.

Weinberg, T. S. (1983). *Gay men, gay selves: The social construction of homosexual identities.* New York: Irvington.

Weinberg, T. S. (1984). Biology, ideology, and the reification of developmental stages in the study of homosexual identities. *Journal of Homosexuality, 10,* 77-85.

Wolf, T. J. (1985). Marriages of bisexual men. *Journal of Homosexuality, 11* (1/2), 135-148.

Index